# THE POLITICAL WRITINGS
## OF ST. AUGUSTINE

184-207
305-317

# THE
# POLITICAL WRITINGS
## OF
# *St. Augustine*

*Edited, with an Introduction,*
*by*
HENRY PAOLUCCI

Including an Interpretative Analysis
by Dino Bigongiari

REGNERY GATEWAY
Washington, D.C.

Photo courtesy of John M. Wing Foundation, The New-
berry Library, Chicago, Illinois. "The Death of Saul."

Library of Congress Cataloging-in-Publication Data
Augustine, ‡Saint, Bishop of Hippo.
    The political writings of St. Augustine.

    Includes bibliographical references.
    1. Political science—early works to 1700—Collected
works.    I. Paolucci, Henry.    II. Bigongiari, Dino.
III. Title.
JC121.A796   1985        320'.01        85-7583
ISBN 0-89526-941-4 (pbk.)

Published in the United States by
Regnery Gateway
1130 17th Street, NW
Washington, DC 20036

Distributed to the trade by
National Book Network
4720-A Boston Way
Lanham, MD 20706

Printed on acid free paper.
Manufactured in the United States of America.

# CONTENTS

# INTRODUCTION

*Dicant nobis Christiani quid boni attulit Christus unde feliciores putent res humanas, quia venit Christus?* [1]

The political ideas of St. Augustine, no less than his ideas on sin, grace, and predestination, have long been an object of controversy. Was the great African bishop a political pessimist—a "precursor" of Machiavelli, as Friedrich Meinecke suggests in his *Die Idee der Staatsräson?*[2] Or was he a prophetic utopian—the chief source of "that ideal of a world society which is haunting the minds of so many today," as Étienne Gilson asserts in his preface to *The City of God* and attempts to demonstrate in *Les Métamorphoses de la Cité de Dieu?* [3] Readers of this volume may explore for themselves the possible meanings of the Augustinian writings upon which the controversy turns.

The works in which St. Augustine defines his political thought were almost without exception provoked by religious controversy, social upheavals, or military disasters. Some were replies to the Manichaeans of his day, who still ranted

1. *Enarrationes in Psalmos,* CXXXVI (Lat.), 9.
2. Friedrich Meinecke, *Die Idee der Staatsräson in der neueren Geschichte,* München und Berlin, 1925, p. 33.
3. Étienne Gilson, foreword to the *Fathers of the Church* edition of *The City of God,* New York, 1950, Vol. I, p. xi; *Les métamorphoses de la Cité de Dieu,* Louvain, 1952, *passim.*

against what they called the crimes, obscenities, calumnies, and absurdities of the Judaic *Old Testament*. Others were intended for the correction of the heretical and ardently nationalistic Donatists of North Africa, who were attacking orthodox Christian communities and rioting against the civil authorities. Still others, written after Alaric's frightful sack of Rome in 410 A.D., were answers to pagan charges that Christ's teachings are obviously "not adaptable to the customs of the state," and that great evils are bound to befall a people "when Christian rulers generally observe the Christian religion." [4]

In all these works, St. Augustine's concern is clearly practical rather than theoretical. Technically precise descriptions of governmental institutions and detailed comparisons of constitutional forms are conspicuously absent from his pages. Yet it by no means follows that we must, as Pierre de Labriolle recently suggested,[5] deny him a political theory in the traditional sense of the term. On the contrary, if the reduction of empirical multiplicity to conceptual unity is the goal of theoretic science, St. Augustine's account of the political regime of the world—which is what he means by the term *civitas terrena*—must be considered a masterpiece of political theory. His primary object, as a Christian bishop and apologist, was no doubt to determine the will and ultimately the conduct of his readers. But he had first to inform the intellect. And to the accomplishment of that distinctly theoretical task he brought a mastery of philosophical discourse and

4. *Epistolae*, CXXXVI, 2.
5. *La Cité de Dieu,* text latin et traduction française, avec un introduction et des notes par Pierre de Labriolle, Paris, 1957, Vol. I, pp. xi-xv.

a depth of psychological insight unsurpassed in the Western World.

From a juridical point of view it may be said, therefore, that St. Augustine's political doctrine has two aspects, one descriptive, or theoretical, the other censorial, or corrective. It is descriptive when the object is to trace the fixed pattern of an inviolable law—empirically ascertainable, like the laws of planetary motions—operating in the sphere of human conduct. It is censorial when it considers the obligations imposed by the various normative laws—natural, divine, and human —that men "ought" to obey, but which they often violate, without, however, in the least disturbing the operation of the fixed higher law that eternally governs "things as they are."

Because of its intimate association with the doctrine of predestination, this distinction between the normative natural, divine, and human laws and the non-normative eternal law has disturbed many students of Augustinian thought. Yet, despite its difficult moral and theological implications, St. Augustine considered it so indispensable a part of his political teaching that he insisted upon it even in sermons addressed to popular audiences. In Sermon CXXV, for instance, he says: "Let us not, because human affairs seem to be in disorder, fancy that there is no governance of human affairs. For all men are ordered to their proper places; but to every man it seems as though they have no order." To illustrate his meaning he offers two simple analogies. "Look," he says, "at a painter. Before him are placed various colours, and he knows where to set each colour on." The sinner, he explains, has no doubt chosen to be the black color. But that does not disturb the painter; he knows how to make use of black. With black he makes the hair, the beard, the eyebrows—though he makes the face of white only. "Look then," St. Augustine concludes, "to that which thou wouldest wish to be; take no care where He may place thee Who cannot err."

The second, more explicit illustration is drawn from the sphere of criminal law. St. Augustine says:

So we see it happen by the common laws of the world. Some man, for instance, has chosen to be a house-breaker: the law of the judge knows that he has acted contrary to the law: the law of the judge knows where to place him; and orders him most properly. He indeed has lived evilly; but not evilly has the law ordered him. From a house-breaker he will be sentenced to the mines; from the labour of such how great works are constructed? The condemned man's punishment is the city's ornament. So then God knoweth where to place thee. Do not think that thou art disturbing the counsel of God, if thou art minded to be disorderly.[6]

Among the selections presented in this volume there are undoubtedly many in which the grand Augustinian vision of a heteronomy of divine ends realized through the autonomy of men receives a much more sophisticated expression; yet the humble words of this popular sermon precisely define the fundamental idea. Not by constraint of human will, which ever remains subject to a hierarchy of normative laws, but by an artful granting or withholding of power to accomplish what has been willed, God's providential design is inexorably realized in human history.

The grand pattern of political and historical development delineated by St. Augustine is

6. *Sermones,* CXXV, 5.

rivalled in comprehensiveness and profundity only by the vast developmental systems of thought of Aristotle and Hegel. His description of the operation of eternal law in the rise and fall of nations is as awe-inspiring as the grandest visions of Hegel on the cunning of reason in history; while his conception of the all-pervading power of erotic love, or *cupiditas* (the love that builds the earthly city) is elaborated no less impressively than the Aristotelian system of nature, in which a single principle, itself unmoved, sustains and moves all things by "being loved."

As used by St. Augustine, the term *cupiditas* has not the restricted meaning of its English derivative. On the contrary, like the Aristotelian *eros,* it comprehends the entire range of erotic desire. In addition to economic greed and sexual appetite, it includes also lust for political rule and that desire to know which the Platonists spoke of as *eros philosophicos.* Comparing and contrasting the erotic inclinations of man with similar tendencies in animals, plants, compounds, and elements, St. Augustine reveals how profoundly, impressed he was by the Aristotelian and Neo-Platonic doctrine. "If we were sheep of some kind," he writes in *The City of God,*

we would love the carnal life of the senses which would be our sufficient good. . . . Likewise, if we were trees, we could not love by any sensuous tendency; nevertheless, there would be a kind of striving for whatever would make us more abundant in our fruitfulness. Again, if we were stones or waves, winds or flames, or anything of this sort which is without sensation or life, we would nevertheless be endowed with a kind of attraction for our proper place in the order of nature. The specific gravity of a body is, as it were, its love, whether it tends upward by its lightness or downward by its weight. For a body is borne by gravity as a spirit by love, whichever way it is moved.[7]

To show how the spirit of man is borne upward by *eros* or *cupiditas,* how it is moved to accomplish or perpetrate all the worldly things it has done, is doing, and shall do in the course of its earthly existence, is the chief burden of St. Augustine's political theory as of his philosophy of history.

Epitomizing his thought on politics and history in a brief paragraph of *The City of God,* St. Augustine begins by noting the obvious truth that, despite the bonds of a common nature, mankind the world over is divided against itself. What all human beings, men, women, and children, ultimately desire is, of course, peace and happiness. Unfortunately, their passions and appetites prompt them to pursue these ends in such a way that the satisfaction of one person often, if not always, involves the frustration of another. Conflicts occur; the strong overcome the weak, and the vanquished, "preferring any sort of peace and safety to freedom itself," readily submit unconditionally to the victors. This is so usual, St. Augustine remarks, that, in all parts of the world, men "who choose to die rather than be slaves have been greatly wondered at." Indeed, it seems as if nature itself speaks as with one voice among all peoples, advising them to submit to a conqueror's will rather than risk total annihilation in prolonged conflict. "Thus it happens," St. Augustine concludes, "(but not without God's

7. *De civitate Dei,* XI, 28. For a fuller comparison of the Augustinian and Aristotelian doctrines of love, see St. Augustine, *The Enchiridion,* ed. H. Paolucci, Chicago, 1961, pp. xi-xviii.

providence) that some are endowed with kingdoms and others are subject to kings." [8]

It is in his account of how political regimes are formed and maintained, or undermined and destroyed, that St. Augustine appears to anticipate the views of Machiavelli on statecraft. Of course, long before St. Augustine's time, very similar views had already been well formulated —though not so shockingly expressed—for political science, particularly by Aristotle and Polybius. To the classical account, St. Augustine adds the insight of Christian pessimism. Like the author of the *Prince,* he tears away the veil of respectability that successful political regimes hang, or try to hang, over their origins. His purpose is not, however, like Machiavelli's, to provide a manual of politically useful maxims for a new "founding father." He means to show how, with all the sweat, blood, and tears, with all the class struggles, ideological arguments, elaborate schemes for insuring domestic tranquillity, providing for the common defense, and promoting the general welfare, at home, by means of law and education, abroad, by means of trade, diplomacy, and war, it is nevertheless not the will of men, but the will of God that is accomplished in history. Machiavelli hints at a similar doctrine in his concept of *fortuna*; but the experience St. Augustine means to provide for his readers is rather that of Spinoza's "insight into necessity," or, more precisely—as has already been suggested —that of Hegel's *"List der Vernumft."* [9]

8. *De civ.,* XVIII, 2.
9. G. W. F. Hegel, *Sämtliche Werke,* ed. J. Hoffmeister, Vol. XVIII, *Vorlesungen über die Philosophie der Weltgeschichte,* I. Teilband, Einleitung: *Die Vernumft in der Geschichte,* Hamburg, 1955, p. 105.

"Passions, private aims, and the satisfaction of selfish desires," Hegel observes in words that might easily be mistaken for St. Augustine's, "are most effective springs of action" because they "respect none of the limitations which justice and morality would impose" and because they exert a "more direct influence over men than the artificial and tedious discipline that tends toward order and self-restraint, law and morality." Yet, when we read the record of history and note the evil and ruin that such passions, aims, and desires have wrought, when we contemplate the "miseries that have overwhelmed the noblest nations and polities, and the finest examples of private virtue," we experience, Hegel acknowledges, "mental torture, allowing no defense or escape but the consideration that what has happened could not be otherwise; that it is a fatality which no intervention could alter." [10] As a Christian apologist constantly combating the materialistic and astrological determinism preached by contemporary pagans, including the Epicureans and Stoics, St. Augustine was not much inclined to speak of "fatality" in the governance of human history. Yet, in Book Five of *The City of God*, after asserting that the rise and fall of nations is governed by God's will, he did not hesitate to write: "If anyone attributes it to fate because he gives the name of fate to God's will or power, let him keep his opinion, but hold his tongue." [11] Centuries later, St. Thomas Aquinas cited these very words (together with an example of the pious compliance of Pope Gregory I) in support of his

10. *Sämtliche Werke*, pp. 79-80 (trans. adapted from J. Sibree's version of *The Philosophy of History*, New York, 1899, pp. 20-21).
11. *De civ.*, V, 1.

own statement that "to deny fate is to deny divine providence." [12]

Like Hegel, St. Augustine found relief for the mental torture occasioned by the tragic spectacle of human history in the consideration that what happened could not have been otherwise. Yet, because of his practical purpose, he dwelt more fully than Hegel was inclined to do on the myriad violations of normative laws and on the individual and collective failures through which the higher reason of history realizes its purposes. Viewed philosophically, in the grand sweep of its historical development, the *civitas terrena,* or worldly civilization of man, is awesome to behold. In its material and intellectual structures are embodied the loftiest aspirations of worldly men. Yet how painful it is for most of us, St. Augustine remarks again and again, to realize that, as an instrument for the pursuit of happiness and peace, the whole thing has been a pathetic failure. Countless individuals, generation upon generation, have gone down into death unwillingly, painfully, clinging to life, yet trampled underfoot by misfortunes. The efforts of earnest men to combat disease, to alleviate poverty, to prevent crime, to banish ignorance, to escape natural disasters, to put an end to wars, are but measures of the actual extent of misery and suffering.

And how colossal have been the collective failures! Whole nations annihilated in war, or constrained for security to order their subjects to go out and commit the worst brutalities, devastating the cities of their enemies, butchering men, women, and children indiscriminately, often only to find when victory has come that they have at-

12. *Summa Contra Gentiles,* III, xciii.

tained, perhaps, the very opposite of what they fought for, losing more in victory than they feared to lose in defeat. No nation—St. Augustine reminds us—desires to perish. Yet, in the past all have gone down, all have proved mortal, like the men who build them. For the common good, for the safety of the republic, brave men have willingly sacrificed all things else they held dear. Great soldiers have silenced their consciences, allowing their hearts to harden, lest they should hesitate, when defeat and victory hang in the balance, to match and surpass, if necessary, the enemy's brutality. And what lies, betrayals of pacts, crimes, low deceptions have statesmen not found it necessary to commit in order to realize the public policy they have pledged themselves to serve!

In other words, according to St. Augustine, the world is such that, at the very top of the social order, in positions of highest trust, men are often required to commit acts of the very kind that civilizing society, with its laws and education, attempts to repress in the conduct of the mass of its members. The sad truth is, obviously, that, considering the mass of men as a whole, not an iota of their self-destructive force is ever really charmed out of them. For if we observe closely, we cannot help seeing that political regimes—whether they be tiny city states or world governments—are able to maintain a semblance of peace and order in the world only by using coercive force, veiled or naked, to restrain coercive force. If the responsible few in public office fail to hold on to the power concentrated in their hands, or neglect to use it effectively when necessary, it will inevitably drain back into the hands of the many. And these, giving vent to their passions, private aims, and selfish desires, will gradually be reduced to a condition of complete unrestraint, which will last until the strong again begin to prevail over the weak, and power is again concentrated, perhaps more tightly than ever before, in the hands of the few who have come to understand what really holds the city of man together.

But what about Christianity? Has not Christ's coming into the world made a difference in its politics? The question was being raised very pointedly in St. Augustine's time. Less than a full generation earlier, Christianity had been proclaimed the official religion of the Roman Empire, and the event had inspired in most faithful minds an irresistible sense of optimism. Even so thoughtful a Churchman as St. Ambrose of Milan had allowed himself to entertain the hope (so movingly expressed in his oration on the death of the elder Theodosius)[13] that the Roman Empire, because of the piety of its rulers, might ever reign in the world, together with the Church, in a partnership of two sovereignties, each with special power and authority from God, each serving to guarantee the safety and well-being of the other. But then Alaric's sack came, just fifteen years after the death of Theodosius, and such optimism was shaken to its very foundations. The city of Rome had not been violated by an enemy in almost eight hundred years of pagan rule, and now —see what befalls it under Christian emperors! *Ubi est deus eorum?*[14] was the contemptuous cry

13. *Sancti Ambrosii Oratio de obitu Theodisii,* ed. and tr. Sister M. D. Mannix, Washington, 1925.
14. *De civ.,* I, 29.

often heard in the streets; while in more polite circles, as St. Augustine reports, pagans were demanding of Christians: "Tell us the reason for Christ's coming; tell us what benefit it has been to the human race. Have not matters been worse upon earth since Christ came, and was it not better in the old days than it is now?" [15]

It had been primarily to answer such questions that St. Augustine undertook to write at length concerning the rise and fall of earthly kingdoms. But he wrote also in order to warn his fellow-Christians not to be misled by the taunts of their enemies into making false claims for Christianity. In letters, sermons, and treatises, he reminded them that Christ's sacrifice on the cross was for the salvation, not of political regimes, but of individual souls; and he especially warned them not to confound the Christian community with Rome or any other worldly state.

Nations, St. Augustine asserts, may boast of having Christian political rule, but in fact their Christianity, like their much-vaunted justice, can be at best only nominal, only a handsomely-colored semblance.[16] Since Christians cannot, in good faith, constitute a kingdom or *polis* of their own in this world, they cannot, in good faith, claim to have a politics of their own. The only politics possible on earth is that of coercive power used to restrain coercive power, which has always characterized the *civitas terrena*.

And the *civitas terrena*, St. Augustine further insists, has absolutely nothing to fear, in the way of political interference, from the pilgrim Christian fellowship living in its midst. In one of his

15. *Enarr.* CXXXVI, 9.
16. Compare *De civ.*, II, 21.

most emphatic utterances on the subject, he thus paraphrases and interprets the words of Jesus before Pilate: "Hear then, ye Jews and Gentiles; hear, O circumcision; hear, O uncircumcision; hear, all ye kingdoms of the earth: I interfere not with your government in the world." Worldly rulers, he says, have Christ's assurance that He and His people constitute no danger to them:

Cherish ye not the utterly vain terror that threw Herod the elder into consternation when the birth of Christ was announced, and led him to the murder of so many infants in the hope of including Christ in the fatal number, made more cruel by his fear than by his anger: "My kingdom," He said, "is not of this world." What would you more? [And] He proved this by saying, "If my kingdom were of this world, then would my servants fight, that I should not be delivered to the Jews." [17]

Because they are not *of* this world, Christians do not interfere with its rule; yet it is plain, from the Scriptures, that they are to remain *in* the world: they are not to attempt to live apart. St. Augustine cites the words of Jesus to the Father: "I pray not that Thou shouldest take them out of the world, but that Thou shouldest keep them from evil";[18] and also St. Peter's admonition to the faithful: "Submit yourselves to every ordinance of man for the Lord's sake; whether it be to the king as supreme; or unto governors, as unto them that are sent for the punishment of evil doers." [19] Christians, he holds, are under religious obligation to coöperate with the earthly city in its efforts to check violence with violence. It is not that they require the restraints of coercive

17. *In Joannis Evangelium*, CXV, 2.
18. *Ibid.*
19. I *Peter*, II, 13.

INTRODUCTION

government for their own discipline. Obviously, if all human beings were truly Christian, loving God wholeheartedly and their neighbors for God's sake, there would be no need of coercive government. Worldly political regimes, St. Augustine holds emphatically, exist for the mutual restraint of the wicked. The peace they enforce is a genuine good—yet clearly a good of the sort that results when the violently insane are bound in straitjackets to prevent them from destroying one another. Such peace is to be accounted a true good even if those who bind are neither less demented nor less violent than those who are bound. It suffices only that they be more powerful.

In the spirit of this grim truth, St. Augustine says of the pilgrim portion of the heavenly city that, so long as it "lives like a captive and stranger" in the world, calling its members out of all nations, it will respect "diversities in the manners, laws, and institutions whereby earthly peace is secured and maintained." For it recognizes that, "however various these are, they all tend to one and the same end of earthly peace." [20]

St. Augustine thus provides us with an explanation, if not a justification, of the fact, noted earlier in this introduction, that descriptions of governmental operations and comparisons of constitutions have little if any place in his political doctrine. The form of political regime under which Christians are called upon to live is, or ought to be, of little consequence to them. Whether they be "kings, princes, judges, soldiers, provincials, rich, poor, free, slave, male, or female," he declares unambiguously, "they are bound to toler-

20. *De civ.*, XIX, 17.

ate even the worst, and if need be, the most atrocious form of government [*etiam pessimam, si ita
necesse est, flagitiosissimamque rem publicam*]."[21]
And it is, he says finally, through just such duti-
ful tolerance—imitating Christ's tolerance of Pilate's power—that true Christians may hope to
enter the republic of heaven, where God's will
is the only law.

The first two chapters of this volume present
selections from *The City of God* on the theory
of coercive government and the law of history
that regulates the rise and fall of nations. For the
reader's convenience, related passages, widely
separated in the original text, are brought together under descriptive headings supplied by the
editor. The third chapter is made up of passages
from the *Reply to Faustus the Manichaean, Expositions on the Book of Psalms, Tractates on the
Gospel According to St. John, Sermons,* and *Letters,* as well as from *The City of God,* in which
St. Augustine considers the responsibilities of
Christians as law-abiding citizens of worldly
states, and especially the grounds of Christian co-
operation in the regulation of civil rights under
human law and in the prosecution of so-called
just wars.

The selections in the fourth chapter, on the
treatment of heretics, and those in the fifth, on
the right of ecclesiastical intercession in the administration of civil justice (drawn from the
*Treatise Concerning the Correction of the Dona-
tists* and the *Letters*) complement one another.
Doctrinaire libertarians are not likely to be persuaded by St. Augustine's arguments supporting

21. *De civ.,* II, 19.

the view that, when civil governments are willing to do so, they have a right to compel heretics to enter the Church. Yet, upon close examination, these arguments seem to stand up rather well as compared or contrasted with, say, President Lincoln's views on compelling the rebellious Southern States to remain in the Federal Union, or the views of those who have justified the use of force to compel integration of the races in American schools, and of the separated provinces in the old Belgian Congo. St. Augustine pleads eloquently for mercy in the administration of civil laws, and demands of Christian public officials that they respect his pleas. Yet, at the same time, he warns all concerned with the maintenance of civil order not to undermine the foundations of society by attempting to "legalize" or "legislate" mercy.

The readings presented in the sixth chapter, from the *Tractates on the Gospel According to St. John, Expositions on the Book of Psalms,* and *Sermons,* are indispensable for a correct appreciation of the essentially Christian aspect of St. Augustine's political theory. Most important in this respect is his interpretation of the fundamental texts of Scripture upon which all Christian political doctrine must ultimately depend. These include the account of Pilate's interrogation of Jesus in the Gospel of St. John and, of course, the utterances of St. Peter and St. Paul on the obligation of Christians to be subject to the higher powers. The sixth chapter ends with St. Augustine's magnificent discourse on the Psalm, "By the Waters of Babylon." His interpretation of the fanaticism of political vengeance with which that extraordinary Psalm ends should be of considerable interest to all who value the Judaic-Christian Scriptures.

Printed in the Appendix is an essay presenting the substance of two lectures on the political ideas of St. Augustine delivered at Columbia University in 1954 by the eminent medievalist, Professor Dino Bigongiari.[22] Readers of this volume will find it an invaluable guide to the interpretation of the texts they have read and also to further study.

22. See notes to the Appendix.

# BIBLIOGRAPHICAL NOTE

The selections in this volume are drawn from the following translations:

THE CITY OF GOD, trs. M. Dods, J. J. Smith, and G. Wilson. Edinburgh: 1872.

EXPOSITIONS ON THE BOOK OF PSALM*S*, Vols. III-VI, eds. C. Marriot and H. Walford, trs. T. Scratton, H. M. Wilkins, and H. Walford. Oxford: 1849-1857.

LECTURES OR TRACTATES ON THE GOSPEL ACCORDING TO ST. JOHN, Vols. I-II, tr. J. Gibb. Edinburgh: 1873, 1874.

LETTERS OF ST. AUGUSTINE, Vols. I-II, tr. J. G. Cunningham. Edinburgh: 1872, 1875.

LETTERS (Fathers of the Church Edition), Vol. III, tr. Sister W. Parsons. New York: 1953. Used with the kind permission of the Catholic University of America Press.

SERMONS ON SELECTED LESSONS OF THE NEW TESTAMENT, Vols. I-II, tr. R. G. Macmullen. Oxford: 1844, 1845.

WRITINGS IN CONNECTION WITH THE DONATIST CONTROVERSY, Vol. III, tr. J. R. King. Edinburgh: 1872.

WRITINGS IN CONNECTION WITH THE MANICHAEAN HERESY, tr. R. Stothert. Edinburgh: 1872.

Many passages of the translations used, especially those from Dods' version of *The City of*

*God,* have been considerably revised to bring them into closer accord with the Latin texts as found in the *Corpus Scriptorum Ecclesiasticorum Latinorum* or Migne's *Patrologiae Cursus Completus: Series Latina.* Slight modifications, consistent with the meaning of the Latin text have occasionally been introduced to facilitate transitions from one selection to the next.

A letter in superscript ([a]) indicates the beginning of a selection, and the source is given in the corresponding footnote.

# CHAPTER I

## ORIGINS OF COERCIVE GOVERNMENT

### A. *Fallen Nature and the Two Cities*

[a]God, desiring not only that the human race might be able by their similarity of nature to associate with one another, but also that they might be bound together in harmony and peace by the ties of relationship, was pleased to derive all men from one individual. And He created men with such a nature that the members of the race should not have died, had not the first two (of whom one was created out of nothing, and the other out of him) merited this with their disobedience; for by them so great a sin was committed, that by it the human nature was altered for the worse, and was transmitted also to their posterity.

[b]That the whole human race has been condemned in its first origin, this life itself, if life it is to be called, bears witness by the host of cruel ills with which it is filled. Is not this proved by the profound and dreadful ignorance which produces all the errors that enfold the children of Adam, and from which no man can be delivered without toil, pain, and fear? Is it not proved by his love of so many vain and hurtful things, which pro-

a. *City of God,* XIV, 1.
b. *Ibid.,* XXII, 22.

duces gnawing cares, disquiet, griefs, fears, wild joys, quarrels, law-suits, wars, treasons, angers, hatreds, deceit, flattery, fraud, theft, robbery, perfidy, pride, ambition, envy, murders, parricides, cruelty, ferocity, wickedness, luxury, insolence, impudence, shamelessness, fornications, adulteries, incests, and the numberless uncleannesses and unnatural acts of both sexes, which it is shameful so much as to mention; sacrileges, heresies, blasphemies, perjuries, oppression of the innocent, calumnies, plots, falsehoods, false witnessings, unrighteous judgments, violent deeds, plunderings, and innumerable other crimes that do not easily come to mind, but that never absent themselves from the actuality of human existence? These are indeed the crimes of wicked men, yet they spring from that root of error and misplaced love which is born with every son of Adam. For who is there that has not observed with what profound ignorance, manifesting itself even in infancy, and with what superfluity of foolish desires, beginning to appear in boyhood, man comes into this life, so that, were he left to live as he pleased, and to do whatever he pleased, he would plunge into all, or certainly into many of those crimes and iniquities which I mentioned, and could not mention?

But because God does not wholly desert those whom He condemns, nor shuts up in His anger His tender mercies, the human race is restrained by law and education, which keep guard against the ignorance that besets us, and oppose the assaults of vice, but are themselves full of labour and sorrow. For what mean those multifarious threats which are used to restrain the folly of children? What mean pedagogues, masters, the birch, the strap, the cane, the schooling which Scripture says must be given a child, "beating him on the sides lest he wax stubborn," [1] and it be hardly possible or not possible at all to subdue him? Why all these punishments, save to overcome ignorance and bridle evil desires—these evils with which we come into the world? For why is it that we remember with difficulty, and without difficulty forget? learn with difficulty, and without difficulty remain ignorant? are diligent with difficulty, and without difficulty are indolent? Does not this show what vitiated nature inclines and tends to by its own weight, and what succour it needs if it is to be delivered? Inactivity, sloth, laziness, negligence, are vices which shun labour, since labour, though useful, is itself a punishment.

But, besides the punishments of childhood, without which there would be no learning of what the parents wish—and the parents rarely wish anything useful to be taught—who can describe, who can conceive the number and severity of the punishments which afflict the human race—pains which are not only the accompaniment of the wickedness of godless men, but are a part of the human condition and the common misery—what fear and what grief are caused by bereavement and mourning, by losses and condemnations, by fraud and falsehood, by false suspicions, and all the crimes and wicked deeds of other men? For at their hands we suffer robbery, captivity, chains, imprisonment, exile, torture, mutilation, loss of sight, the violation of chastity to satisfy the lust of the oppressor, and many other dreadful evils. What numberless casualties threaten our bodies from without—extremes of heat and

1. Ecclus. xxx. 12.

cold, storms, floods, inundations, lightning, thunder, hail, earthquakes, houses falling; or from the stumbling, or shying, or vice of horses; from countless poisons in fruits, water, air, animals; from the painful or even deadly bites of wild animals; from the madness which a mad dog communicates, so that even the animal which of all others is most gentle and friendly to its own master, becomes an object of intenser fear than a lion or dragon, and the man whom it has by chance infected with this pestilential contagion becomes so rabid, that his parents, wife, children, dread him more than any wild beast! What disasters are suffered by those who travel by land or sea! What man can go out of his own house without being exposed on all hands to unforeseen accidents? Returning home sound in limb, he slips on his own door-step, breaks his leg, and never recovers. What can seem safer than a man sitting in his chair? Eli the priest fell from his, and broke his neck. How many accidents do farmers, or rather all men, fear that the crops may suffer from the weather, or the soil, or the ravages of destructive animals? Commonly they feel safe when the crops are gathered and housed. Yet, to my certain knowledge, sudden floods have driven the labourers away, and swept the barns clean of the finest harvest. Is innocence a sufficient protection against the various assaults of demons? That no man might think so, even baptized infants, who are certainly unsurpassed in innocence, are sometimes so tormented, that God, who permits it, teaches us hereby to bewail the calamities of this life, and to desire the felicity of the life to come. As to bodily diseases, they are so numerous that they cannot all be contained even in medical books. And in very many, or almost all of them, the cures and remedies are themselves tortures, so that men are delivered from a pain that destroys by a cure that pains. Has not the madness of thirst driven men to drink human urine, and even their own? Has not hunger driven men to eat human flesh, and that the flesh not of bodies found dead, but of bodies slain for the purpose? Have not the fierce pangs of famine driven mothers to eat their own children, incredibly savage as it seems? In fine, sleep itself, which is justly called repose, how little of repose there sometimes is in it when disturbed with dreams and visions; and with what terror is the wretched mind overwhelmed by the appearances of things which are so presented, and which, as it were, so stand out before the senses, that we cannot distinguish them from realities! How wretchedly do false appearances distract men in certain diseases! With what astonishing variety of appearances are even healthy men sometimes deceived by evil spirits, who produce these delusions for the sake of perplexing the senses of their victims, if they cannot succeed in seducing them to their side!

From this hell upon earth, <sup>c</sup>the deserved penalty of sin would have hurled all headlong even into the second death, of which there is no end, had not the undeserved grace of God saved some therefrom. And thus it has come to pass, that though there are very many and great nations all over the earth, whose rites and customs, speech, arms, and dress, are distinguished by marked differences, yet there are no more than two kinds of human society, which we may justly call two cities, according to the language of our Scriptures. The

c. *City of God,* XIV, 1-2.

one consists of those who wish to live after the flesh, the other of those who wish to live after the spirit.

First, we must see what it is to live after the flesh, and what to live after the spirit. For any one who either does not recollect, or does not sufficiently weigh, the language of sacred Scripture, may, on first hearing what we have said, suppose that the Epicurean philosophers live after the flesh, because they place man's highest good in bodily pleasure; and that those others do so who have been of opinion that in some form or other bodily good is man's supreme good; and that the mass of men do so who, without dogmatizing or philosophizing on the subject, are so prone to lust that they cannot delight in any pleasure save such as they receive from bodily sensations: and he may suppose that the Stoics, who place the supreme good of men in the soul, live after the spirit; for what is man's soul, if not spirit? But in the sense of the divine Scripture both are proved to live after the flesh. For by flesh it means not only the body of a terrestrial and mortal animal, as when it says, "All flesh is not the same flesh, but there is one kind of flesh of men, another flesh of beasts, another of fishes, another of birds," [2] but it uses this word in many other significations. . . . If we are to ascertain what it is to live after the flesh (which is certainly evil, though the nature of flesh is not itself evil), we must carefully examine that passage of the epistle which the Apostle Paul wrote to the Galatians, in which he says, "Now the works of the flesh are manifest, which are these: adultery, fornication, uncleanness, lasciviousness, idolatry, witchcraft, hatred, variance, emulations,

2. I. Cor. xv. 39.

wrath, strife, seditions, heresies, envyings, murders, drunkenness, revellings, and such like: of the which I tell you before, as I have also told you in time past, that they which do such things shall not inherit the kingdom of God." [3] This whole passage of the apostolic epistle being considered, so far as it bears on the matter in hand, will be sufficient to answer the question, what it is to live after the flesh.

[d]In enunciating this proposition of ours, then, that because some live according to the flesh and others according to the spirit there have arisen two diverse and conflicting cities, we might equally well have said, "because some live according to man, others according to God." For Paul says very plainly to the Corinthians, "For whereas there is among you envying and strife, are ye not carnal, and walk according to man?" [4] So that to walk according to man and to be carnal are the same; for by *flesh,* that is, by a part of man, man is meant.

[e]But the character of the human will is of moment; . . . for the man who lives according to God, and not according to man, ought to be a lover of good, and therefore a hater of evil. And since no one is evil by nature, but whosoever is evil is evil by vice, he who lives according to God ought to cherish toward evil men a perfect hatred, so that he shall neither hate the man because of his vice, nor love the vice because of the man. For the vice being cursed, all that ought to be loved, and nothing that ought to be hated, will remain.

3. Gal. v. 19-21.
d. *City of God,* XIV, 4.
4. I. Cor. iii. 3.
e. *City of God,* XIV, 6-7.

He who resolves to love God, and to love his neighbor as himself, not according to man but according to God, is on account of this love said to be of a good will; and this is in Scripture more commonly called charity, but it is also, even in the same books, called love. . . . The right will is, therefore, well-directed love, and the wrong will is ill-directed love. Love yearning to have what is loved, is desire; and having and enjoying it, is joy; fleeing what is opposed to it, is fear; and feeling what is opposed to it, when it has befallen it, is sadness. Now these motions are evil if the love is evil; good if the love is good.

ʳTwo cities have been formed, therefore, by two loves: the earthly by love of self, even to contempt of God; the heavenly by love of God, even to contempt of self. The former glories in itself, the latter in the Lord. For the one seeks glory from men; but the greatest glory of the other is God, the witness of conscience. The one lifts up its head in its own glory; the other says to its God, "Thou art my glory, and the lifter up of mine head." [5] In the one, the princes and the nations it subdues are ruled by the love of ruling; in the other, the princes and the subjects serve one another in love, the latter obeying, while the former take thought for all. The one delights in its own strength, represented in the persons of its rulers; the other says to its God, "I will love Thee, O Lord, my strength." [6] And therefore the wise men of the one city, living according to man, have sought for profit to their own bodies or souls, or both, and those who have known God "glorified Him not as

f. *City of God,* XIV, 28.
5. Ps. iii. 3.
6. Ps. xviii. 1.

God, neither were thankful, but became vain in their imaginations, and their foolish hearts were darkened; professing themselves to be wise"—that is, glorying in their own wisdom, and being possessed by pride—"they became fools, and changed the glory of the incorruptible God into an image made like to corruptible man, and to birds, and four-footed beasts, and creeping things." For they were either leaders or followers of the people in adoring images, "and worshipped and served the creature more than the Creator, who is blessed for ever." [7] But in the other city there is no human wisdom, but only godliness, which offers due worship to the true God, and looks for its reward in the society of the saints, of holy angels as well as holy men, "that God may be all in all." [8] [g]And when these two cities severally achieve what they wish, they live in peace, each after its kind.

[h]Now peace is a good so great, that even in this earthly and mortal life there is no word we hear with such pleasure, nothing we more strongly desire, or enjoy more thoroughly when it comes. So that if we dwell for a little longer on this subject, we shall not, in my opinion, be wearisome to our readers who will bear with us both for the sake of understanding what is the end of this city of which we speak, and for the sake of the sweetness of peace which is dear to all.

Everyone who has observed the conduct of men's affairs and common human nature will agree with me in this: that just as there is no man who does not long for joy, so there is no man who

7. Rom. i. 21-25.
8. I. Cor. xv. 28.
g. *City of God*, XIV, 1.
h. *Ibid.*, XIX, 11-12.

✳ does not long for peace. Even those who want
war, want it really only for victory's sake: that is,
they want to attain a glorious peace by fighting.
For what is victory if not the subjugation of those
who resist us? And when this is done, peace follows.

It is therefore with the desire for peace that wars
are waged, even by those who take pleasure in
exercising their warlike nature in command and
battle. And hence it is obvious that peace is the
end sought for by war. For every man seeks peace
by waging war, but no man seeks war by making
peace. For even they who intentionally interrupt
the peace in which they are living have no hatred
of peace, but only wish it changed into a peace
that suits them better. They do not, therefore,
wish to have no peace, but only one more to their
mind. And in the case of sedition, when men have
separated themselves from the community, they
yet do not effect what they wish, unless they maintain some kind of peace with their fellow-conspir-
ators. And therefore even robbers take care to
maintain peace with their comrades, that they may
with greater effect and greater safety invade the
peace of other men. And if an individual happen
to be of such unrivalled strength, and to be so
jealous of partnership, that he trusts himself with
no comrades, but makes his own plots, and commits depredations and murders on his own account, yet he maintains some shadow of peace
with such persons as he is unable to kill, and from
whom he wishes to conceal his deeds. In his own
home, too, he makes it his aim to be at peace with
his wife and children, and any other members of
his household; for unquestionably their prompt
obedience to his every look is a source of pleasure

to him. And if this be not rendered, he is angry, he chides and punishes; and even by this storm he secures the calm peace of his own home, as occasion demands. For he sees that peace cannot be maintained unless all the members of the same domestic circle be subject to one head, such as he himself is in his own house. And therefore if a city or nation offered to submit itself to him, to serve him in the same style as he had made his household serve him, he would no longer lurk in a brigand's hiding-places, but lift his head in open day as a king, though the same covetousness and wickedness should remain in him. And thus all men desire to have peace with their own circle whom they wish to govern as suits themselves. For even those whom they make war against they wish to make their own, and impose on them the laws of their own peace.

But let us suppose a man such as poetry and mythology speak of—a man so insociable and savage as to be called rather a semi-man than a man. Although, then, his kingdom was the solitude of a dreary cave, and he himself was so singularly bad-hearted that he was named Κακός, which is the Greek word for *bad;* though he had no wife to soothe him with endearing talk, no children to play with, no sons to do his bidding, no friend to enliven him with intercourse, not even his father Vulcan (though in one respect he was happier than his father, not having begotten a monster like himself); although he gave to no man, but took as he wished whatever he could, from whomsoever he could, when he could; yet in that solitary den, the floor of which, as Virgil [9] says, was always reeking with recent slaughter, there was nothing else

9. *Æneid,* viii. 195.

than peace sought, a peace in which no one should molest him, or disquiet him with any assault or alarm. With his own body he desired to be at peace; and he was satisfied only in proportion as he had this peace. For he ruled his members, and they obeyed him; and for the sake of pacifying his mortal nature, which rebelled when it needed anything, and of allaying the sedition of hunger which threatened to banish the soul from the body, he made forays, slew, and devoured, but used the ferocity and savageness he displayed in these actions only for the preservation of his own life's peace. So that, had he been willing to make with other men the same peace which he made with himself in his own cave, he would neither have been called bad, nor a monster, nor a semi-man. Or if the appearance of his body and his vomiting smoky fires frightened men from having any dealings with him, perhaps his fierce ways arose not from a desire to do mischief, but from the necessity of finding a living. But he may have had no existence, or, at least, he was not such as the poets fancifully describe him, for they had to exalt Hercules, and did so at the expense of Cacus. It is better, then, to believe that such a man or semi-man never existed, and that this, in common with many other fancies of the poets, is mere fiction. For the most savage animals (and he is said to have been almost a wild beast) encompass their own species with a ring of protecting peace. They cohabit, beget, produce, suckle, and bring up their young, though very many of them are not gregarious, but solitary—not like sheep, deer, pigeons, starlings, bees, but such as lions, foxes, eagles, bats. For what tigress does not gently purr over her cub, and lay aside her ferocity to fondle them?

What kite, solitary as he is when circling over his
prey, does not seek a mate, build a nest, hatch the
eggs, bring up the young birds, and maintain with
the mother of his family as peaceful a domestic
alliance as he can? How much more powerfully
do the laws of man's nature move him to hold
fellowship and maintain peace with all men so far
as in him lies, since even wicked men wage war
to maintain the peace of their own circle, and wish
that, if possible, all men belonged to them, that
all men and things might serve but one head, and
might, either through love or fear, yield themselves to peace with him!

iBut the dominion of bad men harms themselves
far more than their subjects, for they destroy their
own souls in their greater license to exercise their
lusts; while those who are put under them in service are not hurt except by their own iniquities. For
to the just all the evils imposed on them by unjust
rulers are not the punishment of crime, but the
test of virtue. Therefore the good man, although
he is a slave, is free; but the bad man, even if he
reigns, is a slave, and that not of one man, but,
what is far more grievous, of as many masters as
he has vices; of which vices where the divine
Scripture treats, it says: "Of whatsoever a man is
overcome, to that he is in bondage." [10]

jThis earthly city, which shall not be everlasting
(for it will no longer be a city when it has been
committed to perpetual pains) has all its good in
this world, and rejoices in it with such joy as such
things can afford. kIt is spread throughout the

i. *City of God*, IV, 3.
10. 2 Pet. ii. 19.
j. *City of God*, XIV, 4.
k. *Ibid.*, XVIII, 2.

world in the most diverse places, and, though united by a common nature, is for the most part divided against itself, and the strongest oppress the others, because all follow after their own interests and lusts, while what is longed for either suffices for none, or not for all, because it is not the true good. [1]Each part of it that arms against another desires to be the world's master, whereas it is itself in bondage to vice. If, when it has conquered, it is inflated with pride, its victory is self-destroying; but if it turns its thoughts upon the common casualties of our mortal condition, and is rather anxious concerning the disasters that may befall it than elated with the successes already achieved, this victory, though of a higher kind, is still only short-lived; for it cannot abidingly rule over those whom it has subjugated by conquest. Yet one cannot say that the things this earthly city desires are not good, since it itself is, of its kind, better than all other human things. For it desires earthly peace for the sake of enjoying earthly goods, and it makes war in order to attain this peace; since, if it has conquered, and there remains no one to resist it, it enjoys a peace which it had not while there were opposing parties to contest it for the enjoyment of those things which were too little to satisfy both.

[m]And the vanquished readily succumb to the victors, preferring any sort of peace and safety to freedom itself; so that they who choose to die rather than be slaves have been greatly wondered at. For nature seems to cry out with one voice through all peoples of the world, that it is better to serve the conqueror than be destroyed by war.

1. *City of God*, XV, 4.
m. *Ibid.*, XVIII, 2.

Thus it happens (but not without God'; dence) that some are endowed with kingd< others made subject to kings.

## B. *The City of Man from Cain to Romulus*

ᵃOf the two first parents of the human race, Cain was the first-born, and he belonged to the city of men; after him was born Abel, who belonged to the city of God. For as in the individual the truth of the apostle's statement is discerned, "that is not first which is spiritual, but that which is natural, and afterward that which is spiritual," [1] whence it comes to pass that each man, being derived from a condemned stock, is first of all born of Adam evil and carnal, and becomes good and spiritual only afterwards, when he is grafted into Christ by regeneration: so was it in the human race as a whole. When these two cities began to run their course by a series of deaths and births, the citizen of this world was the first-born, and after him the stranger in this world, the citizen of the city of God, predestinated by grace, elected by grace, by grace a stranger below, and by grace a citizen above. By grace—for so far as regards himself he is sprung from the same mass, all of which is condemned in its origin; but God, like a potter (for this comparison is introduced by the apostle judiciously, and not without thought), of the same lump made one vessel to honour, another to dishonour.[2] But first the vessel to dishonour was made, and after it another to honour. For in each individual, as I have already said, there is first of all that which is reprobate, that from which we

a. *City of God*, XV, 1.
1. I. Cor. xv. 46.
2. Rom. ix. 21.

must begin, but in which we need not necessarily remain; afterwards is that which is well-approved, to which we may by advancing attain, and in which, when we have reached it, we may abide. Not, indeed, that every wicked man shall be good, but that no one will be good who was not first of all wicked; but the sooner any one becomes a good man, the more speedily does he receive this title, and abolish the old name in the new. Accordingly, it is recorded of Cain that he built a city,[3] but Abel, being a sojourner, built none.

[b]And this founder of the earthly city was a fratricide. Overcome with envy, he slew his own brother, a citizen of the eternal city, and a sojourner on earth. So that we cannot be surprised that this first specimen, or, as the Greeks say, archetype of crime, should, long afterwards, find a corresponding crime at the foundation of that city which was destined to reign over so many nations, and be the head of this earthly city of which we speak. For of that city also, as one of their poets has mentioned, "the first walls were stained with a brother's blood," [4] or, as Roman history records, Remus was slain by his brother Romulus. And thus there is no difference between the foundation of this city and of the earthly city, unless it be that Romulus and Remus were both citizens of the earthly city. Both desired to have the glory of founding the Roman republic, but both could not have as much glory as if one only claimed it; for he who wished to have the glory of ruling would certainly rule less if his power were shared by a living consort. In order, therefore,

3. Gen. iv. 17.
b. *City of God,* XV, 5.
4. Lucan, *Phar.* i. 95.

that the whole glory might be enjoyed by one, his consort was removed; and by this crime the empire was made larger indeed, but inferior, while otherwise it would have been less, but better. Now these brothers, Cain and Abel, were not both animated by the same earthly desires, nor did the murderer envy the other because he feared that, by both ruling, his own dominion would be curtailed—for Abel was not solicitous to rule in that city which his brother built—he was moved by that diabolical, envious hatred with which the evil regard the good, for no other reason than because they are good while themselves are evil. For the possession of goodness is by no means diminished by being shared with a partner either permanent or temporarily assumed; on the contrary, the possession of goodness is increased in proportion to the concord and charity of each of those who share it. In short, he who is unwilling to share this possession cannot have it; and he who is most willing to admit others to a share of it will have the greatest abundance to himself. The quarrel, then, between Romulus and Remus shows how the earthly city is divided against itself; that which fell out between Cain and Abel illustrated the hatred that subsists between the two cities, that of God and that of men. The wicked war with the wicked; the good also war with the wicked. But with the good, good men, or at least perfectly good men, cannot war; though, while only going on towards perfection, they war to this extent, that every good man resists others in those points in which he resists himself. And in each individual "the flesh lusteth against the spirit, and the spirit against the flesh." [5] This spiritual lusting, therefore, can be at war with

5. Gal. v. 17.

the carnal lust of another man; or carnal lust may be at war with the spiritual desires of another, in some such way as good and wicked men are at war; or, still more certainly, the carnal lusts of two men, good but not yet perfect, contend together, just as the wicked contend with the wicked, until the health of those who are under the treatment of grace attains final victory.

ᶜScripture may not be reckoned incredible when it relates that one man built a city at a time in which there seem to have been but four men upon earth, or rather indeed but three, after one brother slew the other—to wit, the first man the father of all, and Cain himself, and his son Enoch, by whose name the city was itself called. But they who are moved by this consideration forget to take into account that the writer of the sacred history does not necessarily mention all the men who might be alive at that time, but those only whom the scope of his work required him to name. The design of that writer (who in this matter was the instrument of the Holy Ghost) was to descend to Abraham through the successions of ascertained generations propagated from one man, and then to pass from Abraham's seed to the people of God, in whom, separated as they were from other nations, was prefigured and predicted all that relates to the city whose reign is eternal, and to its king and founder Christ, which things were foreseen in the Spirit as destined to come; yet neither is this object so effected as that nothing is said of the other society of men which we call the earthly city, but mention is made of it so far as seemed needful to enhance the glory of the heavenly city by contrast to its opposite.

c. *City of God*, **XV, 8.**

[d]Yet we are not to suppose that all that is recorded has some signification; but those things which have no signification of their own are interwoven for the sake of the things which are significant. It is only the ploughshare that cleaves the soil; but to effect this, other parts of the plough are requisite. It is only the strings in harps and other musical instruments which produce melodious sounds; but that they may do so, there are other parts of the instrument which are not indeed struck by those who sing, but are connected with the strings which are struck, and produce musical notes. So in this prophetic history some things are narrated which have no significance, but are, as it were, the framework to which the significant things are attached.

[e]Now, among the very many kingdoms of the earth into which, by earthly interest or lust, society is divided (which we call by the general name of the city of this world), we see that two, settled and kept distinct from each other both in time and place, have grown far more famous than the rest, first that of the Assyrians, then that of the Romans. First came the one, then the other. The former arose in the east, and, immediately on its close, the latter in the west. I may speak of other kingdoms and other kings as appendages of these.

Ninus, who succeeded his father Belus, the first king of Assyria, was already the second king of that kingdom when Abraham was born in the land of the Chaldees. There was also at that time a very small kingdom of Sicyon, with which, as from an ancient date, that most universally learned man Marcus Varro begins, in writing of the Roman

d. *City of God,* XVI, 2.
e. *Ibid.,* XVIII, 2.

race. For from these kings of Sicyon he passes to the Athenians, from them to the Latins, and from these to the Romans. Yet very little is related about these kingdoms, before the foundation of Rome, in comparison with that of Assyria. For although even Sallust, the Roman historian, admits that the Athenians were very famous in Greece, yet he thinks they were greater in fame than in fact. For in speaking of them he says, "The deeds of the Athenians, as I think, were very great and magnificent, but yet somewhat less than reported by fame. But because writers of great genius arose among them, the deeds of the Athenians were celebrated throughout the world as very great. Thus the virtue of those who did them was held to be as great as men of transcendent genius could represent it to be by the power of laudatory words." [6] This city also derived no small glory from literature and philosophy, the study of which chiefly flourished there. But as regards empire, none in the earliest times was greater than the Assyrian, or so widely extended. For when Ninus the son of Belus was king, he is reported to have subdued the whole of Asia, even to the boundaries of Libya, which as to number is called the third part, but as to size is found to be the half of the whole world. The Indians in the eastern regions were the only people over whom he did not reign; but after his death Semiramis his wife made war on them. Thus it came to pass that all the people and kings in those countries were subject to the kingdom and authority of the Assyrians, and did whatever they were commanded. Now Abraham was born in that kingdom among the Chaldees, in the time of Ninus. But since Grecian affairs are

6. Sallust, *Bel. Cat.* c. 8.

much better known to us than Assyrian, and those
who have diligently investigated the antiquity of
the Roman nation's origin have followed the order
of time through the Greeks to the Latins, and
from them to the Romans, who themselves are
Latins, we ought on this account, where it is needful, to mention the Assyrian kings, that it may appear how Babylon, like a first Rome, ran its course
along with the city of God, which is a stranger in
this world. But the things proper for insertion in
this work in comparing the two cities, that is, the
earthly and heavenly, ought to be taken mostly
from the Greek and Latin kingdoms, where Rome
herself is like a second Babylon.

At Abraham's birth, then, the second kings of
Assyria and Sicyon respectively were Ninus and
Europs, the first having been Belus and Ægialeus.
But when God promised Abraham, on his departure from Babylonia, that he should become a
great nation, and that in his seed all nations of the
earth should be blessed, the Assyrians had their
seventh king, the Sicyons their fifth; for the son of
Ninus reigned among them after his mother Semiramis, who is said to have been put to death by him
for attempting to defile him by incestuously lying
with him. Some think that she founded Babylon,
and indeed she may have founded it anew. But as
to when and by whom it was actually founded, we
read in Holy Writ: f"The whole earth was of one
lip, and all had one speech. And it came to pass,
as they journeyed from the east, that they found
a plain in the land of Shinar, and dwelt there. And
they said one to another, Come, and let us make
bricks and burn them thoroughly. And they had
bricks for stone, and slime for mortar. And they

f. *City of God,* XVI, 4.

said, Come, and let us build for ourselves a city, and a tower whose top shall reach the sky; and let us make us a name, before we be scattered abroad on the face of all the earth. And the Lord came down to see the city and the tower, which the children of men builded. And the Lord God said, Behold, the people is one, and they have all one language; and this they begin to do: and now nothing will be restrained from them, which they have imagined to do. Come, and let us go down, and confound there their language, that they may not understand one another's speech. And God scattered them thence on the face of all the earth: and they left off to build the city and the tower. Therefore the name of it is called Confusion; because the Lord did there confound the language of all the earth: and the Lord God scattered them thence on the face of all the earth." [7] This city, which was called Confusion, is the same as Babylon, whose wonderful construction Gentile history also notices. For Babylon means Confusion. Whence we conclude that the giant Nimrod was its founder, as had been hinted a little before, where Scripture, in speaking of him, says that the beginning of his kingdom was Babylon, that is, Babylon had a supremacy over the other cities as the metropolis and royal residence; although it did not rise to the grand dimensions designed by its proud and impious founder. The plan was to make it so high that it should reach the sky, whether this was meant of one tower which they intended to build higher than the others, or of all the towers, which might be signified by the singular number, as we speak of "the soldier," meaning the army, and of the frog or the locust, when we

7. Gen. xi. 1-9.

refer to the whole multitude of frogs and locusts in the plagues with which Moses smote the Egyptians.[8] But what did these vain and presumptuous men intend? How did they expect to raise this lofty mass against God, when they had built it above all the mountains and the clouds of the earth's atmosphere? What injury could any spiritual or material elevation do to God? The safe and true way to heaven is made by humility, which lifts up the heart to the Lord, not against Him; as this giant is said to have been a "hunter *against* the Lord." This has been misunderstood by some through the ambiguity of the Greek word, and they have translated it, not "against the Lord," but "before the Lord;" for ἐναντίον means both "before" and "against." In the Psalm this word is rendered, "Let us weep *before* the Lord our Maker."[9] The same word occurs in the book of Job, where it is written, "Thou hast broken into fury *against* the Lord."[10] And so this giant is to be recognised as a "hunter *against* the Lord." And what is meant by the term "hunter" but deceiver, oppressor, and destroyer of the animals of the earth? He and his people, therefore, erected this tower against the Lord, and so gave expression to their impious pride; and justly was their wicked intention punished by God, even though it was unsuccessful. But what was the nature of the punishment? As the tongue is the instrument of domination, in it pride was punished; so that man, who would not understand God when He issued His commands, should be misunderstood when he himself gave orders. Thus was that conspiracy disbanded, for

8. Ex. x.
9. Ps. xcv. 6.
10. Job xv. 13.

each man retired from those he could not understand, and associated with those whose speech was intelligible; and the nations were divided according to their languages, and scattered over the earth as seemed good to God, who accomplished this in ways hidden from and incomprehensible to us.

gWhat is recorded of the land of Shinar which belonged to Nimrod's kingdom, to wit, that Assur went forth from it and built Nineveh and the other cities mentioned with it, happened long after; but the Author of Holy Writ takes occasion to speak of it there on account of the grandeur of the Assyrian kingdom, which was wonderfully extended by Ninus son of Belus, and founder of the great city Nineveh, which was named after him, Nineveh, from Ninus. . . .

hTo be brief, that greatest of all kingdoms, the Assyrian, had its long duration brought to a close at the time of Rome's birth drawing nigh. For the Assyrian empire was transferred to the Medes after nearly thirteen hundred and five years, if we include the reign of Belus. iTroy had already been overthrown and its destruction was everywhere being sung and made well known even to boys; for it was signally published and spread abroad, both by its own greatness and by writers of excellent style.

jAfter the capture and destruction of Troy, Æneas, with twenty ships laden with the Trojan relics, came into Italy, when Latinus reigned there, Menestheus in Athens, Polyphidos in Sicyon, and

g. *City of God*, XVI, 3.
h. *Ibid.*, XVIII, 21.
i. *Ibid.*, XVIII, 16.
j. *Ibid.*, XVIII, 19-22.

Tautanos in Assyria, and Abdon was judge of the Hebrews. On the death of Latinus, Æneas reigned three years, the same kings continuing in the above-named places, except that Pelasgus was now king in Sicyon, and Sampson was judge of the Hebrews, who is thought to be Hercules, because of his wonderful strength. Now the Latins made Æneas one of their gods, because at his death he was nowhere to be found. The Sabines also placed among the gods their first king, Sancus, [Sangus], or Sanctus as some call him. At that time Codrus king of Athens exposed himself *incognito* to be slain by the Peloponnesian foes of that city, and so was slain. In this way, they say, he delivered his country. For the Peloponnesians had received a response from the oracle, that they should over-come the Athenians only on condition that they did not slay their king. Therefore he deceived them by appearing in a poor man's dress, and provok-ing them, by quarrelling, to murder him. Whence Virgil says, "Or the quarrels of Codrus." [11] And the Athenians worshipped this man as a god with sacrificial honours. The fourth king of the Latins was Silvius the son of Æneas, not by Creüsa, of whom Ascanius the third king was born, but by Lavinia the daughter of Latinus, and he is said to have been his posthumous child. Oneus was the twenty-ninth king of Assyria, Melanthus the six-teenth of the Athenians, and Eli the priest was judge of the Hebrews; and the kingdom of Sicyon then came to an end, after lasting, it is said, for nine hundred and fifty-nine years.

At that date those Latin kings began who were surnamed Silvii, having that surname, in addition to their proper name, from their predecessor, that

11. Virgil, *Eclogue,* v. ii.

son of Æneas who was called Silvius; just as, long afterward, the successors of Caesar Augustus were surnamed Caesars. . . . Then also the Athenians ceased to have kings, after the death of Codrus, and began to have a magistracy to rule the republic. . . . Then Alba was built among the Latins, from which thereafter the kings began to be styled kings not of the Latins, but of the Albans, although in the same Latium. . . .

After Æneas, whom they deified, Latium had eleven kings, none of whom was deified. But Aventinus, who was the twelfth after Æneas, having been laid low in war, and buried in that hill still called by his name, was added to the number of such gods as they made for themselves. Some, indeed, were unwilling to write that he was slain in battle, but said he was nowhere to be found, and that it was not from his name, but from the alighting of birds, that hill was called Aventinus.[12] After this no god was made in Latium except Romulus the founder of Rome. But two kings are found between these two, the first of whom I shall describe in the Virgilian verse:

"Next came that Procas, glory of the Trojan race." [13]

Now Procas reigned before Amulius. And Amulius had made his brother Numitor's daughter, Rhea by name, who was also called Ilia, a vestal virgin, who conceived twin sons by Mars, as they will have it, in that way honouring or excusing her adultery, adding as a proof that a she-wolf nursed the infants when exposed. For they think this kind of beast belongs to Mars, so that the she-wolf is

12. Varro, *De Lingua Latina*, v. 43.
13. *Æneid*, vi. 767.

believed to have given her teats to the infants, because she knew they were the sons of Mars her lord; although there are not wanting persons who say that when the crying babies lay exposed, they were first of all picked up by I know not what harlot, and sucked her breasts first (now harlots were called *lupæ,* she-wolves, from which their vile abodes are even yet called *lupanaria*), and that afterwards they came into the hands of the shepherd Faustulus, and were nursed by Acca his wife. Yet what wonder is it, if, to rebuke the king who had cruelly ordered them to be thrown into the water, God was pleased, after divinely delivering them from the water, to succour, by means of a wild beast giving milk, these infants by whom so great a city was to be founded? Amulius was succeeded in the Latian kingdom by his brother Numitor, the grandfather of Romulus; and Rome was founded in the first year of this Numitor, who from that time reigned along with his grandson Romulus.

In short, the city of Rome was founded, like another Babylon, and as it were the daughter of the former Babylon, by which God was pleased to conquer the whole world, and subdue it far and wide by bringing it into one fellowship of government and laws. For there were already powerful and brave peoples and nations trained to arms, who did not easily yield, and whose subjugation necessarily involved great danger and destruction as well as great and horrible labour. For when the Assyrian kingdom subdued almost all Asia, although this was done by fighting, yet the wars could not be very fierce or difficult, because the nations were as yet untrained to resist, and neither so many nor so great as afterward; forasmuch as,

ʳeatest and indeed universal flood, when
ꞑen escaped in Noah's ark, not much
_ ꞥan a thousand years had passed when
Ninus subdued all Asia with the exception of India.
But Rome did not with the same quickness and
facility wholly subdue all those nations of the east
and west which we see brought under the Roman
empire, because, in its gradual increase, in whatever direction it was extended, it found them
strong and warlike.

## C. *True Justice: Not of This World*

[a]Justinus, who wrote Greek or rather foreign
history in Latin, and briefly, like Trogus Pompeius
whom he followed, begins his work thus: "In the
beginning of the affairs of peoples and nations the
government was in the hands of kings, who were
raised to the height of this majesty not by courting
the people, but by the knowledge good men had of
their moderation. The people were held bound by
no laws; the decisions of the princes were instead
of laws. It was the custom to guard rather than to
extend the boundaries of the empire; and kingdoms
were kept within the bounds of each ruler's native
land. Ninus king of the Assyrians first of all,
through new lust of empire, changed the old and,
as it were, ancestral custom of nations. He first
made war on his neighbours, and wholly subdued
as far as to the frontiers of Libya the nations as
yet untrained to resist." And a little after he says:
"Ninus established by constant possession the
greatness of the authority he had gained. Having
mastered his nearest neighbours, he went on to
others, strengthened by the accession of forces,
and by making each fresh victory the instrument

a. *City of God*, IV, 6.

of that which followed, subdued the nations of the whole East." Now, with whatever fidelity to fact either he or Trogus may in general have written —for that they sometimes told lies is shown by other more trustworthy writers—yet it is agreed among other authors, that the kingdom of the Assyrians was extended far and wide by King Ninus. And it lasted so long, that the Roman empire has not yet attained the same age; for, as those write who have treated of chronological history, this kingdom endured for twelve hundred and forty years from the first year in which Ninus began to reign, until it was transferred to the Medes. But to make war on your neighbours, and thence to proceed to others, and through mere lust of dominion to crush and subdue people who do you no harm, what else is this to be called than great robbery?

ᵇIndeed, without justice, what are kingdoms but great robberies? For what are robberies themselves, but little kingdoms? The band itself is made up of men; it is ruled by the authority of a prince, it is knit together by the pact of the confederacy; the booty is divided by the law agreed on. If, by the admittance of abandoned men, this evil increases to such a degree that it holds places, fixes abodes, takes possession of cities, and subdues peoples, it assumes the more plainly the name of a kingdom, because the reality is now manifestly conferred on it, not by the removal of covetousness, but by the addition of impunity. Indeed, that was an apt and true reply which was given to Alexander the Great by a pirate who had been seized. For when that king had asked the man what he meant by keeping hostile possession of the

b. *City of God*, IV, 4.

sea, he answered with bold pride, "What thou meanest by seizing the whole earth; but because I do it with a petty ship, I am called a robber, whilst thou who dost it with a great fleet art styled emperor." [1]

ᶜYet, at the end of the second book of Cicero's *De Republica*, Scipio says: "As, among the different sounds which proceed from lyres, flutes, and the human voice, there must be maintained a certain harmony which a cultivated ear cannot endure to hear disturbed or jarring, but which may be elicited in full and absolute concord by the modulation even of voices very unlike one another; so, where reason is allowed to modulate the diverse elements of the state, there is obtained a perfect concord from the upper, lower, and middle classes as from various sounds; and what musicians call harmony in singing, is concord in matters of state, which is the strictest bond and best security of any republic, and which by no ingenuity can be retained where justice has become extinct." Then, when he had expatiated somewhat more fully, and had more copiously illustrated the benefits of its presence and the ruinous effects of its absence upon a state, Pilus, one of the company present at the discussion, struck in and demanded that the question should be more thoroughly sifted, and that the subject of justice should be freely discussed for the sake of ascertaining what truth there was in the maxim which was then becoming daily more current, that "the republic cannot be governed without injustice." Scipio expressed his willingness to have this maxim discussed and sifted,

1. Nonius Marcell. borrows this anecdote from Cicero, *De Repub.* iii.
   c. *City of God,* II, 21.

and gave it as his opinion that it was baseless, and
that no progress could be made in discussing the
republic unless it was established, not only that
this maxim, that "the republic cannot be governed
without injustice," was false, but also that the
truth is, that it cannot be governed without the
most absolute justice. And the discussion of this
question, being deferred till the next day, is carried on in the third book with great animation. For
Pilus himself undertook to defend the position that
the republic cannot be governed without injustice,
at the same time being at special pains to clear
himself of any real participation in that opinion.
He advocated with great keenness the cause of injustice against justice, and endeavoured by plausible reasons and examples to demonstrate that the
former is beneficial, the latter useless, to the republic. Then, at the request of the company, Læ-
lius attempted to defend justice, and strained every
nerve to prove that nothing is so hurtful to a state
as injustice; and that without justice a republic
can neither be governed, nor even continue to
exist.

When this question has been handled to the satisfaction of the company, Scipio reverts to the
original thread of discourse, and repeats with commendation his own brief definition of a republic,
that it is the weal of the people. "The people" he
defines as being not every assemblage or mob, but
an assemblage associated by a common acknowledgment of law, and by a community of interests.
Then he shows the use of definition in debate; and
from these definitions of his own he gathers that
a republic, or "weal of the people," then exists
only when it is well and justly governed, whether
by a monarch, or an aristocracy, or by the whole

people. But when the monarch is unjust, or, as the Greeks say, a tyrant; or the aristocrats are unjust, and form a faction; or the people themselves are unjust, and become, as Scipio for want of a better name calls them, themselves the tyrant, then the republic is not only blemished (as had been proved the day before), but by legitimate deduction from those definitions, it altogether ceases to be. For it could not be the people's weal when a tyrant factiously lorded it over the state; neither would the people be any longer a people if it were unjust, since it would no longer answer the definition of a people—"an assemblage associated by a common acknowledgment of law, and by a community of interests."

Cicero himself, speaking not in the person of Scipio or any one else, but uttering his own sentiments, uses the following language in the beginning of the fifth book, after quoting a line from the poet Ennius, in which he said, "Rome's severe morality and her citizens are her safeguard." "This verse," says Cicero, "seems to me to have all the sententious truthfulness of an oracle. For neither would the citizens have availed without the morality of the community, nor would the morality of the commons without outstanding men have availed either to establish or so long to maintain in vigour so grand a republic with so wide and just an empire. Accordingly, before our day, the hereditary usages formed our foremost men, and they on their part retained the usages and institutions of their fathers. But our age, receiving the republic as a *chef-d'œuvre* of another age which has already begun to grow old, has not merely neglected to restore the colours of the original, but has not even been at the pains to preserve so much as the general outline and most outstanding features. For what survives of that primitive morality which the poet called Rome's safeguard? It is so obsolete and forgotten, that, far from practising it, one does not even know it. And of the citizens what shall I say? Morality has perished through poverty of great men; a poverty for which we must not only assign a reason, but for the guilt of which we must answer as criminals charged with a capital crime. For it is through our vices, and not by any mishap, that we retain only the name of a republic, and have long since lost the reality."

This is the confession of Cicero, long indeed after the death of Africanus, whom he introduced as an interlocutor in his work *De Republica*. . . . But Rome's admirers have need to inquire whether, even in the days of primitive men and morals, true justice flourished in it; or was it not perhaps even then, to use the casual expression of Cicero, rather a coloured painting than the living reality? If God will, I mean in its own place to show that—according to the definitions in which Cicero himself, using Scipio as his mouthpiece, briefly propounded what a republic is, and what a people is, and according to many testimonies, both of his own lips and of those who took part in that same debate—Rome never was a republic, because true justice had never a place in it.

ᵈAway with deceitful masks, with deluding whitewashes; look at the naked deeds: weigh them naked, judge them naked! ᵉSallust says that "equity and virtue prevailed among the Romans not more by force of laws than of nature." [2] I presume it is

d. *City of God*, III, 14.
e. *Ibid.*, II, 17-18.
2. Sallust, *Cat. Con.* ix.

to this inborn equity and goodness of disposition
we are to ascribe the rape of the Sabine women.
What, indeed, could be more equitable and virtuous, than to carry off by force, as each man was
fit, and without their parents' consent, girls who
were strangers and guests, and who had been de-
coyed and entrapped by the pretence of a spectacle! If the Sabines were wrong to deny their daughters when the Romans asked for them, was it not
a greater wrong in the Romans to carry them off
after that denial? The Romans might more justly
have waged war against the neighbouring nation
for having refused their daughters in marriage
when they first sought them, than for having demanded them back when they had stolen them.
War should have been proclaimed at first: it was
then that Mars should have helped his warlike son,
that he might by force of arms avenge the injury
done him by the refusal of marriage, and might
also thus win the women he desired. There might
have been some appearance of "right of war" in a
victor carrying off, in virtue of this right, the virgins
who had been without any show of right denied
him; whereas there was no "right of peace" en-
titling him to carry off those who were not given
to him, and to wage an unjust war with their justly
enraged parents. One happy circumstance was indeed connected with this act of violence, viz., that
though it was commemorated by the games of the
circus, yet even this did not constitute it a precedent in the city or realm of Rome. If one would
find fault with the results of this act, it must rather
be on the ground that the Romans made Romulus
a god in spite of his perpetrating this iniquity; for
one cannot reproach them with making this deed
any kind of precedent for the rape of women.

Again, I presume it was due to this natural equity and virtue, that after the expulsion of King Tarquin, whose son had violated Lucretia, Junius Brutus the consul forced Lucius Tarquinius Collatinus, Lucretia's husband and his own colleague, a good and innocent man, to resign his office and go into banishment, on the one sole charge that he was of the name and blood of the Tarquins. This injustice was perpetrated with the approval, or at least connivance, of the people, who had themselves raised to the consular office both Collatinus and Brutus. Another instance of this equity and virtue is found in their treatment of Marcus Camillus. This eminent man, after he had rapidly conquered the Veians, at that time the most formidable of Rome's enemies, and who had maintained a ten years' war, in which the Roman army had suffered the usual calamities attendant on bad generalship, after he had restored security to Rome, which had begun to tremble for its safety, and after he had taken the wealthiest city of the enemy, had charges brought against him by the malice of those that envied his success, and by the insolence of the tribunes of the people; and seeing that the city bore him no gratitude for preserving it, and that he would certainly be condemned, he went into exile, and even in his absence was fined 10,000 *asses*. Shortly after, however, his ungrateful country had again to seek his protection from the Gauls. But I cannot now mention all the shameful and iniquitous acts with which Rome was agitated, when the aristocracy attempted to subject the people, and the people resented their encroachments, and the advocates of either party were actuated rather by the love of victory than by any equitable or virtuous consideration.

I will therefore pause, and adduce the testimony of Sallust himself, whose words in praise of the Romans (that "equity and virtue prevailed among them not more by force of laws than of nature") have given occasion to this discussion. He was referring to that period immediately after the expulsion of the kings, in which the city became great in an incredibly short space of time. And yet this same writer acknowledges in the first book of his history, in the very exordium of his work, that even at that time, when a very brief interval had elapsed after the government had passed from kings to consuls, the more powerful men began to act unjustly, and occasioned the defection of the people from the patricians, and other disorders in the city. For after Sallust had stated that the Romans enjoyed greater harmony and a purer state of society between the second and third Punic wars than at any other time, and that the cause of this was not their love of good order, but their fear lest the peace they had with Carthage might be broken (this also Nasica contemplated when he opposed the destruction of Carthage, for he supposed that fear would tend to repress wickedness, and to preserve wholesome ways of living), he then goes on to say: "Yet, after the destruction of Carthage, discord, avarice, ambition, and the other vices which are commonly generated by prosperity, more than ever increased." If they "increased," and that "more than ever," then already they had appeared, and had been increasing. And so Sallust adds this reason for what he said. "For," he says, "the oppressive measures of the powerful, and the consequent secessions of the plebs from the patricians, and other civil dissensions, had existed from the first, and affairs were

administered with equity and well-tempered justice
for no longer a period than the short time after the
expulsion of the kings, while the city was occupied
with the serious Tuscan war and Tarquin's vengeance." You see how, even in that brief period after
the expulsion of the kings, fear, he acknowledges,
was the cause of the interval of equity and good
order. They were afraid, in fact, of the war which
Tarquin waged against them, after he had been
driven from the throne and the city, and had allied
himself with the Tuscans. But observe what he
adds: "After that, the patricians treated the people
as their slaves, ordering them to be scourged or
beheaded just as the kings had done, driving them
from their holdings, and harshly tyrannizing over
those who had no property to lose. The people,
overwhelmed by these oppressive measures, and
most of all by exorbitant usury, and obliged to
contribute both money and personal service to the
constant wars, at length took arms, and seceded
to Mount Aventine and Mount Sacer, and thus
obtained for themselves tribunes and protective
laws. But it was only the second Punic war that
put an end on both sides to discord and strife."
You see what kind of men the Romans were, even
so early as a few years after the expulsion of the
kings; and it is of these men he says, that "equity
and virtue prevailed among them not more by
force of law than of nature."

Now, if these were the days in which the Roman
republic shows fairest and best, what are we to
say or think of the succeeding age, when, to use
the words of the same historian, "changing little
by little from the fair and virtuous city it was, it
became utterly wicked and dissolute?" This was,
as he mentions, after the destruction of Carthage.

Sallust's brief sum and sketch of this period may be read in his own history, in which he shows how the profligate manners which were propagated by prosperity resulted at last even in civil wars. He says: "And from this time the primitive manners, instead of undergoing an insensible alteration as hitherto they had done, were swept away as by a torrent: the young men were so depraved by luxury and avarice, that it may justly be said that no father had a son who could either preserve his own patrimony, or keep his hands off other men's." Sallust adds a number of particulars about the vices of Sylla, and the debased condition of the republic in general; and other writers make similar observations, though in much less striking language.

ʹThis, then, is the place where I should return to Cicero's argument, and explain, as briefly and clearly as possible, that if we are to accept the definitions laid down by Scipio in his *De Republica,* there never was a Roman republic; for he briefly defines a republic as the weal of the people. And if this definition be true, there never was a Roman republic, for the people's weal was never attained among the Romans. For the people, according to his definition, is an assemblage associated by a common acknowledgment of right and by a community of interests. And what he means by a common acknowledgment of right he explains at large, showing that a republic cannot be administered without justice. Where, therefore, there is no true justice there can be no right. For that which is done by right is justly done, and what is unjustly done cannot be done by right. For the unjust inventions of men are neither to be considered

f. *City of God,* XIX, 21-24.

nor spoken of as rights; for even they themselves say that right is that which flows from the fountain of justice, and deny the definition which is commonly given by those who misconceive the matter, that right is that which is useful to the stronger party. Thus, where there is not true justice there can be no assemblage of men associated by a common acknowledgment of right, and therefore there can be no people, as defined by Scipio or Cicero; and if no people, then no weal of the people, but only of some promiscuous multitude unworthy of the name of people. Consequently, if the republic is the weal of the people, and there is no people if it be not associated by a common acknowledgment of right, and if there is no right where there is no justice, then most certainly it follows that there is no republic where there is no justice.

Further, justice is that virtue which gives every one his due. Where, then, is the justice of man, when he deserts the true God and yields himself to impure demons? Is this to give every one his due? Or is he who keeps back a piece of ground from the purchaser, and gives it to a man who has no right to it, unjust, while he who keeps back himself from the God who made him, and serves wicked spirits, is just?

This same book, *De Republica,* advocates the cause of justice against injustice with great force and keenness. The pleading for injustice against justice was first heard, and it was asserted (as we noted earlier) that without injustice a republic could neither increase nor even subsist, for it was laid down as an absolutely unassailable position that it is unjust for some men to rule and some to serve; and yet the imperial city to which the republic belongs cannot rule her provinces without having recourse to this injustice. It was replied in behalf of justice, that this ruling of the provinces is just, because servitude may be advantageous to the provincials, and is so when rightly administered —that is to say, when lawless men are prevented from doing harm. And further, as they became worse and worse so long as they were free, they will improve by subjection. To confirm this reasoning, there is added an eminent example drawn from nature: for "why," it is asked, "does God rule man, the soul the body, the reason the passions and other vicious parts of the soul?" This example leaves no doubt that, to some, servitude is useful; and, indeed, to serve God is useful to all. And it is when the soul serves God that it exercises a right control over the body; and in the soul itself the reason must be subject to God if it is to govern as it ought the passions and other vices. Hence, when a man does not serve God, what justice can we ascribe to him, since in this case his soul cannot exercise a just control over the body, nor his reason over his vices? And if there is no justice in such an individual, certainly there can be none in a community composed of such persons. Here, therefore, there is not that common acknowledgment of right which makes an assemblage of men a people whose affairs we call a republic. And why need I speak of the advantageousness, the common participation in which, according to the definition, makes a people? For although, if you choose to regard the matter attentively, you will see that there is nothing advantageous to those who live godlessly, as every one lives who does not serve God but demons, whose wickedness you

may measure by their desire to receive the worship of men though they are most impure spirits,
yet what I have said of the common acknowledgment of right is enough to demonstrate that, according to the above definition, there can be no
people, and therefore no republic, where there is
no justice. For if they assert that in their republic
the Romans did not serve unclean spirits, but good
and holy gods, must we therefore again reply to
this evasion, though already we have said enough,
and more than enough, to expose it? He must be an
uncommonly stupid, or a shamelessly contentious
person, who . . . can yet question whether the
Romans served wicked and impure demons. But,
not to speak of their character, it is written in the
law of the true God, "He that sacrificeth unto
any god save unto the Lord only, he shall be
utterly destroyed." [3] He, therefore, who uttered
so menacing a commandment decreed that no
worship should be given either to good or bad
gods.

And where there is not that justice whereby the
one supreme God rules the obedient city according to His grace, so that it sacrifices to none but
Him, and whereby, in all the citizens of this obedient city, the soul consequently rules the body and
reason the vices in the rightful order, so that, as
the individual just man, so also the community
and people of the just, live by faith, which works
by love, that love whereby man loves God as He
ought to be loved, and his neighbour as himself—
there, I say, there is not an assemblage associated
by a common acknowledgment of right, and by a
community of interests. But if there is not this,

3. Ex. xxii. 20.

there is not a people, if our definition be true, and therefore there is no republic; for where there is no people there can be no republic.

But if we discard this definition of a people, and, assuming another, say that a people is an assemblage of reasonable beings bound together by a common agreement as to the objects of their love, then, in order to discover the character of any people, we have only to observe what they love. Yet whatever it loves, if only it is an assemblage of reasonable beings and not of beasts, and is bound together by an agreement as to the objects of love, it is reasonably called a people; and it will be a superior people in proportion as it is bound together by higher interests, inferior in proportion as it is bound together by lower. According to this definition of ours, the Roman people is a people, and its weal is without doubt a commonwealth or republic. But what its tastes were in its early and subsequent days, and how it declined into sanguinary seditions and then to social and civil wars, and so burst asunder or rotted off the bond of concord in which the health of a people consists, history shows. . . . Yet I would not on this account say either that it was not a people, or that its administration was not a republic, so long as there remains an assemblage of reasonable beings bound together by a common agreement as to the objects of love. But what I say of this people and of this republic I must be understood to think and say of the Athenians or any Greek state, of the Egyptians, of the early Assyrian Babylon, and of every other nation, great or small, which had a public government. For, in general, the city of the ungodly, which did not obey the command of God that it should offer no sacrifice save to Him alone, and which, therefore, could not give to the soul its proper command over the body, nor to the reason its just authority over the vices, is void of true justice.

For though the soul may seem to rule the body admirably, and the reason the vices, if the soul and reason do not themselves obey God, as God has commanded them to serve Him, they have no proper authority over the body and the vices. For what kind of mistress of the body and the vices can that mind be which is ignorant of the true God, and which, instead of being subject to His authority, is prostituted to the corrupting influences of the most vicious demons? It is for this reason that the virtues which it seems to itself to possess, and by which it restrains the body and the vices that it may obtain and keep what it desires, are rather vices than virtues so long as there is no reference to God in the matter. For although some suppose that virtues which have a reference only to themselves, and are desired only on their own account, are yet true and genuine virtues, the fact is that even then they are inflated with pride, and are therefore to be reckoned vices rather than virtues.

ᵍThus, in fact, true justice has no existence save in that republic whose founder and ruler is Christ, if at least any choose to call this a republic; and indeed we cannot deny that it is the people's weal. But if perchance this name, which has become familiar in other connections, be considered alien to our common parlance, we may at all events say that in this city is true justice; the city of which Holy Scripture says, "Glorious things are said of thee, O city of God."

g. *City of God*, II, 21.

# CHAPTER II

## THE RISE AND FALL OF NATIONS

### A. *An End to All Earthly Kingdoms*

[a]I am aware what ability is requisite to persuade the proud how great is the virtue of humility, which raises us, not by a quite human arrogance, but by a divine grace, above all earthly dignities that totter on this shifting scene. For the King and Founder of this city of which we speak has in Scripture uttered to His people a dictum of the divine law in these words: "God resisteth the proud, but giveth grace unto the humble." [1] But this, which is God's prerogative, the inflated ambition of a proud spirit also affects, and dearly loves that this be numbered among its attributes:

To spare the lowly, and strike down the proud.[2] And therefore, as the plan of this work we have undertaken requires, and as occasion offers, we must speak also of the earthly city, which, though it be mistress of the nations, is itself ruled by its lust of rule.

For to this earthly city belong the enemies against whom I have to defend the city of God. Many of them, indeed, being reclaimed from their ungodly error, have become sufficiently creditable

a. *City of God*, I, Preface-1.
1. Jas. iv. 6 and I Pet. v. 5.
2. Virgil, *Æneid*, vi. 854.

citizens of this city; but many are so inflamed with hatred against it, and are so ungrateful to its Redeemer for His signal benefits, as to forget that they would now be unable to utter a single word to its prejudice, had they not found in its sacred places, as they fled from the enemy's steel, that life in which they now boast themselves. Are not those very Romans, who were spared by the barbarians through their respect for Christ, become enemies to the name of Christ? The reliquaries of the martyrs and the churches of the apostles bear witness to this; for in the sack of the city they were open sanctuary for all who fled to them, whether Christian or Pagan. To their very threshold the bloodthirsty enemy raged; there his murderous fury owned a limit. Thither did such of the enemy as had any pity convey those to whom they had given quarter, lest any less mercifully disposed might fall upon them. And, indeed, when even those murderers who everywhere else showed themselves pitiless came to these spots where that was forbidden which the licence of war permitted in every other place, their furious rage for slaughter was bridled, and their eagerness to take prisoners was quenched. Thus escaped multitudes who now reproach the Christian religion, and impute to Christ the ills that have befallen their city; but the preservation of their own life—a boon which they owe to the respect entertained for Christ by the barbarians—they attribute not to our Christ, but to their own good luck. They ought rather, had they any right perceptions, to attribute the severities and hardships inflicted by their enemies, to that divine providence which is wont to reform the depraved manners of men by chastisement, and which exercises with similar afflictions the righteous and praiseworthy—either translating them, when they have passed through the trial, to a better world, or detaining them still on earth for ulterior purposes. And they ought to attribute it to the spirit of these Christian times, that, contrary to the custom of war, these blood-thirsty barbarians spared them, and spared them for Christ's sake, whether this mercy was actually shown in promiscuous places, or in those places specially dedicated to Christ's name, and of which the very largest were selected as sanctuaries, that full scope might thus be given to the expansive compassion which desired that a large multitude might find shelter there. Therefore ought they to give God thanks, and with sincere confession flee for refuge to His name, that so they may escape the punishment of eternal fire—they who with lying lips took upon them this name, that they might escape the punishment of present destruction. For of those whom you see insolently and shamelessly insulting the servants of Christ, there are numbers who would not have escaped that destruction and slaughter had they not pretended that they themselves were Christ's servants. Yet now, in ungrateful pride and most impious madness, and at the risk of being punished in everlasting darkness, they perversely oppose that name under which they fraudulently protected themselves for the sake of enjoying the light of this brief life.

[b]See, they say, in Christian times it is that Rome perishes. Perhaps, Rome is not perishing; perhaps she is only scourged, not utterly destroyed; perhaps she is chastened, not brought to nought. It may be so; Rome will not perish, if the Romans

b. *Sermons,* XXXI, 9.

do not perish. And perish they will not if they praise God; perish they will, if they blaspheme Him. For what is Rome, but the Romans? For the question is not of her wood and stones, of her lofty insulated palaces, and all her spacious walls. All this was made only on this condition that it should fall some other day. When man built it, he laid stone on stone; and when man destroyed it, he removed stone from stone. Man made it, man destroyed it. Is any injury done to Rome, because it is said, *She is falling?* No, not to Rome, but to her builder perhaps. Do we then its builder any injury, because we say, Rome is falling, which Romulus built? This world itself will be burnt with fire, which God built. But neither does what man has made fall to ruin, except when God wills it; nor what God has made, except when He wills. For if the work of man fall not without God's will, how can God's work fall by the will of man? Yet God both made the world that was one day to fall for thee; and therefore made He thee as one who was one day to die. Man himself, the city's ornament, man himself the city's inhabitant, ruler, governor, comes on this condition that he may go, is born on this condition that he may die, entered into the world on this condition that he may pass away; *Heaven and earth shall pass away:*[3] what wonder ᶜthat the kingdoms of the earth are perishing? Therefore hath a heavenly kingdom been promised thee, that thou mightest not perish with the kingdoms of the earth. For it was foretold, foretold distinctly, that they should perish. For we cannot deny that it was foretold. Thy Lord for Whom thou art waiting, hath told thee, *Nation*

3. Matt. xxiv. 35.
c. Sermons, LV, 9-13.

*shall rise up against nation, and kingdom against kingdom.*[4] The kingdoms of the earth have their changes; He will come of Whom it is said, *and of His kingdom there shall be no end.*[5]

They who have promised this to earthly kingdoms have not been guided by truth, but have lied through flattery. A certain poet of theirs has introduced Jupiter speaking, and he says of the Romans;

> To them no bounds of empire I assign,
> Nor term of years to their immortal line.[6]

Most certainly truth makes no such answer. This empire which thou hast given "without term of years," is it on earth, or in heaven? On earth assuredly. And even if it were in heaven, yet *heaven and earth shall pass away.*[7] Those things shall pass away which God hath Himself made; how much more rapidly shall that pass away which Romulus founded! Perhaps if we had a mind to press Virgil on this point, and tauntingly to ask him why he said it; he would take us aside privately, and say to us, "I know this as well as you, but what could I do who was selling words to the Romans, if by this kind of flattery I did not promise something which was false? And yet even in this very instance I have been cautious, when I said, "I assigned to them an empire without term of years," I introduced their Jupiter to say it. I did not utter this falsehood in my own person, but put upon Jupiter the character of untruthfulness: as the god was false, the poet was

4. Mark xiii. 8.
5. Luke i. 33.
6. Virgil, *Æneid,* i, 282-3.
7. Luke xxi. 33.

false. For would ye know that I well knew the
truth of it? In another place, when I did not
introduce this stone, called Jupiter, but spoke in
my own person, I said,

Th' impending ruin of the Roman state.[8]

See how I spoke of the impending ruin of the
state. I spoke of its impending ruin. I did not
suppress it." When he spoke in truth he was not
silent as to its ruin; when in flattery, he promised
that it should abide for ever.

Let us not then faint, my Brethren: an end
there will be to all earthly kingdoms. If that end
be now, God knoweth. For peradventure it is not
yet, and we, through some infirmity, or merciful-
ness, or misery, are wishing that it may not be yet;
nevertheless will it not therefore some day be? Fix
your hope in God, desire the things eternal, wait
for the things eternal. Ye are Christians, Brethren,
we are all Christians. Christ did not come down
into the flesh that we might live softly; let us endure rather than love the things present; manifest
is the harm of adversity, deceitful is the soft blan-
dishment of prosperity. Fear the sea, even when it
is a calm. On no account let us hear in vain, *Let
us lift up our hearts*. Why place we our hearts in
the earth, when we see that the earth is being
turned upside down? We cannot but exhort you,
that ye may have something to say and answer in
defence of your hope against the deriders and
blasphemers of the Christian name. Let no one by
his murmuring turn you back from waiting for the
things to come. All who by reason of these adversities blaspheme our Christ, are the *scorpion's*

8. *Georg.* ii. 489.

tail. Let us put our egg under the wings of that Hen of the Gospel, Which crieth out to that false and abandoned city, *O Jerusalem, Jerusalem, how often would I have gathered thy children together, even as a hen her chickens, and thou wouldest not!* Let it not be said to us, *How often would I, and thou wouldest not!* [9] For that Hen is the Divine Wisdom; but It assumed flesh to accommodate Itself to its chickens. See the hen with feathers bristling, with wings hanging down, with voice broken, and tremulous, and faint, and languid, accommodating herself to her little ones. Our egg then, that is, our hope, let us place beneath the wings of this Hen.

Ye have noticed, it may be, how a hen will tear a scorpion in pieces. O then that the Hen of the Gospel would tear in pieces and devour these blasphemers, creeping out of their holes, and inflicting hurtful stings, would pass them over into Her Body, and turn them into an egg. Let them not be angry; we seem to be excited; but we do not return curses for curses. *We are cursed, and we bless, being defamed, we intreat.*[10] But "let him not speak of Rome, it is said of me: O that he would hold his tongue about Rome;" as though I were insulting it, and not rather entreating the Lord for it, and exhorting you all, unworthy as I am. Be it far from me to insult it! The Lord avert this from my heart, and from the grief of my conscience. Have we not had many brethren there? have we not still? Does not a large portion of the pilgrim city Jerusalem live there? has it not endured there temporal afflictions? but it has not lost the things eternal. What can I say then, when

9. Matt. xxiii. 37.
10. I Cor. iv. 12-13.

I speak of Rome, but that that is false, which they say of our Christ, that He is Rome's destroyer, and that the gods of wood and stone were her defenders? Add what is more costly, "gods of brass." Add what is costlier still, "of silver and gold:" the *idols of the nations are silver and gold.*[11] He did not say, *stone;* he did not say, *wood;* he did not say, *clay;* but, what they value highly, *silver and gold.* Yet these silver and golden idols *have eyes, and see not.* The gods of gold, of wood, are as regards their costliness unequal; but as to *having eyes, and seeing not,* they are equal. See to what sort of guardians learned men have entrusted Rome, to those *who have eyes, and see not.* Or if they were able to preserve Rome, why did they first perish themselves? They say; "Rome perished at the same time." Nevertheless they perished. "No," they say, "they did not perish themselves, but their statues." Well, how then could they keep your houses, who were not able to keep their own statues? Alexandria once lost such gods as these. Constantinople some time since, ever since it was made a grand city, for it was made so by a Christian Emperor, lost its false gods; and yet it has increased, and still increases, and remains. And remain it will, as long as God pleases. For we do not to this city either promise an eternal duration because we say this. Carthage remains now in its possession of the Name of Christ, yet once on a time its goddess Cælestis was overthrown; because celestial she was not, but terrestrial.

And that which they say is not true, that immediately on losing her gods Rome has been taken and ruined. It is not true at all; their im-

11. Ps. cxv. 4.

ages were overthrown before; and even so were
the Goths with Rhadagaisus conquered. Remember, my Brethren, remember; it is no long time
since, but a few years, call it to mind. When all
the images in the city of Rome had been overthrown, Rhadagaisus king of the Goths came
with a large army, much more numerous than
that of Alaric was. Rhadagaisus was a Pagan;
he sacrificed to Jupiter every day. Everywhere
it was announced, that Rhadagaisus did not cease
from sacrificing. Then said they all, "Lo, we do
not sacrifice, he does sacrifice, we, who are not
allowed to sacrifice must be conquered by him who
does sacrifice." But God making proof that not
even temporal deliverance, nor the preservation of
these earthly kingdoms, consist in these sacrifices,
Rhadagaisus, by the Lord's help, was marvellously
overcome. Afterwards came other Goths who did
not sacrifice, they came, who though they were
not Catholics in the Christian faith, were yet
hostile and opposed to idols, and they took Rome;
they conquered those who put their trust in idols,
who were still seeking after the idols they had lost,
and desiring still to sacrifice to the lost gods. And
amongst them too were some of our brethren, and
these were afflicted also: but they had learnt to
say, *I will bless the Lord at all times*.[12] They were
involved in the afflictions of their earthly kingdom: but they lost not the kingdom of heaven;
yea, rather, they were made the better for obtaining it through the exercise of tribulations. And if
they did not in their tribulations blaspheme, they
came out as sound vessels from the furnace, and
were filled with the blessing of the Lord. Whereas
those blasphemers, who follow and long after

12. Ps. xxxiv. 1.

earthly things, who place their hope in earthly things, when these they have lost, whether they will or no, what shall they retain? where shall they abide? Nothing without, nothing within; an empty coffer, an emptier conscience.

ᵈThe whole family of God, most high and most true, has therefore a consolation of its own—a consolation which cannot deceive, and which has in it a surer hope than the tottering and falling affairs of earth can afford. They will not refuse the discipline of this temporal life, in which they are schooled for life eternal; nor will they lament their experience of it, for the good things of earth they use as pilgrims who are not detained by them, and its ills either prove or improve them. As for those who insult them in their trials, and when ills befall them say, "Where is thy God?" [13] we may ask them where their gods are when they suffer the very calamities for the sake of avoiding which they worship their gods, or maintain they ought to be worshipped; for the family of Christ is furnished with its reply: our God is everywhere present, wholly everywhere; not confined to any place. He can be present unperceived, and be absent without moving; when He exposes us to adversities, it is either to prove our perfections or correct our imperfections; and in return for our patient endurance of the sufferings of time, He reserves for us an everlasting reward.

ᵉBut the worshippers and admirers of pagan gods delight in imitating their scandalous iniquities, and are nowise concerned that the republic be less depraved and licentious. Only let it remain

d. *City of God*, I, 29.
13. Ps. xlii. 10.
e. *City of God*, II, 20.

undefeated, they say, only let it flourish and abound in resources; let it be glorious by its victories, or still better, secure in peace; and what matters it to us? This is our concern, that every man be able to increase his wealth so as to supply his daily prodigalities, and so that the powerful may subject the weak for their own purposes. Let the poor court the rich for a living, and that under their protection they may enjoy a sluggish tranquillity; and let the rich abuse the poor as their dependants, to minister to their pride. Let the people applaud not those who protect their interests, but those who provide them with pleasure. Let no severe duty be commanded, no impurity forbidden. Let kings estimate their prosperity, not by the righteousness, but by the servility of their subjects. Let the provinces stand loyal to the kings, not as moral guides, but as lords of their possessions and purveyors of their pleasures; not with a hearty reverence, but a crooked and servile fear. Let the laws take cognizance rather of the injury done to another man's property, than of that done to one's own person. If a man be a nuisance to his neighbour, or injure his property, family, or person, let him be actionable; but in his own affairs let every one with impunity do what he will in company with his own family, and with those who willingly join him. Let there be a plentiful supply of public prostitutes for every one who wishes to use them, but specially for those who are too poor to keep one for their private use. Let there be erected houses of the largest and most ornate description: in these let there be provided the most sumptuous banquets, where every one who pleases may, by day or night, play, drink, vomit, dissipate. Let there be everywhere heard the rustling of dancers, the loud, immodest laughter of the theatre; let a succession of the most cruel and the most voluptuous pleasures maintain a perpetual excitement. If such happiness is distasteful to any, let him be branded as a public enemy; and if any attempt to modify or put an end to it, let him be silenced, banished, put an end to. Let these be reckoned the true gods, who procure for the people this condition of things, and preserve it when once possessed. Let them be worshipped as they wish; let them demand whatever games they please, from or with their own worshippers; only let them secure that such felicity be not imperilled by foe, plague, or disaster of any kind.

'If the famous Scipio Nasica were now alive, who was once your pontiff, and was unanimously chosen by the senate, when, in the panic created by the Punic war, they sought for the best citizen to entertain the Phrygian goddess, he would curb this shamelessness of yours, though you would perhaps scarcely dare to look upon the countenance of such a man. For why in your calamities do you complain of Christianity, unless because you desire to enjoy your luxurious licence unrestrained, and to lead an abandoned and profligate life without the interruption of any uneasiness or disaster? For certainly your desire for peace, and prosperity, and plenty is not prompted by any purpose of using these blessings honestly, that is to say, with moderation, sobriety, temperance, and piety; for your purpose rather is to run riot in an endless variety of sottish pleasures, and thus to generate from your prosperity a moral pestilence which will prove a thousandfold more

f. *City of God*, I, 30.

disastrous than the fiercest enemies. It was such a calamity as this that Scipio, your chief pontiff, your best man in the judgment of the whole senate, feared when he refused to agree to the destruction of Carthage, Rome's rival; and opposed Cato, who advised its destruction. He feared security, that enemy of weak minds, and he perceived that a wholesome fear would be a fit guardian for the citizens. And he was not mistaken: the event proved how wisely he had spoken.

ᵍO infatuated men, what is this blindness, or rather madness, which possesses you? How is it that while, as we hear, even the eastern nations are bewailing your ruin, and while powerful states in the most remote parts of the earth are mourning your fall as a public calamity, ye yourselves should be crowding to the theatres, should be pouring into them and filling them; and, in short, be playing a madder part now than ever before? This was the foul plague-spot, this the wreck of virtue and honour that Scipio sought to preserve you from when he prohibited the construction of theatres; this was his reason for desiring that you might still have an enemy to fear, seeing as he did how easily prosperity would corrupt and destroy you. He did not consider that republic flourishing whose walls stand, but whose morals are in ruins. But the seductions of evil-minded devils had more influence with you than the precautions of prudent men. Hence the injuries you do, you will not permit to be imputed to you; but the injuries you suffer, you impute to Christianity. Depraved by good fortune, and not chastened by adversity, what you desire in the restoration of a peaceful and secure state, is not the tranquillity of

g. *City of God,* I, 33.

the commonwealth, but the impunity
vicious luxury. Scipio wished you
pressed by an enemy, that you migl
yourselves to luxurious manners; but so au...
are you, that not even when crushed by the enemy
is your luxury repressed. You have missed the
profit of your calamity; you have been made most
wretched, and have remained most profligate.

## B. *Brief History of the Misfortunes of Pagan Rome*

[a]Of moral and spiritual evils, which are above
all others to be deprecated, I think enough has
already been said to show that the false gods took
no steps to prevent the people who worshipped
them from being overwhelmed by such calamities,
but rather aggravated the ruin. I see I must now
speak of those evils which alone are dreaded by
the heathen—famine, pestilence, war, pillage, captivity, massacre, and the like calamities, already
enumerated. For evil men account those things
alone evil which do not make men evil; neither do
they blush to praise good things, and yet to remain
evil among the good things they praise. It grieves
them more to own a bad house than a bad life, as
if it were man's greatest good to have everything
good but himself. But not even such evils as were
alone dreaded by the heathen were warded off by
their gods, even when they were most unrestrict-
edly worshipped. For in various times and places
before the advent of our Redeemer, the human
race was crushed with numberless and sometimes
incredible calamities; and at that time what gods
but those did the world worship, if you except the
one nation of the Hebrews, and, beyond them,

a. *City of God*, III, 1.

such individuals as the most secret and most just
judgment of God counted worthy of divine grace?
But that I may not be prolix, I will be silent regarding the heavy calamities that have been suffered by any other nations, and will speak only
of what happened to Rome and the Roman empire, by which I mean Rome properly so called,
and those lands which already, before the coming
of Christ, had by alliance or conquest become, as
it were, members of the body of the state.

ᵇIt is believed that it was by the help of the gods
that the successor of Romulus, Numa Pompilius,
enjoyed peace during his entire reign, and shut
the gates of Janus, which are customarily kept
open during war. And it is supposed he was thus
requited for appointing many religious observances
among the Romans. Certainly that king would
have commanded our congratulations for so rare a
leisure, had he been wise enough to spend it on
wholesome pursuits, and, subduing a pernicious
curiosity, had sought out the true God with true
piety. But as it was, the gods were not the authors
of his leisure; but possibly they would have deceived him less had they found him busier. For the
more disengaged they found him, the more they
themselves occupied his attention. Varro informs
us of all his efforts, and of the arts he employed
to associate these gods with himself and the city;
and in its own place, if God will, I shall discuss
these matters. Meanwhile, as we are speaking of
the benefits conferred by the gods, I have already
admitted that peace is a great benefit; but it is a
benefit of the true God, which, like the sun, the
rain, and other supports of life, is frequently conferred on the ungrateful and wicked. But if this

b. *City of God,* III, 9-10.

great boon was conferred on Rome and Pompilius by their gods, why did they never afterwards grant it to the Roman empire during even more. meritorious periods? Were the sacred rites more efficient at their first institution than during their subsequent celebration? But they had no existence in Numa's time, until he added them to the ritual; whereas afterwards they had already been celebrated and preserved, that benefit might arise from them. How, then, is it that those forty-three, or as others prefer it, thirty-nine years of Numa's reign, were passed in unbroken peace, and yet that afterwards, when the worship was established, and the gods themselves, who were invoked by it, were the recognised guardians and patrons of the city, we can with difficulty find during the whole period, from the building of the city to the reign of Augustus, one year—that, viz., which followed the close of the first Punic war—in which, for a marvel, the Romans were able to shut the gates of war?

Do they reply that the Roman empire could never have been so widely extended, nor so glorious, save by constant and unintermitting wars? A fit argument, truly! Why must a kingdom be distracted in order to be great? In this little world of man's body, is it not better to have a moderate stature, and health with it, than to attain the huge dimensions of a giant by unnatural torments, and when you attain it to find no rest, but to be pained the more in proportion to the size of your members? What evil would have resulted, or rather what good would not have resulted, had those times continued which Sallust sketched, when he says, "At first the kings (for that was the first title of empire in the world) were divided in their sentiments: part cultivated the mind, others the body: at that time the life of men was led without covetousness; every one was sufficiently satisfied with his own!" [1] Was it requisite, then, for Rome's prosperity, that the state of things which Virgil reprobates should succeed:

> At length stole on a baser age,
> And war's indomitable rage,
> And greedy lust of gain? [2]

But obviously the Romans have a plausible defence for undertaking and carrying on such disastrous wars—to wit, that the pressure of their enemies forced them to resist, so that they were compelled to fight, not by any greed of human applause, but by the necessity of protecting life and liberty. Well, let that pass. Here is Sallust's account of the matter: "For when their state, enriched with laws, institutions, territory, seemed abundantly prosperous and sufficiently powerful, according to the ordinary law of human nature, opulence gave birth to envy. Accordingly, the neighbouring kings and states took arms and assaulted them. A few allies lent assistance; the rest, struck with fear, kept aloof from dangers. But the Romans, watchful at home and in war, were active, made preparations, encouraged one another, marched to meet their enemies—protected by arms their liberty, country, parents. Afterwards, when they had repelled the dangers by their bravery, they carried help to their allies and friends, and procured alliances more by conferring than by receiving favours." [3] This was to build up

1. Sall. *Cat. Conj.* ii.
2. *Æneid*, viii. 326-7.
3. Sall. *Cat. Conj.* vi.

Rome's greatness by honourable means. But, in Numa's reign, I would know whether the long peace was maintained in spite of the incursions of wicked neighbours, or if these incursions were discontinued that the peace might be maintained? For if even then Rome was harassed by wars, and yet did not meet force with force, the same means she then used to quiet her enemies without conquering them in war, or terrifying them with the onset of battle, she might have used always, and have reigned in peace with the gates of Janus shut. And if this was not in her power, then Rome enjoyed peace not at the will of her gods, but at the will of her neighbours round about, and only so long as they cared to provoke her with no war, unless perhaps these pitiful gods will dare to sell to one man as their favour what lies not in their power to bestow, but in the will of another man. ᶜAnd what happened after Numa's reign, when the Albans were provoked into war, with sad results not to themselves alone, but also to the Romans? The long peace of Numa had become tedious; and with what endless slaughter and detriment of both states did the Roman and Alban armies bring it to an end! For Alba, which had been founded by Ascanius, son of Æneas, and which was more properly the mother of Rome than Troy herself, was provoked to battle by Tullus Hostilius, king of Rome, and in the conflict both inflicted and received such damage, that at length both parties wearied of the struggle. It was then devised that the war should be decided by the combat of three twin-brothers from each army: from the Romans the three Horatii stood forward, from the Albans the three Curiatii. Two of the

c. *City of God*, III, 14-17.

Horatii were overcome and disposed of by the Curiatii; but by the remaining Horatius the three Curiatii were slain. Thus Rome remained victorious, but with such a sacrifice that only one survivor returned to his home. Whose was the loss on both sides? Whose the grief, but of the offspring of Æneas, the descendants of Ascanius, the progeny of Venus, the grandsons of Jupiter? For this, too, was a "worse than civil" war, in which the belligerent states were mother and daughter. And to this combat of the three twin-brothers there was added another atrocious and horrible catastrophe. For as the two nations had formerly been friendly (being related and neighbours), the sister of the Horatii had been betrothed to one of the Curiatii; and she, when she saw her brother wearing the spoils of her betrothed, burst into tears, and was slain by her own brother in his anger. To me, this one girl seems to have been more humane than the whole Roman people. I cannot think her to blame for lamenting the man to whom already she had plighted her troth, or, as perhaps she was doing, for grieving that her brother should have slain him to whom he had promised his sister. For why do we praise the grief of Æneas (in Virgil[4]) over the enemy cut down even by his own hand? Why did Marcellus shed tears over the city of Syracuse, when he recollected, just before he destroyed, its magnificence and meridian glory, and thought upon the common lot of all things? I demand, in the name of humanity, that if men are praised for tears shed over enemies conquered by themselves, a weak girl should not be counted criminal for bewailing her lover slaughtered by the hand of her brother. While, then, that

4. *Æneid*, x. 821.

maiden was weeping for the death of her betrothed inflicted by her brother's hand, Rome was rejoicing that such devastation had been wrought on her mother state, and that she had purchased a victory with such an expenditure of the common blood of herself and the Albans.

Why allege to me the mere names and words of "glory" and "victory?" . . . Let the charge be brought against Alba, as Troy was charged with adultery. There is no such charge, none like it found: the war was kindled only in order that there

> Might sound in languid ears the cry
> Of Tallus and of victory[5]

This vice of restless ambition was the sole motive to that social and parricidal war—a vice which Sallust brands in passing; for when he has spoken with brief but hearty commendation of those primitive times in which life was spent without covetousness, and every one was sufficiently satisfied with what he had, he goes on: "But after Cyrus in Asia, and the Lacedemonians and Athenians in Greece, began to subdue cities and nations, and to account the lust of sovereignty a sufficient ground for war, and to reckon that the greatest glory consisted in the greatest empire;" [6] and so on, as I need not now quote. This lust of sovereignty disturbs and consumes the human race with frightful ills. By this lust Rome was overcome when she triumphed over Alba, and praising her own crime, called it glory. For, as our Scriptures say, "the wicked boasteth of his

5. *Æneid,* vi. 813.
6. Sallust, *Cat. Conj.* ii.

heart's desire, and blesseth the covetous, whom the Lord abhorreth." [7] . . . Let no man tell me that this and the other was a "great" man, because he fought and conquered so and so. Gladiators fight and conquer, and this barbarism has its need of praise; but I think it were better to take the consequences of any sloth, than to seek the glory won by such arms. And if two gladiators entered the arena to fight, one being father, the other his son, who would endure such a spectacle? who would not be revolted by it? How, then, could that be a glorious war which a daughter-state waged against its mother? Or did it constitute a difference, that the battlefield was not an arena, and that the wide plains were filled with the carcasses not of two gladiators, but of many of the flower of two nations; and that those contests were viewed not by the amphitheatre, but by the whole world, and furnished a profane spectacle both to those alive at the time, and to their posterity, so long as the fame of it is handed down?

Yet those gods, guardians of the Roman empire, and, as it were, theatric spectators of such contests as these, were not satisfied until the sister of the Horatii was added by her brother's sword as a third victim from the Roman side, so that Rome herself, though she won the day, should have as many deaths to mourn. Afterwards, as a fruit of the victory, Alba was destroyed, though it was there the Trojan gods had formed a third asylum after Ilium had been sacked by the Greeks, and after they had left Lavinium, where Æneas had founded a kingdom in a land of banishment. But probably Alba was destroyed because from it too

7. Ps. x. 3.

the gods had migrated, in their usual fashion, as
Virgil says:

> Gone from each fane, each sacred shrine,
> Are those who made this realm divine.[8]

Gone, indeed, and from now their third asylum,
that Rome might seem all the wiser in committing
herself to them after they had deserted three other
cities. Alba, whose king Amulius had banished
his brother, displeased them; Rome, whose king
Romulus had slain his brother, pleased them. But
before Alba was destroyed, its population, they
say, was amalgamated with the inhabitants of
Rome, so that the two cities were one. Well, admitting it was so, yet the fact remains that the
city of Ascanius, the third retreat of the Trojan
gods, was destroyed by the daughter-city. Besides,
to effect this pitiful conglomerate of the war's
leavings, much blood was spilt on both sides. And
how shall I speak in detail of the same wars, so
often renewed in subsequent reigns, though they
seemed to have been finished by great victories;
and of wars that time after time were brought
to an end by great slaughters, and which yet time
after time were renewed by the posterity of those
who had made peace and struck treaties? Of this
calamitous history we have no small proof, in the
fact that no subsequent king closed the gates of
war; and therefore, with all their tutelar gods, no
one of them reigned in peace.

And what was the end of the kings themselves?
Of Romulus, a flattering legend tells us that he
was assumed into heaven. But certain Roman

8. *Æneid,* iii. 351-2.

historians relate that he was torn in pieces by the senate for his ferocity, and that a man, Julius Proculus, was suborned to give out that Romulus had appeared to him, and through him commanded the Roman people to worship him as a god; and that in this way the people, who were beginning to resent the action of the senate, were quieted and pacified. . . .

The other kings of Rome, too, with the exception of Numa Pompilius and Ancus Marcius, who died natural deaths, what horrible ends they had! Tullus Hostilius, the conqueror and destroyer of Alba, was, as I said, himself and all his house consumed by lightning. Priscus Tarquinius was slain by his predecessor's son. Servius Tullius was foully murdered by his son-in-law Tarquinius Superbus, who succeeded him on the throne. Nor did so flagrant a parricide committed against Rome's best king drive from their altars and shrines those gods who were said to have been moved by Paris' adultery to treat poor Troy in this style, and abandon it to the fire and sword of the Greeks. Nay, the very Tarquin who had murdered, was allowed to succeed his father-in-law. And this infamous parricide, during the reign he had secured by murder, was allowed to triumph in many victorious wars, and to build the Capitol from their spoils; the gods meanwhile not departing, but abiding, and abetting, and suffering their king Jupiter to preside and reign over them in that very splendid Capitol, the work of a parricide. For he did not build the Capitol in the days of his innocence, and then suffer banishment for subsequent crimes; but to that reign during which he built the Capitol, he won his way by unnatural crime. And when he was afterwards banished by the

Romans, and forbidden the City, it was not for his
own but his son's wickedness in the affair of
Lucretia—a crime perpetrated not only without
his cognizance, but in his absence. For at that
time he was besieging Ardea, and fighting Rome's
battles; and we cannot say what he would have
done had he been aware of his son's crime. Notwithstanding, though his opinion was neither inquired into nor ascertained, the people stripped
him of royalty; and when he returned to Rome
with his army, it was admitted, but he was ex-
cluded, abandoned by his troops, and the gates
shut in his face. And yet, after he had appealed
to the neighbouring states, and tormented the
Romans with calamitous but unsuccessful wars,
and when he was deserted by the ally on whom he
most depended, despairing of regaining the kingdom, he lived a retired and quiet life for fourteen
years, as it is reported, in Tusculum, a Roman
town, where he grew old in his wife's company,
and at last terminated his days in a much more
desirable fashion than his father-in-law, who had
perished by the hand of his son-in-law; his own
daughter abetting, if report be true. And this Tarquin the Romans called, not the Cruel, nor the
Infamous, but the Proud; their own pride perhaps
resenting his tyrannical airs. So little did they make
of his murdering their best king, his own father-
in-law, that they elected him their own king. I
wonder if it was not even more criminal in them
to reward so bountifully so great a criminal. And
yet there was no word of the gods abandoning the
altars; unless, perhaps, some one will say in defence of the gods, that they remained at Rome
for the purpose of punishing the Romans, rather
than of aiding and profiting them, seducing them

by empty victories, and wearing them out by severe wars. Such was the life of the Romans under the kings during the much-praised epoch of the state which extends to the expulsion of Tarquinius Superbus in the 243d year, during which all those victories, which were bought with so much blood and such disasters, hardly pushed Rome's dominion twenty miles from the city; a territory which would by no means bear comparison with that of any petty Gætulian state.

To this epoch let us add also that of which Sallust says, that it was ordered with justice and moderation, while the fear of Tarquin and of a war with Etruria was impending. For so long as the Etrurians aided the efforts of Tarquin to regain the throne, Rome was convulsed with distressing war. And therefore he says that the state was ordered with justice and moderation, through the pressure of fear, not through the influence of equity. And in this very brief period, how calamitous a year was that in which consuls were first created, when the kingly power was abolished! They did not fulfil their term of office. For Junius Brutus deprived his colleague Lucius Tarquinius Collatinus, and banished him from the city; and shortly after he himself fell in battle, at once slaying and slain, having formerly put to death his own sons and his brothers-in-law, because he had discovered that they were conspiring to restore Tarquin. It is this deed that Virgil shudders to record, even while he seems to praise it; for when he says,

> And call his own rebellious seed
> For menaced liberty to bleed,

he immediately exclaims,

Unhappy father! howsoe'er
The deed be judged by after days;

that is to say, let posterity judge the deed as they
please, let them praise and extol the father who
slew his sons, he is unhappy. And then he adds, as
if to console so unhappy a man:

His country's love shall all o'erbear,
And unextinguished thirst of praise.[9]

In the tragic end of Brutus, who slew his own
sons, and though he slew his enemy, Tarquin's
son, yet could not survive him, but was survived
by Tarquin the elder, does not the innocence of
his colleague Collatinus seem to be vindicated,
who, though a good citizen, suffered the same
punishment as Tarquin himself, when that tyrant
was banished? For Brutus himself is said to have
been a relative of Tarquin. But Collatinus had
the misfortune to bear not only the blood, but
the name of Tarquin. To change his name, then,
not his country, would have been his fit penalty:
to abridge his name by this word, and be called
simply L. Collatinus. But he was not compelled
to lose what he could lose without detriment, but
was stripped of the honour of the first consulship,
and was banished from the land he loved. Is this,
then, the glory of Brutus—this injustice, alike detestable and profitless to the republic? Was it to
this he was driven by "his country's love, and unextinguished thirst of praise?"

When Tarquin the tyrant was expelled, L. Tarquinius Collatinus, the husband of Lucretia, was
created consul along with Brutus. How justly the

9. *Æneid*, vi. 820, etc.

people acted, in looking more to the character than the name of a citizen! How unjustly Brutus acted, in depriving of honour and country his colleague in that new office, whom he might have deprived of his name, if it were so offensive to him! Such were the ills, such the disasters, which fell out when the government was "ordered with justice and moderation." Lucretius, too, who succeeded Brutus, was carried off by disease before the end of that same year. So P. Valerius, who succeeded Collatinus, and M. Horatius, who filled the vacancy occasioned by the death of Lucretius, completed that disastrous and funereal year, which had five consuls. Such was the year in which the Roman republic inaugurated the new honour and office of the consulship.

After this, when their fears were gradually diminished—not because the wars ceased, but because they were not so furious—that period in which things were "ordered with justice and moderation" drew to an end, and there followed that state of matters which Sallust thus briefly sketches: "Then began the patricians to oppress the people as slaves, to condemn them to death or scourging, as the kings had done, to drive them from their holdings, and to tyrannize over those who had no property to lose. The people, overwhelmed by these oppressive measures, and most of all by usury, and obliged to contribute both money and personal service to the constant wars, at length took arms and seceded to Mount Aventine and Mount Sacer, and thus secured for themselves tribunes and protective laws. But it was only the second Punic war that put an end on both sides to discord and strife." [10] But why should I spend

10. *Hist.* i.

time in writing such things, or make others spend it in reading them? Let the terse summary of Sallust suffice to intimate the misery of the republic through all that long period till the second Punic war—how it was distracted from without by unceasing wars, and torn with civil broils and dissentions.

<sup>d</sup>In the Punic wars, when victory hung so long in the balance between the two kingdoms, when two powerful nations were straining every nerve and using all their resources against one another, how many smaller kingdoms were crushed, how many large and flourishing cities were demolished, how many states were overwhelmed and ruined, how many districts and lands far and near were desolated! How often were the victors on either side vanquished! What multitudes of men, both of those actually in arms and of others, were destroyed! What huge navies, too, were crippled in engagements, or were sunk by every kind of marine disaster! Were we to attempt to recount or mention these calamities, we should become writers of history. At that period Rome was mightily perturbed, and resorted to vain and ludicrous expedients. On the authority of the Sibylline books, the secular games were reappointed, which had been inaugurated a century before, but had faded into oblivion in happier times. The games consecrated to the infernal gods were also renewed by the pontiffs; for they, too, had sunk into disuse in the better times. And no wonder; for when they were renewed, the great abundance of dying men made all hell rejoice at its riches, and give itself up to sport: for certainly the ferocious wars, and disastrous quarrels, and bloody

d. *City of God,* III, 18-31.

victories—now on one side, and now on the other—though most calamitous to men, afforded great sport and a rich banquet to the devils. But in the first Punic war there was no more disastrous event than the Roman defeat in which Regulus was taken. We made mention of him in the two former books as an incontestably great man, who had before conquered and subdued the Carthaginians, and who would have put an end to the first Punic war, had not an inordinate appetite for praise and glory prompted him to impose on the worn-out Carthaginians harder conditions than they could bear. If the unlooked-for captivity and unseemly bondage of this man, his fidelity to his oath, and his surpassingly cruel death, do not bring a blush to the face of the gods, it is true that they are brazen and bloodless. . . .

As to the second Punic war, it were tedious to recount the disasters it brought on both the nations engaged in so protracted and shifting a war, that (by the acknowledgment even of those writers who have made it their object not so much to narrate the wars as to eulogize the dominion of Rome) the people who remained victorious were less like conquerors than conquered. For, when Hannibal poured out of Spain over the Pyrenees, and overran Gaul, and burst through the Alps, and during his whole course gathered strength by plundering and subduing as he went, and inundated Italy like a torrent, how bloody were the wars, and how continuous the engagements, that were fought! How often were the Romans vanquished! How many towns went over to the enemy, and how many were taken and subdued! What fearful battles there were, and how often did the defeat of the Romans shed lustre on the arms of Hannibal!

And what shall I say of the wonderfully crushing defeat at Cannæ, where even Hannibal, cruel as he was, was yet sated with the blood of his bitterest enemies, and gave orders that they be spared? From this field of battle he sent to Carthage three bushels of gold rings, signifying that so much of the rank of Rome had that day fallen, that it was easier to give an idea of it by measure than by numbers; and that the frightful slaughter of the common rank and file whose bodies lay undistinguished by the ring, and who were numerous in proportion to their meanness, was rather to be conjectured than accurately reported. In fact, such was the scarcity of soldiers after this, that the Romans impressed their criminals on the promise of impunity, and their slaves by the bribe of liberty, and out of these infamous classes did not so much recruit as create an army. But these slaves, or, to give them all their titles, these freedmen who were enlisted to do battle for the republic of Rome, lacked arms. And so they took arms from the temples, as if the Romans were saying to their gods: Lay down those arms you have held so long in vain, if by chance our slaves may be able to use to purpose what you, our gods, have been impotent to use. At that time, too, the public treasury was too low to pay the soldiers, and private resources were used for public purposes; and so generously did individuals contribute of their property, that, saving the gold ring and bulla which each wore, the pitiful mark of his rank, no senator, and much less any of the other orders and tribes, reserved any gold for his own use. But if in our day they were reduced to this poverty, who would be able to endure their reproaches, barely endurable as they are now, when more money is spent on actors for the sake of a superfluous gratification, than was then disbursed to the legions?

But among all the disasters of the second Punic war, there occurred none more lamentable, or calculated to excite deeper complaint, than the fate of the Saguntines. This city of Spain, eminently friendly to Rome, was destroyed by its fidelity to the Roman people. For when Hannibal had broken treaty with the Romans, he sought occasion for provoking them to war, and accordingly made a fierce assault upon Saguntum. When this was reported at Rome, ambassadors were sent to Hannibal, urging him to raise the siege; and when this remonstrance was neglected, they proceeded to Carthage, lodged complaint against the breaking of the treaty, and returned to Rome without accomplishing their object. Meanwhile the siege went on; and in the eighth or ninth month, this opulent but ill-fated city, dear as it was to its own state and to Rome, was taken, and subjected to treatment which one cannot read, much less narrate, without horror. And yet, because it bears directly on the matter in hand, I will briefly touch upon it. First, then, famine wasted the Saguntines, so that even human corpses were eaten by some: so at least it is recorded. Subsequently, when thoroughly worn out, that they might at least escape the ignominy of falling into the hands of Hannibal, they publicly erected a huge funeral pile, and cast themselves into its flames, while at the same time they slew their children and themselves with the sword. Could these gods, these debauchees and gourmands, whose mouths water for fat sacrifices, and whose lips utter lying divinations—could they not do anything in a case like this? Could they not interfere for the preservation of a city closely allied to the Roman people, or prevent it perishing for its fidelity to that alliance of which they themselves had been the mediators? Saguntum, faithfully keeping the treaty it had entered into before these gods, and to which it had firmly bound itself by an oath, was besieged, taken, and destroyed by a perjured person. If afterwards, when Hannibal was close to the walls of Rome, it was the gods who terrified him with lightning and tempest, and drove him to a distance, why, I ask, did they not thus interfere before? For I make bold to say, that this demonstration with the tempest would have been more honourably made in defence of the allies of Rome—who were in danger on account of their reluctance to break faith with the Romans, and had no resources of their own—than in defence of the Romans themselves, who were fighting in their own cause, and had abundant resources to oppose Hannibal. If, then, they had been the guardians of Roman prosperity and glory, they would have preserved that glory from the stain of this Saguntine disaster; and how silly it is to believe that Rome was preserved from destruction at the hands of Hannibal by the guardian care of those gods who were unable to rescue the city of Saguntum from perishing through its fidelity to the alliance of Rome. If the population of Saguntum had been Christian, and had suffered as it did for the Christian faith (though, of course, Christians would not have used fire and sword against their own persons), they would have suffered with that hope which springs from faith in Christ—the hope not of a brief temporal reward, but of unending and eternal bliss. What, then, will the advocates and apologists of these gods say in their defence, when charged with the blood of these Saguntines; for they are professedly worshipped and invoked for this very purpose of securing prosperity in this fleeting and transitory life? . . .

Omitting many things, that I may not exceed the limits of the work I have proposed to myself, I come to the epoch between the second and last Punic wars, during which, according to Sallust, the Romans lived with the greatest virtue and concord. Now, in this period of virtue and harmony, the great Scipio, the liberator of Rome and Italy, who had with surprising ability brought to a close the second Punic war—that horrible, destructive, dangerous contest—who had defeated Hannibal and subdued Carthage, and whose whole life is said to have been dedicated to the gods, and cherished in their temples—this Scipio, after such a triumph, was obliged to yield to the accusations of his enemies, and to leave his country, which his valour had saved and liberated, to spend the remainder of his days in the town of Liternum, so indifferent to a recall from exile, that he is said to have given orders that not even his remains should lie in his ungrateful country. It was at that time also that the proconsul Cn. Manlius, after subduing the Galatians, introduced into Rome the luxury of Asia, more destructive than all hostile armies. It was then that iron bedsteads and expensive carpets were first used; then, too, that female singers were admitted at banquets, and other licentious abominations were introduced. But at present I meant to speak, not of the evils men voluntarily practise, but of those they suffer in spite of themselves. So that the case of Scipio, who succumbed to his enemies, and died in exile from the country he had rescued, was mentioned by me as being pertinent to the present discussion; for this was the reward he received from those Roman gods whose temples he saved from Hannibal, and who are worshipped only for the sake of securing temporal happiness. But since Sallust, as we have seen, declares that the manners of Rome were never better than at that time, I therefore judged it right to mention the Asiatic luxury then introduced, that it might be seen that what he says is true, only when that period is compared with the others, during which the morals were certainly worse, and the factions more violent. For at that time—I mean between the second and third Punic war—that notorious Lex Voconia was passed, which prohibited a man from making a woman, even an only daughter, his heir; than which law I am at a loss to conceive what could be more unjust. It is true that in the interval between these two Punic wars the misery of Rome was somewhat less. Abroad, indeed, their forces were consumed by wars, yet also consoled by victories; while at home there were not such disturbances as at other times. But when the last Punic war had terminated in the utter destruction of Rome's rival, which quickly succumbed to the other Scipio, who thus earned for himself the surname of Africanus, then the Roman republic was overwhelmed with such a host of ills, which sprang from the corrupt manners induced by prosperity and security, that the sudden overthrow of Carthage is seen to have injured Rome more seriously than her long-continued hostility. During the whole subsequent period down to the time of Cæsar Augustus, who seems to have entirely deprived the Romans of liberty—a liberty, indeed, which in their own judgment was no longer glorious, but full of broils and dangers, and which now was quite enervated and languishing—and who submitted all things again to the will of a monarch, and infused as it were a new life into the sickly old age of the republic, and inaugurated a fresh *régime;*—during this whole period, I say, many military disasters were sustained on a variety of occasions, all of which I here pass by. There was specially the treaty of Numantia, blotted as it was with extreme disgrace; for the sacred chickens, they say, flew out of the coop, and thus augured disaster to Mancinus the consul; just as if, during all these years in which that little city of Numantia had withstood the besieging army of Rome, and had become a terror to the republic, the other generals had all marched against it under unfavourable auspices.

These things, I say, I pass in silence; but I can by no means be silent regarding the order given by Mithridates, king of Asia, that on one day all Roman citizens residing anywhere in Asia (where great numbers of them were following their private business) should be put to death: and this order was executed. How miserable a spectacle was then presented, when each man was suddenly and treacherously murdered wherever he happened to be, in the field or on the road, in the town, in his own home, or in the street, in market or temple, in bed or at table! Think of the groans of the dying, the tears of the spectators, and even of the executioners themselves. For how cruel a necessity was it that compelled the hosts of these victims, not only to see these abominable butcheries in their own houses, but even to perpetrate them: to change their countenance suddenly from the bland kindliness of friendship, and in the midst of peace set about the business of war; and, shall I say, give and receive wounds  the slain being pierced in body, the slayer in spirit! Had all these murdered persons, then, despised auguries? Had they neither public nor household gods to consult when they left their homes and set out on that fatal journey? If they had not, our adversaries have no reason to complain of these Christian times in this particular, since long ago the Romans despised auguries as idle. If, on the other hand, they did consult omens, let them tell us what good they got thereby, even when such things were not prohibited, but authorized, by human, if not by divine law.

But let us now mention, as succinctly as possible, those disasters which were still more vexing, because nearer home; I mean those discords which are erroneously called civil, since they destroy civil interests. The seditions had now become urban wars, in which blood was freely shed, and in which parties raged against one another, not with wrangling and verbal contention, but with physical force and arms. What a sea of Roman blood was shed, what desolations and devastations were occasioned in Italy by wars social, wars servile, wars civil! Before the Latins began the social war against Rome, all the animals used in the service of man —dogs, horses, asses, oxen, and all the rest that are subject to man—suddenly grew wild, and forgot their domesticated tameness, forsook their stalls and wandered at large, and could not be closely approached either by strangers or their own masters without danger. If this was a portent, how serious a calamity must have been portended by a plague which, whether portent or no, was in itself a serious calamity! Had it happened in our day, the heathen would have been more rabid against us than their animals were against them.

The civil wars originated in the seditions which

the Gracchi excited regarding the agrarian laws;
for they were minded to divide among the people
the lands which were wrongfully possessed by the
nobility. But to reform an abuse of so long standing was an enterprise full of peril, or rather, as the
event proved, of destruction. For what disasters
accompanied the death of the elder Gracchus!
what slaughter ensued when, shortly after, the
younger brother met the same fate! For noble and
ignoble were indiscriminately massacred; and this
not by legal authority and procedure, but by mobs
and armed rioters. After the death of the younger
Gracchus, the consul Lucius Opimius, who had
given battle to him within the city, and had defeated and put to the sword both himself and his
confederates, and had massacred many of the citizens, instituted a judicial examination of others,
and is reported to have put to death as many as
3000 men. From this it may be gathered how many
fell in the riotous encounters, when the result even
of a judicial investigation was so bloody. The
assassin of Gracchus himself sold his head to the
consul for its weight in gold, such being the previous agreement. In this massacre, too, Marcus Ful-
vius, a man of consular rank, with all his children,
was put to death.

A pretty decree of the senate it was, truly, by
which the temple of Concord was built on the spot
where that disastrous rising had taken place, and
where so many citizens of every rank had fallen.
. . . But they supposed that, in erecting the temple of Concord within the view of the orators, as
a memorial of the punishment and death of the
Gracchi, they were raising an effectual obstacle to
sedition. How much effect it had, is indicated by
the still more deplorable wars that followed. For

after this the orators endeavoured not to avoid the example of the Gracchi, but to surpass their projects; as did Lucius Saturninus, a tribune of the people, and Caius Servilius the prætor, and some time after Marcus Drusus, all of whom stirred seditions which first of all occasioned bloodshed, and then the social wars by which Italy was grievously injured, and reduced to a piteously desolate and wasted condition. Then followed the servile war and the civil wars; and in them what battles were fought, and what blood was shed, so that almost all the peoples of Italy, which formed the main strength of the Roman empire, were conquered as if they were barbarians! Then even historians themselves find it difficult to explain how the servile war was begun by a very few, certainly less than seventy gladiators, what numbers of fierce and cruel men attached themselves to these, how many of the Roman generals this band defeated, and how it laid waste many districts and cities. And that was not the only servile war: the province of Macedonia, and subsequently Sicily and the sea-coast, were also depopulated by bands of slaves. And who can adequately describe either the horrible atrocities which the pirates first committed, or the wars they afterwards maintained against Rome?

But when Marius, stained with the blood of his fellow-citizens, whom the rage of party had sacrificed, was in his turn vanquished and driven from the city, it had scarcely time to breathe freely, when, to use the words of Cicero, "Cinna and Marius together returned and took possession of it. Then, indeed, the foremost men in the state were put to death, its lights quenched. Sylla afterwards avenged this cruel victory; but we need not say with what loss of life, and with what ruin to the republic." [11] For of this vengeance, which was more destructive than if the crimes which it punished had been committed with impunity, Lucan says: "The cure was excessive, and too closely resembled the disease. The guilty perished, but when none but the guilty survived, then private hatred and anger, unbridled by law, were allowed free indulgence." [12] In that war between Marius and Sylla, besides those who fell in the field of battle, the city, too, was filled with corpses in its streets, squares, markets, theatres, and temples; so that it is not easy to reckon whether the victors slew more before or after victory, that they might be, or because they were, victors. As soon as Marius triumphed, and returned from exile, besides the butcheries everywhere perpetrated, the head of the consul Octavius was exposed on the rostrum; Cæsar and Fimbria were assassinated in their own houses; the two Crassi, father and son, were murdered in one another's sight; Bebius and Numitorius were disembowelled by being dragged with hooks; Catulus escaped the hands of his enemies by drinking poison; Merula, the flamen of Jupiter, cut his veins and made a libation of his own blood to his god. Moreover, every one whose salutation Marius did not answer by giving his hand, was at once cut down before his face.

Then followed the victory of Sylla, the so-called avenger of the cruelties of Marius. But not only was his victory purchased with great bloodshed; but when hostilities were finished, hostility survived, and the subsequent peace was bloody as the war. To the former and still

11. Cicero, *in Catilin. iii. sub. fin.*
12. Lucan, *Pharsal.* ii. 142-146.

recent massacres of the elder Marius, the younger Marius and Carbo, who belonged to the same party, added greater atrocities. For when Sylla approached, and they despaired not only of victory, but of life itself, they made a promiscuous massacre of friends and foes. And, not satisfied with staining every corner of Rome with blood they besieged the senate, and led forth the senators to death from the curia as from a prison. Mucius Scævola the pontiff was slain at the altar of Vesta, which he had clung to because no spot in Rome was more sacred than her temple; and his blood well-nigh extinguished the fire which was kept alive by the constant care of the virgins. Then Sylla entered the city victorious, after having slaughtered in the Villa Publica, not by combat, but by an order, 7000 men who had surrendered, and were therefore unarmed; so fierce was the rage of peace itself, even after the rage of war was extinct. Moreover, throughout the whole city every partisan of Sylla slew whom he pleased, so that the number of deaths went beyond computation, till it was suggested to Sylla that he should allow some to survive, that the victors might not be destitute of subjects. Then this furious and promiscuous licence to murder was checked, and much relief was expressed at the publication of the proscription list, containing though it did the death-warrant of two thousand men of the highest ranks, the senatorial and equestrian. The large number was indeed saddening, but it was consolatory that a limit was fixed; nor was the grief at the numbers slain so great as the joy that the rest were secure. But this very security, hard-hearted as it was, could not but bemoan the exquisite torture applied to some of those who had been doomed to die. For one was torn to pieces by the unarmed hands of the executioners; men treating a living man more savagely than wild beasts are used to tear an abandoned corpse. Another had his eyes dug out, and his limbs cut away bit by bit, and was forced to live a long while, or rather to die a long while, in such torture. Some celebrated cities were put up to auction, like farms; and one was collectively condemned to slaughter, just as an individual criminal would be condemned to death. These things were done in peace when the war was over, not that victory might be more speedily obtained, but that after being obtained, it might not be thought lightly of. Peace vied with war in cruelty, and surpassed it; for while war overthrew armed hosts, peace slew the defenceless. War gave liberty to him who was attacked, to strike if he could; peace granted to the survivors not life, but an unresisting death.

What fury of foreign nations, what barbarian ferocity, can compare with this victory of citizens over citizens? Which was more disastrous, more hideous, more bitter to Rome: the recent Gothic and the old Gallic invasion, or the cruelty displayed by Marius and Sylla and their partisans against men who were members of the same body as themselves? The Gauls, indeed, massacred all the senators they found in any part of the city except the Capitol, which alone was defended; but they at least sold life to those who were in the Capitol, though they might have starved them out if they could not have stormed it. The Goths, again, spared so many senators, that it is the more surprising that they killed any. But Sylla, while Marius was still living, established himself as conqueror in the Capitol, which the Gauls had not violated, and thence issued his death-warrants; and when Marius had escaped by flight, though destined to return more fierce and bloodthirsty than ever, Sylla issued from the Capitol even decrees of the senate for the slaughter and confiscation of the property of many citizens. Then, when Sylla left, what did the Marian faction hold sacred or spare, when they gave no quarter even to Mucius, a citizen, a senator, a pontiff, and though clasping in piteous embrace the very altar in which, they say, reside the destinies of Rome? And that final proscription list of Sylla's, not to mention countless other massacres, despatched more senators than the Goths could even plunder.

With what effrontery, then, with what assurance, with what impudence, with what folly, or rather insanity, do they refuse to impute these disasters to their own gods, and impute the present to our Christ! These bloody civil wars, more distressing, by the avowal of their own historians, than any foreign wars, and which were pronounced to be not merely calamitous, but absolutely ruinous to the republic, began long before the coming of Christ, and gave birth to one another; so that a concatenation of unjustifiable causes led from the wars of Marius and Sylla to those of Sertorius and Catiline, of whom the one was proscribed, the other brought up by Sylla; from this to the war of Lepidus and Catulus, of whom the one wished to rescind, the other to defend the acts of Sylla; from this to the war of Pompey and Cæsar, of whom Pompey had been a partisan of Sylla, whose power he equalled or even surpassed, while Cæsar condemned Pompey's power because it was not his own, and yet exceeded it when Pompey was defeated and slain. From him the chain of civil wars

extended to the second Cæsar, afterwards called
Augustus, and in whose reign Christ was born.
For even Augustus himself waged many civil wars;
and in these wars many of the foremost men perished, among them that skilful manipulator of the
republic, Cicero. Caius [Julius] Cæsar, when he
had conquered Pompey, though he used his victory
with clemency, and granted to men of the opposite faction both life and honours, was suspected
of aiming at royalty, and was assassinated in the
curia by a party of noble senators, who had conspired to defend the liberty of the republic. His
power was then coveted by Antony, a man of very
different character, polluted and debased by every
kind of vice, who was strenuously resisted by
Cicero on the same plea of defending the liberty
of the republic. At this juncture that other Cæsar,
the adopted son of Caius, and afterwards, as I
said, known by the name of Augustus, had made
his *début* as a young man of remarkable genius.
This youthful Cæsar was favoured by Cicero, in
order that his influence might counteract that of
Antony; for he hoped that Cæsar would overthrow and blast the power of Antony, and establish
a free state—so blind and unaware of the future
was he: for that very young man, whose advance-
ment and influence he was fostering, allowed
Cicero to be killed as the seal of an alliance with
Antony, and subjected to his own rule the very
liberty or the republic in defence of which he had
made so many orations.

Let those who have no gratitude to Christ for
His great benefits, blame their own gods for these
heavy disasters. For certainly when these occurred
the altars of the gods were kept blazing, and there
rose the mingled fragrance of "Sabæan incense

and fresh garlands;" [13] the priests were clothed
with honour, the shrines were maintained in splen-
dour; sacrifices, games, sacred ecstasies, were common in the temples; while the blood of the citizens
was being so freely shed, not only in remote places,
but among the very altars of the gods. Cicero did
not choose to seek sanctuary in a temple, because
Mucius had sought it there in vain. But they who
most unpardonably calumniate this Christian era,
are the very men who either themselves fled for
asylum to the places specially dedicated to Christ,
or were led there by the barbarians that they might
be safe. In short, not to recapitulate the many
instances I have cited, and not to add to their
number others which it were tedious to enumerate,
this one thing I am persuaded of, and this every
impartial judgment will readily acknowledge, that
if the human race had received Christianity before
the Punic wars, and if the same desolating calamities which these wars brought upon Europe and
Africa had followed the introduction of Christianity, there is no one of those who now accuse us
who would not have attributed them to our religion. How intolerable would their accusations
have been, at least so far as the Romans are concerned, if the Christian religion had been received
and diffused prior to the invasion of the Gauls,
or to the ruinous floods and fires which desolated
Rome, or to those most calamitous of all events,
the civil wars! And those other disasters, which
were of so strange a nature that they were reckoned prodigies, . . . which of them, suppose they
happened now, would not be attributed to the
Christian religion by those who thus thoughtlessly
accuse us, and whom we are compelled to answer?

13. *Æneid,* i. 417.

And yet to their own gods they attribute none of
these things, though they worship them for the
sake of escaping lesser calamities of the same kind,
and do not reflect that they who formerly worshipped them were not preserved from these serious disasters.

### C. *God's Governance and Roman Political Virtue*

[a]But that God supreme and true, with His Word
and Holy Spirit (which three are one), one God
omnipotent, creator and maker of every soul and
of every body; by whose gift all are happy who are
happy through verity and not through vanity; who
made man a rational animal consisting of soul
and body, who, when he sinned, neither permitted
him to go unpunished, nor left him without mercy;
who has given to the good and to the evil, being
in common with stones, vegetable life in common
with trees, sensuous life in common with brutes,
intellectual life in common with angels alone; from
whom is every mode, every species, every order;
from whom are measure, number, weight; from
whom is everything which has an existence in nature, of whatever kind it be, and of whatever
value; from whom are the seeds of forms and the
forms of seeds, and the motion of seeds and of
forms; who gave also to flesh its origin, beauty,
health, reproductive fecundity, disposition of members, and the salutary concord of its parts; who
also to the irrational soul has given memory, sense,
appetite, but to the rational soul, in addition to
these, has given intelligence and will; who has not
left, not to speak of heaven and earth, angels and
men, but not even the entrails of the smallest and
most contemptible animal, or the feather of a bird,

a. *City of God,* V, 11.

or the little flower of a plant, or the leaf of a tree, without an harmony, and, as it were, a mutual peace among all its parts—that God can never be believed to have left the kingdoms of men, their dominations and servitudes, outside of the laws of His providence.

Wherefore let us go on to consider what virtues of the Romans they were which the true God, in whose power are also the kingdoms of the earth, condescended to help in order to raise the empire, and also for what reason He did so; ᵇthat this was not effected by that multitude of false gods which they worshipped, we have both already adduced, and shall, as occasion offers, yet adduce considerable proof.

ᶜThe ancient and primitive Romans, though their history shows us that, like all the other nations, with the sole exception of the Hebrews, they worshipped false gods, and sacrificed victims, not to God, but to demons, have nevertheless this commendation bestowed on them by their historian, that they were "greedy of praise, prodigal of wealth, desirous of great glory, and content with a moderate fortune."[1] Glory they most ardently loved: for it they wished to live, for it they did not hesitate to die. Every other desire was repressed by the strength of their passion for that one thing. At length their country itself, because it seemed inglorious to serve, but glorious to rule and to command, they first earnestly desired to be free, and then to be mistress. Hence it was that, not enduring the domination of kings, they put the government into the hands of two chiefs, holding

b. *City of God,* V, Preface.
c. *Ibid.,* V, 12.
1. Sallust, *Cat.* vii.

office for a year, who were called consuls, not kings or lords. But royal pomp seemed inconsistent with the administration of a ruler (*regentis*), or the benevolence of one who consults (that is, for the public good) (*consulentis*), but rather with the haughtiness of a lord (*dominantis*). King Tarquin, therefore, having been banished, and the consular government having been instituted, it followed, as the same author already alluded to says in his praises of the Romans, that "the state grew with amazing rapidity after it had obtained liberty, so great a desire of glory had taken possession of it." That eagerness for praise and desire of glory, then, was that which accomplished those many wonderful things, laudable, doubtless, and glorious according to human judgment. The same Sallust praises the great men of his own time, Marcus Cato, and Caius Cæsar, saying that for a long time the republic had no one great in virtue, but that within his memory there had been these two men of eminent virtue, and very different pursuits. Now, among the praises which he pronounces on Cæsar he put this, that he wished for a great empire, an army, and a new war, that he might have a sphere where his genius and virtue might shine forth. Thus it was ever the prayer of men of heroic character that Bellona would excite miserable nations to war, and lash them into agitation with her bloody scourge, so that there might be occasion for the display of their valour. This, forsooth, is what that desire of praise and thirst for glory did. Wherefore, by the love of liberty in the first place, afterwards also by that of domination and through the desire of praise and glory, they achieved many great things; and their most eminent poet testifies to their having been prompted by all these motives:

> Porsenna there, with pride elate,
> Bids Rome to Tarquin ope her gate;
> With arms he hems the city in,
> Æneas' sons stand firm to win.[2]

At that time it was their greatest ambition either to die bravely or to live free; but when liberty was obtained, so great a desire of glory took possession of them, that liberty alone was not enough unless domination also should be sought, their great ambition being that which the same poet puts into the mouth of Jupiter:

> Nay, Juno's self, whose wild alarms
> Set ocean, earth, and heaven in arms,
> Shall change for smiles her moody frown,
> And vie with me in zeal to crown
> Rome's sons, the nation of the gown.
> So stands my will. There comes a day,
> While Rome's great ages hold their way,
> When old Assaracus' sons
> Shall quit them on the myrmidons,
> O'er Phthia and Mycenæ reign,
> And humble Argos to their chain.[3]

Which things, indeed, Virgil makes Jupiter predict as future, whilst, in reality, he was only himself passing in review in his own mind things which were already done, and which were beheld by him as present realities. But I have mentioned them with the intention of showing that, next to liberty, the Romans so highly esteemed domination, that

2. *Æneid*, viii. 646.
3. *Ibid.*, i. 279.

it received a place among those things on which they bestowed the greatest praise. Hence also it is that that poet, preferring to the arts of other nations those arts which peculiarly belong to the Romans, namely, the arts of ruling and commanding, and of subjugating and vanquishing nations, says,

> Others, belike, with happier grace,
> From bronze or stone shall call the face,
> Plead doubtful causes, map the skies,
> And tell when planets set or rise;
> But Roman thou, do thou control
>     The nations far and wide;
> Be this thy genius, to impose
> The rule of peace on vanquished foes,
> Show pity to the humbled soul,
>     And crush the sons of pride.[4]

[d]Wherefore, when the kingdoms of the East had been illustrious for a long time, it pleased God that there should also arise a Western empire, which, though later in time, should be more illustrious in extent and greatness. And, in order that it might overcome the grievous evils which existed among other nations, He purposely granted it to such men as, for the sake of honour, and praise, and glory, consulted well for their country, in whose glory they sought their own, and whose safety they did not hesitate to prefer to their own, suppressing the desire of wealth and many other vices for this one vice, namely, the love of praise. For he has the soundest perception who recognises that even the love of praise is a vice; nor has this escaped the perception of the poet Horace, who says,

4. *Æneid*, vi. 847.
d. *City of God*, V, 13.

You're bloated by ambition? take advice:
Yon book will ease you if you read it thrice.[5]

And the same poet, in a lyric song, hath thus spoken with the desire of repressing the passion for domination:

Rule an ambitious spirit, and thou hast
A wider kingdom than if thou shouldst join
To distant Gades Lybia, and thus
Shouldst hold in service either Carthaginian.[6]

Nevertheless, they who restrain baser lusts, not by the power of the Holy Spirit obtained by the faith of piety, or by the love of intelligible beauty, but by desire of human praise, or, at all events, restrain them better by the love of such praise, are not indeed yet holy, but only less base. Still, ᵉwith regard to those to whom God did not purpose to give eternal life with His holy angels in His own celestial city . . . if He had also withheld from them the terrestrial glory of that most excellent empire, a reward would not have been rendered to their good arts—that is, their virtues—by which they sought to attain so great glory. For as to those who seem to do some good that they may receive glory from men, the Lord also says, "Verily I say unto you, they have received their reward." [7] So also these despised their own private affairs for the sake of the republic, and for its treasury resisted avarice, consulted for the good of their country with a spirit of freedom, addicted neither to what their laws pronounced to be crime nor to

5. Horace, *Epist.* i. 1. 36, 37.
6. Hor. *Carm.* ii. 2.
e. *Ibid.,* V, 15-22.
7. Matt. vi. 2.

lust. By all these acts, as by the true way, they pressed forward to honours, power, and glory; they were honoured among almost all nations; they imposed the laws of their empire upon many nations; and at this day, both in literature and history, they are glorious among almost all nations. There is no reason why they should complain against the justice of the supreme and true God —"they have received their reward."

But the reward of the saints is far different, who even here endured reproaches for that city of God which is hateful to the lovers of this world. That city is eternal. There none are born, for none die. There is true and full felicity—not a goddess, but a gift of God. Thence we receive the pledge of faith, whilst on our pilgrimage we sigh for its beauty. There rises not the sun on the good and the evil, but the Sun of Righteousness protects the good alone. There no great industry shall be expended to enrich the public treasury by suffering privations at home, for there is the common treasury of truth. And, therefore, it was not only for the sake of recompensing the citizens of Rome that her empire and glory had been so signally extended, but also that the citizens of that eternal city, during their pilgrimage here, might diligently and soberly contemplate these examples, and see what a love they owe to the supernal country on account of life eternal, if the terrestrial country was so much beloved by its citizens on account of human glory.

For, as far as this life of mortals is concerned, which is spent and ended in a few days, what does it matter under whose government a dying man lives, if they who govern do not force him to impiety and iniquity? Did the Romans at all harm those nations, on whom, when subjugated, they imposed their laws, except in as far as that was accomplished with great slaughter in war? Now, had it been done with consent of the nations, it would have been done with greater success, but there would have been no glory of conquest, for neither did the Romans themselves live exempt from those laws which they imposed on others. Had this been done without Mars and Bellona, so that there should have been no place for victory, no one conquering where no one had fought, would not the condition of the Romans and of the other nations have been one and the same, especially if that had been done at once which afterwards was done most humanely and most acceptably, namely, the admission of all to the rights of Roman citizens who belonged to the Roman empire, and if that had been made the privilege of all which was formerly the privilege of a few, with this one condition, that the humbler class who had no lands of their own should live at the public expense—an alimentary impost, which would have been paid with a much better grace by them into the hands of good administrators of the republic, of which they were members, by their own hearty consent, than it would have been paid with had it to be extorted from them as conquered men? For I do not see what it makes for the safety, good morals, and certainly not for the dignity, of men, that some have conquered and others have been conquered, except that it yields them that most insane pomp of human glory, in which "they have received their reward," who burned with excessive desire of it, and carried on most eager wars. For do not their lands pay tribute? Have they any privilege of learning what the others are not privileged to learn? Are there not many senators in the other countries who do not even know Rome by sight? Take away outward show, and what are all men after all but men? But even though the perversity of the age should permit that all the better men should be more highly honoured than others, neither thus should human honour be held at a great price, for it is smoke which has no weight. But let us avail ourselves even in these things of the kindness of God. Let us consider how great things they despised, how great things they endured, what lusts they subdued for the sake of human glory, who merited that glory, as it were, in reward for such virtues; and let this be useful to us even in suppressing pride, so that, as that city in which it has been promised us to reign as far surpasses this one as heaven is distant from the earth, as eternal life surpasses temporal joy, solid glory empty praise, or the society of angels the society of mortals, or the glory of Him who made the sun and moon the light of the sun and moon, the citizens of so great a country may not seem to themselves to have done anything very great, if, in order to obtain it, they have done some good works or endured some evils, when those men for this terrestrial country already obtained, did such great things, suffered such great things. And especially are all these things to be considered, because the remission of sins which collects citizens to the celestial country has something in it to which a shadowy resemblance is found in that asylum of Romulus, whither to escape from the punishment of all manner of crimes congregated that multitude with which the state was to be founded.

What great thing, therefore, is it for that eternal and celestial city to despise all the charms of this world, however pleasant, if for the sake of this terrestrial city Brutus could even put to death his son—a sacrifice which the heavenly city compels no one to make? But certainly it is more difficult to put to death one's sons, than to do what is required to be done for the heavenly country, even to distribute to the poor those things which were looked upon as things to be amassed and laid up for one's children, or to let them go, if there arise any temptation which compels us to do so, for the sake of faith and righteousness. For it is not earthly riches which make us or our sons happy; for they must either be lost by us in our lifetime, or be possessed when we are dead, by whom we know not, or perhaps by whom we would not. But it is God who makes us happy, who is the true riches of minds. But of Brutus, even the poet who celebrates his praises testifies that it was the occasion of unhappiness to him that he slew his son, for he says,

> And call his own rebellious seed
> For menaced liberty to bleed.
> Unhappy father! howsoe'er
> The deed be judged by after days.[8]

But in the following verse he consoles him in his unhappiness, saying,

> His country's love shall all o'erbear.

There are those two things, namely, liberty and the desire of human praise, which compelled the Romans to admirable deeds. If, therefore, for the liberty of dying men, and for the desire of human

8. *Æneid,* vi. 820.

praise which is sought after by mortals, sons could be put to death by a father, what great thing is it, if, for the true liberty which has made us free from the dominion of sin, and death, and the devil —not through the desire of human praise, but through the earnest desire of freeing men, not from King Tarquin, but from demons and the prince of the demons—we should, I do not say put to death our sons, but reckon among our sons Christ's poor ones? If, also, another Roman chief, surnamed Torquatus, slew his son, not because he fought against his country, but because, being challenged by an enemy, he through youthful impetuosity fought, though for his country, yet contrary to orders which he his father had given as general; and this he did, notwithstanding that his son was victorious, lest there should be more evil in the example of authority despised, than good in the glory of slaying an enemy;—if, I say, Torquatus acted thus, wherefore should they boast themselves, who, for the laws of a celestial country, despise all earthly good things, which are loved far less than sons? If Furius Camillus, who was condemned by those who envied him, notwithstanding that he had thrown off from the necks of his countrymen the yoke of their most bitter enemies, the Veientes, again delivered his ungrateful country from the Gauls, because he had no other in which he could have better opportunities for living a life of glory;—if Camillus did thus, why should he be extolled as having done some great thing, who, having, it may be, suffered in the church at the hands of carnal enemies most grievous and dishonouring injury, has not betaken himself to heretical enemies, or himself raised some heresy against her, but has rather defended

her, as far as he was able, from the most pernicious perversity of heretics, since there is not another church, I say not in which one can live a
life of glory, but in which eternal life can be obtained? If Mucius, in order that peace might be
made with King Porsenna, who was pressing the
Romans with a most grievous war, when he did
not succeed in slaying Porsenna, but slew another
by mistake for him, reached forth his right hand
and laid it on a red-hot altar, saying that many
such as he saw him to be had conspired for his
destruction, so that Porsenna, terrified at his daring, and at the thought of a conspiracy of such as
he, without any delay recalled all his warlike purposes, and made peace;—if, I say, Mucius did this,
who shall speak of his meritorious claims to the
kingdom of heaven, if for it he may have given to
the flames not one hand, but even his whole body,
and that not by his own spontaneous act, but because he was persecuted by another? If Curtius,
spurring on his steed, threw himself all armed into
a precipitous gulf, obeying the oracles of their
gods, which had commanded that the Romans
should throw into that gulf the best thing which
they possessed, and they could only understand
thereby that, since they excelled in men and arms,
the gods had commanded that an armed man
should be cast headlong into that destruction;—if
he did this, shall we say that that man has done
a great thing for the eternal city who may have
died by a like death, not, however, precipitating
himself spontaneously into a gulf, but having suffered this death at the hands of some enemy of his
faith, more especially when he has received from
his Lord, who is also King of his country, a more
certain oracle, "Fear not them who kill the body,

but cannot kill the soul"? [9] If the Decii dedicated themselves to death, consecrating themselves in a form of words, as it were, that falling, and pacifying by their blood the wrath of the gods, they might be the means of delivering the Roman army; —if they did this, let not the holy martyrs carry themselves proudly, as though they had done some meritorious thing for a share in that country where are eternal life and felicity, if even to the shedding of their blood, loving not only the brethren for whom it was shed, but, according as had been commanded them, even their enemies by whom it was being shed, they have vied with one another in faith of love and love of faith. If Marcus Pulvillus, when engaged in dedicating a temple to Jupiter, Juno, and Minerva, received with such indifference the false intelligence which was brought to him of the death of his son, with the intention of so agitating him that he should go away, and thus the glory of dedicating the temple should fall to his colleague;—if he received that intelligence with such indifference that he even ordered that his son should be cast out unburied, the love of glory having overcome in his heart the grief of bereavement, how shall any one affirm that he has done a great thing for the preaching of the gospel, by which the citizens of the heavenly city are delivered from divers errors, and gathered together from divers wanderings, to whom his Lord has said, when anxious about the burial of his father, "Follow me, and let the dead bury their dead"? [10] Regulus, in order not to break his oath, even with his most cruel enemies, returned to them from Rome itself, because (as he is said to have replied

9. Matt. x. 28.
10. Matt. viii. 22.

**to** the Romans when they wished to retain him) he could not have the dignity of an honourable citizen at Rome after having been a slave to the Africans, and the Carthaginians put him to death with the utmost tortures, because he had spoken against them in the senate. If Regulus acted thus, what tortures are not to be despised for the sake of good faith toward that country to whose beatitude faith itself leads? Or what will a man have rendered to the Lord for all He has bestowed upon him, if, for the faithfulness he owes to Him, he shall have suffered such things as Regulus suffered at the hands of his most ruthless enemies for the good faith which he owed to them? And how shall a Christian dare vaunt himself of his voluntary poverty, which he has chosen in order that during the pilgrimage of this life he may walk the more disencumbered on the way which leads to the country where the true riches are, even God Himself;—how, I say, shall he vaunt himself for this, when he hears or reads that Lucius Valerius, who died when he was holding the office of consul, was so poor that his funeral expenses were paid with money collected by the people?—or when he hears that Quintius Cincinnatus, who, possessing only four acres of land, and cultivating them with his own hands, was taken from the plough to be made dictator—an office more honourable even than that of consul—and that, after having won great glory by conquering the enemy, he preferred notwithstanding to continue in his poverty? Or how shall he boast of having done a great thing, who has not been prevailed upon by the offer of any reward of this world to renounce his connection with that heavenly and eternal country, when he hears that Fabricius could not be prevailed on

to forsake the Roman city by the great gifts offered
to him by Pyrrhus king of the Epirots, who promised him the fourth part of his kingdom, but preferred to abide there in his poverty as a private individual? For if, when their republic—that is, the
interest of the people, the interest of the country,
the common interest—was most prosperous and
wealthy, they themselves were so poor in their own
houses, that one of them, who had already been
twice a consul, was expelled from that senate of
poor men by the censor, because he was discovered to possess ten pounds weight of silver-plate
—since, I say, those very men by whose triumphs
the public treasury was enriched were so poor,
ought not all Christians, who make common property of their riches with a far nobler purpose, even
that (according to what is written in the Acts of
the Apostles) they may distribute to each one according to his need, and that no one may say that
anything is his own, but that all things may be
their common possession[11]—ought they not to understand that they should not vaunt themselves,
because they do that to obtain the society of angels,
when those men did well-nigh the same thing to
preserve the glory of the Romans?

How could these, and whatever like things are
found in the Roman history, have become so
widely known, and have been proclaimed by so
great a fame, had not the Roman empire, extend-
ing far and wide, been raised to its greatness by
magnificent successes? Wherefore, through that
empire, so extensive and of so long continuance,
so illustrious and glorious also through the virtues
of such great men, the reward which they sought
was rendered to their earnest aspirations, and also

11. Acts ii. 45.

examples are set before us, containing necessary
admonition, in order that we may be stung with
shame if we shall see that we have not held fast
those virtues for the sake of the most glorious city
of God, which are, in whatever way, resembled by
those virtues which they held fast for the sake of
the glory of a terrestrial city, and that, too, if we
shall feel conscious that we have held them fast,
we may not be lifted up with pride, because, as the
apostle says, "The sufferings of the present time
are not worthy to be compared to the glory which
shall be revealed in us." [12] But so far as regards
human and temporal glory, the lives of these ancient Romans were reckoned sufficiently worthy.
Therefore, also, we see, in the light of that truth
which, veiled in the Old Testament, is revealed in
the New, namely, that it is not in view of terrestrial and temporal benefits, which divine providence grants promiscuously to good and evil, that
God is to be worshipped, but in view of eternal
life, everlasting gifts, and of the society of the
heavenly city itself;—in the light of this truth we
see that the Jews were most righteously given as
a trophy to the glory of the Romans; for we see
that these Romans, who rested on earthly glory,
and sought to obtain it by virtues, such as they
were, conquered those, who, in their great deprav-
ity, slew and rejected the Giver of true glory, and
of the eternal city.

There is assuredly a difference between the desire of human glory and the desire of domination;
for, though he who has an overweening delight in
human glory will be also very prone to aspire
earnestly after domination, nevertheless they who
desire the true glory even of human praise strive

12. Rom. viii. 18.

not to displease those who judge well of them. For there are many good moral qualities, of which many are competent judges, although they are not possessed by many; and by those good moral qualities those men press on to glory, honour, and domination, of whom Sallust says, "But they press on by the true way."

But whosoever, without possessing that desire of glory which makes one fear to displease those who judge his conduct, desires domination and power, very often seeks to obtain what he loves by most open crimes. Therefore he who desires glory presses on to obtain it either by the true way, or certainly by deceit and artifice, wishing to appear good when he is not. Therefore to him who possesses virtues it is a great virtue to despise glory; for contempt of it is seen by God, but is not manifest to human judgment. For whatever any one does before the eyes of men in order to show himself to be a despiser of glory, if they suspect that he is doing it in order to get greater praise—that is, greater glory—he has no means of demonstrating to the perceptions of those who suspect him that the case is really otherwise than they suspect it to be. But he who despises the judgment of praisers, despises also the rashness of suspectors. Their salvation, indeed, he does not despise, if he is truly good; for so great is the righteousness of that man who receives his virtues from the Spirit of God, that he loves his very enemies, and so loves them that he desires that his haters and detractors may be turned to righteousness, and become his associates, and that not in an earthly but in a heavenly country. But with respect to his praisers, though he sets little value on their praise, he does not set little value on their love; neither does he elude their praise, lest he should forfeit their love. And, therefore, he strives earnestly to have their praises directed to Him from whom every one receives whatever in him is truly praiseworthy. But he who is a despiser of glory, but is greedy of domination, exceeds the beasts in the vices of cruelty and luxuriousness. Such, indeed, were certain of the Romans, who, wanting the love of esteem, wanted not the thirst for domination; and that there were many such, history testifies. But it was Nero Cæsar who was the first to reach the summit, and, as it were, the citadel, of this vice; for so great was his luxuriousness, that one would have thought there was nothing manly to be dreaded in him, and such his cruelty, that, had not the contrary been known, no one would have thought there was anything effeminate in his character. Nevertheless power and domination are not given even to such men save by the providence of the most high God, when He judges that the state of human affairs is worthy of such lords. The divine utterance is clear on this matter; for the Wisdom of God thus speaks: "By me kings reign, and tyrants possess the land." [13] But, that it may not be thought that by "tyrants" is meant, not wicked and impious kings, but brave men, in accordance with the ancient use of the word, as when Virgil says,

> For know that treaty may not stand
> Where king greets king and joins not hand,[14]

in another place it is most unambiguously said of God, that He "maketh the man who is an hypo-

13. Prov. viii. 15.
14. *Æneid,* vii. 266.

crite to reign on account of the perversity of the people." [15] Wherefore, though I have, according to my ability, shown for what reason God, who alone is true and just, helped forward the Romans, who were good according to a certain standard of an earthly state, to the acquirement of the glory of so great an empire, there may be, nevertheless, a more hidden cause, known better to God than to us, depending on the diversity of the merits of the human race. Among all who are truly pious, it is at all events agreed that no one without true piety —that is, true worship of the true God—can have true virtue; and that it is not true virtue which is the slave of human praise. Though, nevertheless, they who are not citizens of the eternal city, which is called the city of God in the sacred Scriptures, are more useful to the earthly city when they possess even that virtue than if they had not even that. But there could be nothing more fortunate for human affairs than that, by the mercy of God, they who are endowed with true piety of life, if they have the skill for ruling people, should also have the power. But such men, however great virtues they possess in this life, attribute it solely to the grace of God that He has bestowed it on them —willing, believing, seeking. And, at the same time, they understand how far they are short of that perfection of righteousness which exists in the society of those holy angels for which they are striving to fit themselves. But however much that virtue may be praised and cried up, which without true piety is the slave of human glory, it is not at all to be compared even to the feeble beginnings of the virtue of the saints, whose hope is placed in the grace and mercy of the true God.

15. Job xxxiv. 30.

Philosophers—who place the end of human good in virtue itself, in order to put to shame certain other philosophers, who indeed approve of the virtues, but measure them all with reference to the end of bodily pleasure, and think that this pleasure is to be sought for its own sake, but the virtues on account of pleasure—are wont to paint a kind of word-picture, in which Pleasure sits like a luxurious queen on a royal seat, and all the virtues are subjected to her as slaves, watching her nod, that they may do whatever she shall command. She commands Prudence to be ever on the watch to discover how Pleasure may rule, and be safe. Justice she orders to grant what benefits she can, in order to secure those friendships which are necessary for bodily pleasure; to do wrong to no one, lest, on account of the breaking of the laws, Pleasure be not able to live in security. Fortitude she orders to keep her mistress, that is, Pleasure, bravely in her mind, if any affliction befall her body which does not occasion death, in order that by remembrance of former delights she may mitigate the poignancy of present pain. Temperance she commands to take only a certain quantity even of the most favourite food, lest, through immoderate use, anything prove hurtful by disturbing the health of the body, and thus Pleasure, which the Epicureans make to consist chiefly in the health of the body, be grievously offended. Thus the virtues, with the whole dignity of their glory, will be the slaves of Pleasure, as of some imperious and disreputable woman.

There is nothing, say our philosophers, more disgraceful and monstrous than this picture, and which the eyes of good men can less endure. And they say the truth. But I do not think that the picture would be sufficiently becoming, even if it were made so that the virtues should be represented as the slaves of human glory; for, though that glory be not a luxurious woman, it is nevertheless puffed up, and has much vanity in it. Wherefore it is unworthy of the solidity and firmness of the virtues to represent them as serving this glory, so that Prudence shall provide nothing, Justice distribute nothing, Temperance moderate nothing, except to the end that men may be pleased and vainglory served. Nor will they be able to defend themselves from the charge of such baseness, whilst they, by way of being despisers of glory, disregard the judgment of other men, seem to themselves wise, and please themselves. For their virtue—if, indeed, it is virtue at all—is only in another way subjected to human praise; for he who seeks to please himself seeks still to please man. But he who, with true piety towards God, whom he loves, believes, and hopes in, fixes his attention more on those things in which he displeases himself, than on those things, if there are any such, which please himself, or rather, not himself, but the truth, does not attribute that by which he can now please the truth to anything but to the mercy of Him whom he has feared to displease, giving thanks for what in him is healed, and pouring out prayers for the healing of that which is yet unhealed.

These things being so, we do not attribute the power of giving kingdoms and empires to any save to the true God, who gives happiness in the kingdom of heaven to the pious alone, but gives kingly power on earth both to the pious and the impious, as it may please Him, whose good pleasure is always just. For though we have said something about the principles which guide His administration, in so far as it has seemed good to Him to explain it, nevertheless it is too much for us, and far surpasses our strength, to discuss the hidden things of men's hearts, and by a clear examination to determine the merits of various kingdoms. He, therefore, who is the one true God, who never leaves the human race without just judgment and help, gave a kingdom to the Romans when He would, and as great as He would, as He did also to the Assyrians, and even the Persians, by whom, as their own books testify, only two gods are worshipped, the one good and the other evil—to say nothing concerning the Hebrew people, of whom I have already spoken as much as seemed necessary, who, as long as they were a kingdom, worshipped none save the true God. The same, therefore, who gave to the Persians harvests, though they did not worship the goddess Segetia, who gave the other blessings of the earth, though they did not worship the many gods which the Romans supposed to preside, each one over some particular thing, or even many of them over each several thing—He, I say, gave the Persians dominion, though they worshipped none of those gods to whom the Romans believed themselves indebted for the empire. And the same is true in respect of men as well as nations. He who gave power to Marius gave it also to Caius Cæsar; He who gave it to Augustus gave it also to Nero; He also who gave it to the most benignant emperors, the Vespasians, father and son, gave it also to the cruel Domitian; and, finally, to avoid the necessity of going over them all, He who gave it to the Christian Constantine gave it also to the apostate Julian, whose gifted mind was deceived by a sacrilegious and detestable curiosity, stimulated by the love of power. And it was because he was addicted through curiosity to vain oracles, that, confident of victory, he burned the ships which were laden with the provisions necessary for his army, and therefore, engaging with hot zeal in rashly audacious enterprises, he was soon slain, as the just consequence of his recklessness, and left his army unprovisioned in an enemy's country, and in such a predicament that it never could have escaped, save by altering the boundaries of the Roman empire, in violation of that omen of the god Terminus of which I have spoken elsewhere; for the god Terminus yielded to necessity, though he had not yielded to Jupiter. Manifestly these things are ruled and governed by the one God according as He pleases; and if His motives are hid, are they therefore unjust?

Thus also the durations of wars are determined by Him as He may see meet, according to His righteous will, and pleasure, and mercy, to afflict or to console the human race, so that they are sometimes of longer, sometimes of shorter duration. The war of the Pirates and the third Punic war were terminated with incredible celerity. Also the war of the fugitive gladiators, though in it many Roman generals and the consuls were defeated, and Italy was terribly wasted and ravaged, was nevertheless ended in the third year, having itself been, during its continuance, the end of much. The Picentes, the Marsi, and the Peligni, not distant but Italian nations, after a long and most loyal servitude under the Roman yoke, attempted to raise their heads into liberty, though many nations had now been subjected to the Roman power, and Carthage had been overthrown. In this

Italian war the Romans were very often defeated, and two consuls perished, besides other noble senators; nevertheless this calamity was not protracted over a long space of time, for the fifth year put an end to it. But the second Punic war, lasting for the space of eighteen years, and occasioning the greatest disasters and calamities to the republic, wore out and well-nigh consumed the strength of the Romans; for in two battles about seventy thousand Romans fell. The first Punic war was terminated after having been waged for three-and-twenty years. The Mithridatic war was waged for forty years. And that no one may think that in the early and much belauded times of the Romans they were far braver and more able to bring wars to a speedy termination, the Samnite war was protracted for nearly fifty years; and in this war the Romans were so beaten that they were even put under the yoke. But because they did not love glory for the sake of justice, but seemed rather to have loved justice for the sake of glory, they broke the peace and the treaty which had been concluded. These things I mention, because many, ignorant of past things, and some also dissimulating what they know, if in Christian times they see any war protracted a little longer than they expected, straightway make a fierce and insolent attack on our religion, exclaiming that, but for it, the deities would have been supplicated still, according to ancient rites; and then, by that bravery of the Romans, which, with the help of Mars and Bellona, speedily brought to an end such great wars, this war also would be speedily terminated. Let them, therefore, who have read history recollect what long-continued wars, having various issues and entailing woful slaughter, were waged by the ancient Romans, in accordance with the general truth that the earth, like the tempestuous deep, is subject to agitations from tempests— tempests of such evils, in various degrees—and let them sometimes confess what they do not like to own, and not, by madly speaking against God, destroy themselves and deceive the ignorant.

ᶠBy no means would we say that certain Christian emperors were therefore happy because they ruled a long time, or, dying a peaceful death, left their sons to succeed them in the empire, or subdued the enemies of the republic, or were able both to guard against and to suppress the attempt of hostile citizens rising against them. These and other gifts or comforts of this sorrowful life even certain worshippers of demons have merited to receive, who do not belong to the kingdom of God to which these belong; and this is to be traced to the mercy of God, who would not have those who believe in Him desire such things as the highest good. But we say that they are happy if they rule justly; if they are not lifted up amid the praises of those who pay them sublime honours, and the obsequiousness of those who salute them with an excessive humility, but remember that they are men; if they make their power the handmaid of His majesty by using it for the greatest possible extension of His worship; if they fear, love, worship God; if more than their own they love that kingdom in which they are not afraid to have partners; if they are slow to punish, ready to pardon; if they apply that punishment as necessary to government and defence of the republic, and not in order to gratify their own enmity; if they grant pardon, not that iniquity may go unpunished, but

f. *City of God*, V, 24-26.

with the hope that the transgressor may amend his ways; if they compensate with the lenity of mercy and the liberality of benevolence for whatever severity they may be compelled to decree; if their luxury is as much restrained as it might have been unrestrained; if they prefer to govern depraved desires rather than any nation whatever; and if they do all these things, not through ardent desire of empty glory, but through love of eternal felicity, not neglecting to offer to the true God, who is their God, for their sins, the sacrifices of humility, contrition, and prayer. Such Christian emperors, we say, are happy in the present time by hope, and are destined to be so in the enjoyment of the reality itself, when that which we wait for shall have arrived.

For the good God, lest men, who believe that He is to be worshipped with a view to eternal life, should think that no one could attain to all this high estate, and to this terrestrial dominion, unless he should be a worshipper of the demons—supposing that these spirits have great power with respect to such things—for this reason He gave to the Emperor Constantine, who was not a worshipper of demons, but of the true God Himself, such fulness of earthly gifts as no one would even dare wish for. To him also He granted the honour of founding a city, a companion to the Roman empire, the daughter, as it were, of Rome itself, but without any temple or image of the demons. He reigned for a long period as sole emperor, and unaided held and defended the whole Roman world. In conducting and carrying on wars he was most victorious; in overthrowing tyrants he was most successful. He died at a great age, of sickness and old age, and left his sons to succeed him in the empire. But again, lest any emperor should become a Christian in order to merit the happiness of Constantine, when every one should be a Christian for the sake of eternal life, God took away Jovian far sooner than Julian, and permitted that Gratian should be slain by the sword of a tyrant. But in his case there was far more mitigation of the calamity than in the case of the great Pompey, for he could not be avenged by Cato, whom he had left, as it were, heir to the civil war. But Gratian, though pious minds require not such consolations, was avenged by Theodosius, whom he had associated with himself in the empire, though he had a little brother of his own, being more desirous of a faithful alliance than of extensive power.

And on this account, Theodosius not only preserved during the lifetime of Gratian that fidelity which was due to him, but also, after his death, he, like a true Christian, took his little brother Valentinian under his protection, as joint emperor, after he had been expelled by Maximus, the murderer of his father. He guarded him with paternal affection, though he might without any difficulty have got rid of him, being entirely destitute of all resources, had he been animated with the desire of extensive empire, and not with the ambition of being a benefactor. It was therefore a far greater pleasure to him, when he had adopted the boy, and preserved to him his imperial dignity, to console him by his very humanity and kindness. Afterwards, when that success was rendering Maximus terrible, Theodosius, in the midst of his perplexing anxieties, was not drawn away to follow the suggestions of a sacrilegious and unlawful curiosity, but sent to John, whose abode was in the desert of Egypt—for he had learned that this servant of God (whose fame was spreading abroad) was endowed with the gift of prophecy—and from him he received assurance of victory. Immediately the slayer of the tyrant Maximus, with the deepest feelings of compassion and respect, restored the boy Valentinianus to his share in the empire from which he had been driven. Valentinianus being soon after slain by secret assassination, or by some other plot or accident, Theodosius, having again received a response from the prophet, and placing entire confidence in it, marched against the tyrant Eugenius, who had been unlawfully elected to succeed that emperor, and defeated his very powerful army, more by prayer than by the sword. Some soldiers who were at the battle reported to me that all the missiles they were throwing were snatched from their hands by a vehement wind, which blew from the direction of Theodosius' army upon the enemy; nor did it only drive with greater velocity the darts which were hurled against them, but also turned back upon their own bodies the darts which they themselves were throwing. And therefore the poet Claudian, although an alien from the name of Christ, nevertheless says in his praises of him, "O prince, too much beloved by God, for thee Æolus pours armed tempests from their caves; for thee the air fights, and the winds with one accord obey thy bugles." [16] But the victor, as he had believed and predicted, overthrew the statues of Jupiter, which had been, as it were, consecrated by I know not what kind of rites against him, and set up in the Alps. And the thunderbolts of these statues, which were made of gold, he mirthfully

16. *Panegyr. de tertio Honorii consulatu.*

and graciously presented to his couriers, who (as the joy of the occasion permitted) were jocularly saying that they would be most happy to be struck by such thunderbolts. The sons of his own enemies, whose fathers had been slain not so much by his orders as by the vehemence of war, having fled for refuge to a church, though they were not yet Christians, he was anxious, taking advantage of the occasion, to bring over to Christianity, and treated them with Christian love. Nor did he deprive them of their property, but, besides allowing them to retain it, bestowed on them additional honours. He did not permit private animosities to affect the treatment of any man after the war. He was not like Cinna, and Marius, and Sylla, and other such men, who wished not to finish civil wars even when they were finished, but rather grieved that they had arisen at all, than wished that when they were finished they should harm any one. Amid all these events, from the very commencement of his reign, he did not cease to help the troubled church against the impious by most just and merciful laws, which the heretical Valens, favouring the Arians, had vehemently afflicted. Indeed, he rejoiced more to be a member of this church than he did to be a king upon the earth. The idols of the Gentiles he everywhere ordered to be overthrown, understanding well that not even terrestrial gifts are placed in the power of demons, but in that of the true God. And what could be more admirable than his religious humility, when, compelled by the urgency of certain of his intimates, he avenged the grievous crime of the Thessalonians, which at the prayer of the bishops he had promised to pardon, and, being laid hold of by the discipline of the church, did penance in such a way that the sight of his imperial loftiness prostrated made the people who were interceding for him weep more than the consciousness of offence had made them fear it when enraged? These and other similar good works, which it would be long to tell, he carried with him from this world of time, where the greatest human nobility and loftiness are but vapour. Of these works the reward is eternal happiness, of which God is the giver, though only to those who are sincerely pious. But all other blessings and privileges of this life, as the world itself, light, air, earth, water, fruits, and the soul of man himself, his body, senses, mind, life, He lavishes on good and bad alike. And among these blessings is also to be reckoned the possession of an empire, whose extent He regulates according to the requirements of His providential government at various times.

# CHAPTER III

## SECURING THE PEACE OF BABYLON

### A. *Empty Dreams and Reality*

[a]I see that I have still to explain, so far as the limits of this work allow me, the reasonings by which men have attempted to make for themselves a happiness in this unhappy life, in order that it may be evident, not only from divine authority, but·also from such reasons as can be adduced to unbelievers, how the empty dreams of the philosophers differ from the hope which God gives to us, and from the substantial fulfilment of it which He will give us as our blessedness. Philosophers have expressed a great variety of diverse opinions regarding the ends of goods and of evils, and this question they have eagerly canvassed, that they might, if possible, discover what makes a man happy. [b]But, of course, the philosophers have this in common with us also. For if I were to ask of you why ye have believed in Christ, why ye have been made Christians; every man answers me truly, "For a happy life." The aiming therefore after a happy life is common to philosophers and Christians. But where the thing as to which there is such agreement may be found, herein is the question, from this point the separation. For to

a. *City of God*, XIX, 1.
b. *Sermons*, CL, 4-5.

aim after a happy life, to wish for a happy life, to desire a happy life, to long for it, to make pursuit for it, is, I suppose, the case of all men. Wherefore I see that I have not said enough, that this aiming after a happy life is common to philosophers and Christians; for I ought to say, common to all men, to all men whatsoever, good and bad. For both he who is good, is therefore good that he may be happy; and he who is bad, would not be bad, if he did not hope that he might be happy thereby. As touching the good, the question is an easy one, that they are therefore good, because they seek a happy life. As touching the bad, some peradventure doubt, whether they too seek a happy life. But if I could interrogate the bad, separate and divided from the good, and say, "Do you wish to be happy?" no one would say, "I do not wish it." For instance, suppose a thief: I ask of him, "Why do you commit theft?" "That I may have," he says, "what I had not." "Why do you wish to have what you had not?" "Because it is wretched not to have." If then it is wretched not to have, he thinks it happy to have. But let us leave these apart; perhaps it will be in place to return to them, when we shall have fulfilled what we have purposed touching the philosophers.

cAlthough philosophers have erred in a variety of ways, yet natural insight has prevented them from wandering from the truth so far that they have not placed the supreme good and evil, some in the soul, some in the body, and some in both. From this tripartite distribution of the sects of philosophy, Marcus Varro, in his book *De Philosophia,* has drawn so large a variety of opinions, that, by a subtle and minute analysis of distinc-

c. *City of God,* XIX, 1.

tions, he numbers without difficulty as many as 288 sects—not that these have actually existed, but sects which are possible.

To illustrate briefly what he means, I must begin with his own introductory statement in the abovementioned book, that there are four things which men desire, as it were by nature without a master, without the help of any instruction, without industry or the art of living which is called virtue, and which is certainly learned: either pleasure, which is an agreeable stirring of the bodily sense; or repose, which excludes every bodily inconvenience; or both these, which Epicurus calls by the one name, pleasure; or the primary objects of nature, which comprehend the things already named and other things, either bodily, such as health, and safety, and integrity of the members, or spiritual, such as the greater and less mental gifts that are found in men. Now these four things —pleasure, repose, the two combined, and the primary objects of nature—exist in us in such sort that we must either desire virtue on their account, or them for the sake of virtue, or both for their own sake; and consequently there arise from this distinction twelve sects, for each is by this consideration tripled. I will illustrate this in one instance, and, having done so, it will not be difficult to understand the others. According, then, as bodily pleasure is subjected, preferred, or united to virtue, there are three sects. It is subjected to virtue when it is chosen as subservient to virtue. Thus it is a duty of virtue to live for one's country, and for its sake to beget children, neither of which can be done without bodily pleasure. For there is pleasure in eating and drinking, pleasure also in sexual intercourse. But when it is preferred to virtue, it is desired for its own sake, and virtue is chosen only for its sake, and to effect nothing else than the attainment or preservation of bodily pleasure. And this, indeed, is to make life hideous; for where virtue is the slave of pleasure it no longer deserves the name of virtue. Yet even this disgraceful distortion has found some philosophers to patronize and defend it. Then virtue is united to pleasure when neither is desired for the other's sake, but both for their own. And therefore, as pleasure, according as it is subjected, preferred, or united to virtue, makes three sects, so also do repose, pleasure and repose combined, and the prime natural blessings, make their three sects each. For as men's opinions vary, and these four things are sometimes subjected, sometimes preferred, and sometimes united to virtue, there are produced twelve sects. But this number again is doubled by the addition of one difference, viz. the social life; for whoever attaches himself to any of these sects does so either for his own sake alone, or for the sake of a companion, for whom he ought to wish what he desires for himself. And thus there will be twelve of those who think some one of these opinions should be held for their own sakes, and other twelve who decide that they ought to follow this or that philosophy not for their own sakes only, but also for the sake of others whose good they desire as their own. These twenty-four sects again are doubled, and become forty-eight by adding a difference taken from the New Academy. For each of these four and twenty sects can hold and defend their opinion as certain, as the Stoics defended the position that the supreme good of man consisted solely in virtue; or they can be held as probable, but not certain, as the New Academics did. There are, therefore, twenty-four who hold their philosophy as certainly true, other twenty-four who hold their opinions as probable, but not certain. Again, as each person who attaches himself to any of these sects may adopt the mode of life either of the Cynics or of the other philosophers, this distinction will double the number, and so make ninety-six sects. Then, lastly, as each of these sects may be adhered to either by men who love a life of ease, as those who have through choice or necessity addicted themselves to study, or by men who love a busy life, as those who while philosophizing, have been much occupied with state affairs and public business, or by men who choose a mixed life, in imitation of those who have apportioned their time partly to erudite leisure, partly to necessary business: by these differences the number of the sects is tripled, and becomes 288.

I have thus, as briefly and lucidly as I could, given in my own words the opinions which Varro expresses in his book. But how he refutes all the rest of these sects, and chooses one, the Old Academy, instituted by Plato, and continuing to Polemo, the fourth teacher of that school of philosophy which held that their system was certain; and how on this ground he distinguishes it from the New Academy, which began with Polemo's successor Arcesilaus, and held that all things are uncertain; and how he seeks to establish that the Old Academy was as free from error as from doubt—all this, I say, were too long to enter upon in detail.

dThat the system of the Old Academy is true and to be adopted, Varro attempts to show in the

d. *City of God*, **XIX**, 3-10.

following manner. As it is the supreme good, not
of a tree, or of a beast, or of a god, but of man,
that philosophy is in quest of, he thinks that, first
of all, we must define man. He is of opinion that
there are two parts in human nature, body and
soul, and makes no doubt that of these two the
soul is the better and by far the more worthy part.
But whether the soul alone is the man, so that the
body holds the same relation to it as a horse to the
horseman, this he thinks has to be ascertained.
The horseman is not a horse and a man, but only a
man, yet he is called a horseman, because he is in
some relation to the horse. Again, is the body alone
the man, having a relation to the soul such as the
cup has to the drink? For it is not the cup and the
drink it contains which are called the cup, but the
cup alone; yet it is so called because it is made to
hold the drink. Or, lastly, is it neither the soul
alone nor the body alone, but both together, which
are man, the body and the soul being each a part,
but the whole man being both together, as we call
two horses yoked together a pair, of which pair the
near and the off horse is each a part, but we do not
call either of them, no matter how connected with
the other, a pair, but only both together? Of these
three alternatives, then, Varro chooses the third,
that man is neither the body alone, nor the soul
alone, but both together. And therefore the highest good, in which lies the happiness of man, is
composed of goods of both kinds, both bodily
and spiritual. And consequently he thinks that
the primary objects of nature are to be sought for
their own sake, and that virtue, which is the art of
living, and can be communicated by instruction, is
the most excellent of spiritual goods. This virtue,
then, or art of regulating life, when it has received

these primary objects of nature which existed independently of it, and prior to any instruction, seeks them all, and itself also, for its own sake; and it uses them, as it also uses itself, that from them all it may derive profit and enjoyment, greater or less, according as they are themselves greater or less; and while it takes pleasure in all of them, it despises the less that it may obtain or retain the greater when occasion demands. Now, of all goods, spiritual or bodily, there is none at all to compare with virtue. For virtue makes a good use both of itself and of all other goods in which lies man's happiness; and where it is absent, no matter how many good things a man has, they are not for his good, and consequently, should not be called good things while they belong to one who makes them useless by using them badly. The life of man, then, is called happy when it enjoys virtue and these other spiritual and bodily good things without which virtue is impossible. It is called happier if it enjoys some or many other good things which are not essential to virtue; and happiest of all, if it lacks not one of the good things which pertain to the body and the soul. For life is not the same thing as virtue, since not every life, but a wisely regulated life, is virtue; and yet, while there can be life of some kind without virtue, there cannot be virtue without life. This I might apply to memory and reason, and such mental faculties; for these exist prior to instruction, and without them there cannot be any instruction, and consequently no virtue, since virtue is learned. But bodily advantages, such as swiftness of foot, beauty, or strength, are not essential to virtue, neither is virtue essential to them, and yet they are good things; and, according to our philosophers, even these advantages are desired by virtue for its own sake, and are used and enjoyed by it in a becoming manner.

They say that this happy life is also social, and loves the advantages of its friends as its own, and for their sake wishes for them what it desires for itself, whether these friends live in the same family, as a wife, children, domestics; or in the locality where one's home is, as the citizens of the same town; or in the world at large, as the nations bound in common human brotherhood; or in the universe itself, comprehended in the heavens and the earth, as those whom they call gods, and provide as friends for the wise man, and whom we more familiarly call angels. Moreover, they say that, regarding the supreme good and evil, there is no room for doubt, and that they therefore differ from the New Academy in this respect, and they are not concerned whether a philosopher pursues those ends which they think true in the Cynic dress and manner of life or in some other. And, lastly, in regard to the three modes of life, the contemplative, the active, and the composite, they declare in favour of the third. That these were the opinions and doctrines of the Old Academy, Varro asserts on the authority of Antiochus, Cicero's master and his own, though Cicero makes him out to have been more frequently in accordance with the Stoics than with the Old Academy. But of what importance is this to us, who ought to judge the matter on its own merits, rather than to understand accurately what different men have thought about it?

If, then, we be asked what the city of God has to say upon these points, and, in the first place, what its opinion regarding the supreme good and evil is, it will reply that life eternal is the supreme good, death eternal the supreme evil, and that to obtain the one and escape the other we must live rightly. And thus it is written, "The just lives by faith," [1] for we do not as yet see our good, and must therefore live by faith; neither have we in ourselves power to live rightly, but can do so only if He who has given us faith to believe in His help do help us when we believe and pray. As for those who have supposed that the sovereign good and evil are to be found in this life, and have placed it either in the soul or the body, or in both, or, to speak more explicitly, either in pleasure or in virtue, or in both; in repose or in virtue, or in both; in pleasure and repose, or in virtue, or in all combined; in the primary objects of nature, or in virtue, or in both—all these have, with a marvellous shallowness, sought to find their blessedness in this life and in themselves. Contempt has been poured upon such ideas by the Truth, saying by the prophet, "The Lord knoweth the thoughts of men" (or, as the Apostle Paul cites the passage, "The Lord knoweth the thoughts of the *wise*") "that they are vain." [2]

For what flood of eloquence can suffice to detail the miseries of this life? Cicero, in the *Consolation* on the death of his daughter, has spent all his ability in lamentation; but how inadequate was even his ability here? For when, where, how, in this life can these primary objects of nature be possessed so that they may not be assailed by unforeseen accident? Is the body of the wise man exempt from any pain which may dispel pleasure,

1. Hab. ii. 4.
2. Ps. xciv. 11, and I Cor. iii. 20.

from any disquietude which may banish repose? The amputation or decay of the members of the body puts an end to its integrity, deformity blights its beauty, weakness its health, lassitude its vigour, sleepiness or sluggishness its activity—and which of these is it that may not assail the flesh of the wise man? Comely and fitting attitudes and movements of the body are numbered among the prime natural blessings; but what if some sickness makes the members tremble? What if a man suffers from curvature of the spine to such an extent that his hands reach the ground, and he goes upon all-fours like a quadruped? Does not this destroy all beauty and grace in the body, whether at rest or in motion? What shall I say of the fundamental blessings of the soul, sense and intellect, of which the one is given for the perception, and the other for the comprehension of truth? But what kind of sense is it that remains when a man becomes deaf and blind? where are reason and intellect when disease makes a man delirious? We can scarcely, or not at all, refrain from tears, when we think of or see the actions and words of such frantic persons, and consider how different from and even opposed to their own sober judgment and ordinary conduct their present demeanour is. And what shall I say of those who suffer from demoniacal possession? Where is their own intelligence hidden and buried while the malignant spirit is using their body and soul according to his own will? And who is quite sure that no such thing can happen to the wise man in this life? Then, as to the perception of truth, what can we hope for even in this way while in the body, as we read in the true book of Wisdom, "The corruptible body weigheth down the soul, and the earthly tabernacle presseth down the mind that museth upon many things"? [3] And eagerness, or desire of action, if this is the right meaning to put upon the Greek ὁρμή, is also reckoned among the primary advantages of nature; and yet is it not this which produces those pitiable movements of the insane, and those actions which we shudder to see, when sense is deceived and reason deranged?

In fine, virtue itself, which is not among the primary objects of nature, but succeeds to them as the result of learning, though it holds the highest place among human good things, what is its occupation save to wage perpetual war with vices—not those that are outside of us, but within; not other men's, but our own—a war which is waged especially by that virtue which the Greeks call σωφροσύνη, and we temperance,[4] and which bridles carnal lusts, and prevents them from winning the consent of the spirit to wicked deeds? For we must not fancy that there is no vice in us, when, as the apostle says, "The flesh lusteth against the spirit;" [5] for to this vice there is a contrary virtue, when, as the same writer says, "The spirit lusteth against the flesh." "For these two," he says, "are contrary one to the other, so that you cannot do the things which you would." But what is it we wish to do when we seek to attain the supreme good, unless that the flesh should cease to lust against the spirit, and that there be no vice in us against which the spirit may lust? And as we cannot attain to this in the present life, however ardently we desire it, let us by God's help accomplish at least this, to preserve

3. Wisdom ix. 15.
4. Cicero, *Tusc. Quæst.* iii. 8.
5. Gal. v. 17.

the soul from succumbing and yielding to the flesh that lusts against it, and to refuse our consent to the perpetration of sin. Far be it from us, then, to fancy that while we are still engaged in this intestine war, we have already found the happiness which we seek to reach by victory. And who is there so wise that he has no conflict at all to maintain against his vices?

What shall I say of that virtue which is called prudence? Is not all its vigilance spent in the discernment of good from evil things, so that no mistake may be admitted about what we should desire and what avoid? And thus it is itself a proof that we are in the midst of evils, or that evils are in us; for it teaches us that it is an evil to consent to sin, and a good to refuse this consent. And yet this evil, to which prudence teaches and temperance enables us not to consent, is removed from this life neither by prudence nor by temperance. And justice, whose office it is to render to every man his due, whereby there is in man himself a certain just order of nature, so that the soul is subjected to God, and the flesh to the soul, and consequently both soul and flesh to God—does not this virtue demonstrate that it is as yet rather labouring towards its end than resting in its finished work? For the soul is so much the less subjected to God as it is less occupied with the thought of God; and the flesh is so much the less subjected to the spirit as it lusts more vehemently against the spirit. So long, therefore, as we are beset by this weakness, this plague, this disease, how shall we dare to say that we are safe? and if not safe, then how can we be already enjoying our final beatitude? Then that virtue which goes by the name of fortitude is the plainest proof of the ills of life, for it is these ills which it is compelled to bear patiently. And this holds good, no matter though the ripest wisdom co-exists with it. And I am at a loss to understand how the Stoic philosophers can presume to say that these are no ills, though at the same time they allow the wise man to commit suicide and pass out of this life if they become so grievous that he cannot or ought not to endure them. But such is the stupid pride of these men who fancy that the supreme good can be found in this life, and that they can become happy by their own resources, that their wise man, or at least the man whom they fancifully depict as such, is always happy, even though he become blind, deaf, dumb, mutilated, racked with pains, or suffer any conceivable calamity such as may compel him to make away with himself; and they are not ashamed to call the life that is beset with these evils happy. O happy life, which seeks the aid of death to end it! If it is happy, let the wise man remain in it; but if these ills drive him out of it, in what sense is it happy? Or how can they say that these are not evils which conquer the virtue of fortitude, and force it not only to yield, but so to rave that it in one breath calls life happy and recommends it to be given up? For who is so blind as not to see that if it were happy it would not be fled from? And if they say we should flee from it on account of the infirmities that beset it, why then do they not lower their pride and acknowledge that it is miserable? Was it, I would ask, fortitude or weakness which prompted Cato to kill himself? for he would not have done so had he not been too weak to endure Cæsar's victory. Where, then, is his fortitude? It has yielded, it has succumbed, it has been so thoroughly over-

come as to abandon, forsake, flee this happy life.
Or was it no longer happy? Then it was miserable.
How, then, were these not evils which made life
miserable, and a thing to be escaped from?

And therefore those who admit that these are
evils, as the Peripatetics do, and the Old Academy,
the sect which Varro advocates, express a more
intelligible doctrine; but theirs also is a surprising
mistake, for they contend that this is a happy life
which is beset by these evils, even though they be
so great that he who endures them should commit
suicide to escape them. "Pains and anguish of
body," says Varro, "are evils, and so much the
worse in proportion to their severity; and to escape
them you must quit this life." What life, I pray?
This life, he says, which is oppressed by such
evils. Then it is happy in the midst of these very
evils on account of which you say we must quit
it? Or do you call it happy because you are at
liberty to escape these evils by death? What, then,
if by some secret judgment of God you were held
fast and not permitted to die, nor suffered to live
without these evils? In that case, at least, you
would say that such a life was miserable. It is
soon relinquished, no doubt, but this does not
make it not miserable; for were it eternal, you
yourself would pronounce it miserable. Its brevity,
therefore, does not clear it of misery; neither
ought it to be called happiness because it is a
brief misery. Certainly there is a mighty force in
these evils which compel a man—according to
them, even a wise man—to cease to be a man that
he may escape them, though they say, and say
truly, that it is as it were the first and strongest
demand of nature that a man cherish himself, and
naturally therefore avoid death, and should so

stand his own friend as to wish and vehemently aim at continuing to exist as a living creature, and subsisting in this union of soul and body. There is a mighty force in these evils to overcome this natural instinct by which death is by every means and with all a man's efforts avoided, and to overcome it so completely that what was avoided is desired, sought after, and if it cannot in any other way be obtained, is inflicted by the man on himself. There is a mighty force in these evils which make fortitude a homicide—if, indeed, that is to be called fortitude which is so thoroughly overcome by these evils, that it not only cannot preserve by patience the man whom it undertook to govern and defend, but is itself obliged to kill him. The wise man, I admit, ought to bear death with patience, but when it is inflicted by another. If, then, as these men maintain, he is obliged to inflict it on himself, certainly it must be owned that the ills which compel him to this are not only evils, but intolerable evils. The life, then, which is either subject to accidents, or environed with evils so considerable and grievous, could never have been called happy, if the men who give it this name had condescended to yield to the truth, and to be conquered by valid arguments, when they inquired after the happy life, as they yield to unhappiness, and are overcome by overwhelming evils, when they put themselves to death, and if they had not fancied that the supreme good was to be found in this mortal life; for the very virtues of this life, which are certainly its best and most useful possessions, are all the more telling proofs of its miseries in proportion as they are helpful against the violence of its dangers, toils, and woes. For if these are true virtues—and such cannot exist save in those who have true piety—they do not profess to be able to deliver the men who possess them from all miseries; for true virtues tell no such lies, but they profess that by the hope of the future world this life, which is miserably involved in the many and great evils of this world, is happy as it is also safe. For if not yet safe, how could it be happy? And therefore the Apostle Paul, speaking not of men without prudence, temperance, fortitude, and justice, but of those whose lives were regulated by true piety, and whose virtues were therefore true, says, "For we are saved by hope: now hope which is seen is not hope; for what a man seeth, why doth he yet hope for? But if we hope for that we see not, then do we with patience wait for it." [6] As, therefore, we are saved, so we are made happy by hope. And as we do not as yet possess a present, but look for a future salvation, so is it with our happiness, and this "with patience;" for we are encompased with evils, which we ought patiently to endure, until we come to the ineffable enjoyment of unmixed good when there shall be no longer anything to endure. Salvation, such as it shall be in the world to come, shall itself be our final happiness. And this happiness these philosophers refuse to believe in, because they do not see it, and attempt to fabricate for themselves a happiness in this life, based upon a virtue which is as deceitful as it is proud.

We give a much more unlimited approval to their idea that the life of the wise man must be social. For how could the city of God (concerning which we have already written so many pages) either take a beginning or be developed, or attain its proper destiny, if the life of the saints were not

6. Rom. viii. 24.

a social life? But who can enumerate all the great grievances with which human society abounds in the misery of this mortal state? Who can weigh them? Hear how one of their comic writers makes one of his characters express the common feelings of all men in this matter: "I am married; this is one misery. Children are born to me; they are additional cares." [7] What shall I say of the miseries of love which Terence also recounts—"slights, suspicions, quarrels, war to-day, peace to-morrow"? [8] Is not human life full of such things? Do they not often occur even in honourable friendships? On all hands we experience these slights, suspicions, quarrels, war, all of which are undoubted evils; while, on the other hand, peace is a doubtful good, because we do not know the heart of our friend, and though we did know it to-day, we should be ignorant of what it might be to-morrow. Who ought to be, or who are more friendly than those who live in the same family? And yet who can rely even upon this friendship, seeing that secret treachery has often broken it up, and produced enmity as bitter as the amity was sweet, or seemed sweet by the most perfect dissimulation? It is on this account that the words of Cicero so move the heart of every one, and provoke a sigh: "There are no snares more dangerous than those which lurk under the guise of duty or the name of relationship. For the man who is your declared foe you can easily baffle by precaution; but this hidden, intestine, and domestic danger not merely exists, but overwhelms you before you can foresee and examine it." [9] It is also to this that allu-

7. Terent. *Adelph.* v. 4.
8. *Eunuch.* i. 1.
9. *In Verrem,* ii. 1. 15.

sion is made by the divine saying, "A man's foes are those of his own household" [10]—words which one cannot hear without pain; for though a man have sufficient fortitude to endure it with equanimity, and sufficient sagacity to baffle the malice of a pretended friend, yet if he himself is a good man, he cannot but be greatly pained at the discovery of the perfidy of wicked men, whether they have always been wicked and merely feigned goodness, or have fallen from a better to a malicious disposition. If, then, home, the natural refuge from the ills of life, is itself not safe, what shall we say of the city, which, as it is larger, is so much the more filled with lawsuits civil and criminal, and is never free from the fear, if sometimes from the actual outbreak, of disturbing and bloody insurrections and civil wars?

What shall I say of these judgments which men pronounce on men, and which are necessary in communities, whatever outward peace they enjoy? Melancholy and lamentable judgments they are, since the judges are men who cannot discern the consciences of those at their bar, and are therefore frequently compelled to put innocent witnesses to the torture to ascertain the truth regarding the crimes of other men. What shall I say of torture applied to the accused himself? He is tortured to discover whether he is guilty, so that, though innocent, he suffers most undoubted punishment for crime that is still doubtful, not because it is proved that he committed it, but because it is not ascertained that he did not commit it. Thus the ignorance of the judge frequently involves an innocent person in suffering. And what is still more unendurable—a thing, indeed, to be bewailed, and,

10. Matt. x. 36.

if that were possible, watered with fountains of tears—is this, that when the judge puts the accused to the question, that he may not unwittingly put an innocent man to death, the result of this lamentable ignorance is that this very person, whom he tortured that he might not condemn him if innocent, is condemned to death both tortured and innocent. For if he has chosen, in obedience to the philosophical instructions to the wise man, to quit this life rather than endure any longer such tortures, he declares that he has committed the crime which in fact he has not committed. And when he has been condemned and put to death, the judge is still in ignorance whether he has put to death an innocent or a guilty person, though he put the accused to the torture for the very purpose of saving himself from condemning the innocent; and consequently he has both tortured an innocent man to discover his innocence and has put him to death without discovering it. If such darkness shrouds social life, will a wise judge take his seat on the bench or no? Beyond question he will. For human society, which he thinks it a wickedness to abandon, constrains him and compels him to this duty. And he thinks it no wickedness that innocent witnesses are tortured regarding the crimes of which other men are accused; or that the accused are put to the torture, so that they are often overcome with anguish, and, though innocent, make false confessions regarding themselves, and are punished; or that, though they be not condemned to die, they often die during, or in consequence of, the torture; or that sometimes the accusers, who perhaps have been prompted by a desire to benefit society by bringing criminals to justice, are themselves condemned through the ignorance of the judge, because they are unable to prove the truth of their accusations though they are true, and because the witnesses lie, and the accused endures the torture without being moved to confession. These numerous and important evils he does not consider sins; for the wise judge does these things, not with any intention of doing harm, but because his ignorance compels him, and because human society claims him as a judge. But though we therefore acquit the judge of malice, we must none the less condemn human life as miserable. And if he is compelled to torture and punish the innocent because his office and his ignorance constrain him, is he a happy as well as a guiltless man? Surely it were proof of more profound considerateness and finer feeling were he to recognise the misery of these necessities, and shrink from his own implication in that misery; and had he any piety about him, he would cry to God, "From my necessities deliver Thou me." [11]

After the state or city comes the world, the third circle of human society—the first being the house, and the second the city. And the world, as it is larger, so it is fuller of dangers, as the greater sea is the more dangerous. And here, in the first place, man is separated from man by the difference of languages. For if two men, each ignorant of the other's language, meet, and are not compelled to pass, but, on the contrary, to remain in company, dumb animals, though of different species, would more easily hold intercourse than they, human beings though they be. For their common nature is no help to friendliness when they are prevented by diversity of language from conveying their sentiments of one another; so that a man would more

11. Ps. xxv. 17.

readily hold intercourse with his dog than with a foreigner. But the imperial city has endeavoured to impose on subject nations not only her yoke, but her language, as a bond of peace, so that interpreters, far from being scarce, are numberless. This is true; but how many great wars, how much slaughter and bloodshed, have provided this unity! And though these are past, the end of these miseries has not yet come. For though there have never been wanting, nor are yet wanting, hostile nations beyond the empire, against whom wars have been and are waged, yet, supposing there were no such nations, the very extent of the empire itself has produced wars of a more obnoxious description—social and civil wars—and with these the whole race has been agitated, either by the actual conflict or the fear of a renewed outbreak. If I attempted to give an adequate description of these manifold disasters, these stern and lasting necessities, though I am quite unequal to the task, what limit could I set? But, say they, the wise man will wage just wars. As if he would not all the rather lament the necessity of just wars, if he remembers that he is a man; for if they were not just he would not wage them, and would therefore be delivered from all wars. For it is the wrong-doing of the opposing party which compels the wise man to wage just wars; and this wrong-doing, even though it gave rise to no war, would still be matter of grief to man because it is man's wrong-doing. Let every one, then, who thinks with pain on all these great evils, so horrible, so ruthless, acknowledge that this is misery. And if any one either endures or thinks of them without mental pain, this is a more miserable plight still, for he thinks himself happy because he has lost human feeling.

In our present wretched condition we frequently mistake a friend for an enemy, and an enemy for a friend. And if we escape this pitiable blindness, is not the unfeigned confidence and mutual love of true and good friends our one solace in human society, filled as it is with misunderstandings and calamities? And yet the more friends we have, and the more widely they are scattered, the more numerous are our fears that some portion of the vast masses of the disasters of life may light upon them. For we are not only anxious lest they suffer from famine, war, disease, captivity, or the inconceivable horrors of slavery, but we are also affected with the much more painful dread that their friendship may be changed into perfidy, malice, and injustice. And when these contingencies actually occur—as they do the more frequently the more friends we have, and the more widely they are scattered—and when they come to our knowledge, who but the man who has experienced it can tell with what pangs the heart is torn? We would, in fact, prefer to hear that they were dead, although we could not without anguish hear of even this. For if their life has solaced us with the charms of friendship, can it be that their death should affect us with no sadness? He who will have none of this sadness must, if possible, have no friendly intercourse. Let him interdict or extinguish friendly affection; let him burst with ruthless insensibility the bonds of every human relationship; or let him contrive so to use them that no sweetness shall distil into his spirit. But if this is utterly impossible, how shall we contrive to feel no bitterness in the death of those whose life has been sweet to us? Hence arises that grief which affects the tender heart like a wound or a bruise, and which is healed by the application of kindly consolation. For though the cure is affected all the more easily and rapidly the better condition the soul is in, we must not on this account suppose that there is nothing at all to heal. Although, then, our present life is afflicted, sometimes in a milder, sometimes in a more painful degree, by the death of those very dear to us, and especially of useful public men, yet we would prefer to hear that such men were dead rather than to hear or perceive that they had fallen from the faith, or from virtue—in other words, that they were spiritually dead. Of this vast material for misery the earth is full, and therefore it is written, "Is not human life upon earth a trial?" [12] And with the same reference the Lord says, "Woe to the world because of offences!" [13] and again, "Because iniquity abounded, the love of many shall wax cold." [14] And hence we enjoy some gratification when our good friends die; for though their death leaves us in sorrow, we have the consolatory assurance that they are beyond the ills by which in this life even the best of men are broken down or corrupted, or are in danger of both results.

The philosophers who wished us to have the gods for our friends rank the friendship of the holy angels in the fourth circle of society, advancing now from the three circles of society on earth to the universe, and embracing heaven itself. And in this friendship we have indeed no fear that the angels will grieve us by their death or deterioration. But as we cannot mingle with them as familiarly as with men (which itself is one of the griev-

12. Job vii. 1.
13. Matt. xvii. 7.
14. Matt. xxiv. 12.

ances of this life), and as Satan, as we read,[15] sometimes transforms himself into an angel of light, to tempt those whom it is necessary to discipline, or just to deceive, there is great need of God's mercy to preserve us from making friends of demons in disguise, while we fancy we have good angels for our friends; for the astuteness and deceitfulness of these wicked spirits is equalled by their hurtfulness. And is this not a great misery of human life, that we are involved in such ignorance as, but for God's mercy, makes us a prey to these demons? And it is very certain that the philosophers of the godless city, who have maintained that the gods were their friends, had fallen a prey to the malignant demons who rule that city, and whose eternal punishment is to be shared by it. For the nature of these beings is sufficiently evinced by the sacred or rather sacrilegious observances which form their worship, and by the filthy games in which their crimes are celebrated, and which they themselves originated and exacted from their worshippers as a fit propitiation.

But for the saints and faithful worshippers of the one true and most high God . . . in this abode of weakness, and in these wicked days, this state of anxiety has its use, stimulating us to seek with keener longing for that security where peace is complete and unassailable. There we shall enjoy the gifts of nature, that is to say, all that God the Creator of all natures has bestowed upon ours— gifts not only good, but eternal—not only of the spirit, healed now by wisdom, but also of the body renewed by the resurrection. There the virtues shall no longer be struggling against any vice or evil, but shall enjoy the reward of victory, the eter-

15. II Cor. xi. 14.

nal peace which no adversary shall disturb. This is the final blessedness, this the ultimate consummation, the unending end. Here, indeed, we are said to be blessed when we have such peace as can be enjoyed in a good life; but such blessedness is mere misery compared to that final felicity. When we mortals possess such peace as this mortal life can afford, virtue, if we are living rightly, makes a right use of the advantages of this peaceful condition; and when we have it not, virtue makes a good use even of the evils a man suffers. But this is true virtue, when it refers all the advantages it makes a good use of, and all that it does in making good use of good and evil things, and itself also, to that end in which we shall enjoy the best and greatest peace possible.

eHe, then, who prefers what is right to what is wrong, and what is well-ordered to what is perverted, sees that the peace of unjust men is not worthy to be called peace in comparison with the peace of the just. And yet even what is perverted must of necessity be in harmony with, and in dependence on, and in some part of the order of things, for otherwise it would have no existence at all. Suppose a man hangs with his head downwards, this is certainly a perverted attitude of body and arrangement of its members; for that which nature requires to be above is beneath, and *vice versâ*. This perversity disturbs the peace of the body, and is therefore painful. Nevertheless the spirit is at peace with its body, and labours for its preservation, and hence the suffering; but if it is banished from the body by its pains, then, so long as the bodily framework holds together, there is in the remains a kind of peace among the members, and

e. *City of God,* XIX, 12-17.

hence the body remains suspended. And inasmuch as the earthy body tends towards the earth, and rests on the bond by which it is suspended, it tends thus to its natural peace, and the voice of its own weight demands a place for it to rest; and though now lifeless and without feeling, it does not fall from the peace that is natural to its place in creation, whether it already has it, or is tending towards it. For if you apply embalming preparations to prevent the bodily frame from mouldering and dissolving, a kind of peace still unites part to part, and keeps the whole body in a suitable place on the earth—in other words, in a place that is at peace with the body. If, on the other hand, the body receive no such care, but be left to the natural course, it is disturbed by exhalations that do not harmonize with one another, and that offend our senses; for it is this which is perceived in putrefaction until it is assimilated to the elements of the world, and particle by particle enters into peace with them. Yet throughout this process the laws of the most high Creator and Governor are strictly observed, for it is by Him the peace of the universe is administered. For although minute animals are produced from the carcase of a larger animal, all these little atoms, by the law of the same Creator, serve the animals they belong to in peace. And although the flesh of dead animals be eaten by others, no matter where it be carried, nor what it be brought into contact with, nor what it be converted and changed into, it still is ruled by the same laws which pervade all things for the conservation of every mortal race, and which bring things that fit one another into harmony.

The peace of the body then consists in the duly proportioned arrangement of its parts. The peace of the irrational soul is the harmonious repose of the appetites, and that of the rational soul the harmony of knowledge and action. The peace of body and soul is the well-ordered and harmonious life and health of the living creature. Peace between man and God is the well-ordered obedience of faith to eternal law. Peace between man and man is well-ordered concord. Domestic peace is the well-ordered concord between those of the family who rule and those who obey. Civil peace is a similar concord among the citizens. The peace of the celestial city is the perfectly ordered and harmonious enjoyment of God, and of one another in God. The peace of all things is the tranquillity of order. Order is the distribution which allots things equal and unequal, each to its own place. And hence, though the miserable, in so far as they are such, do certainly not enjoy peace, but are severed from that tranquillity of order in which there is no disturbance, nevertheless, inasmuch as they are deservedly and justly miserable, they are by their very misery connected with order. They are not, indeed, conjoined with the blessed, but they are disjoined from them by the law of order. And though they are disquieted, their circumstances are notwithstanding adjusted to them, and consequently they have some tranquillity of order, and therefore some peace. But they are wretched because, although not wholly miserable, they are not in that place where any mixture of misery is impossible. They would, however, be more wretched if they had not that peace which arises from being in harmony with the natural order of things. When they suffer, their peace is in so far disturbed; but their peace continues in so far as they do not suffer, and in so far as their nature continues to exist. As, then, there may be life without pain, while there cannot be pain without some kind of life, so there may be peace without war, but there cannot be war without some kind of peace, because war supposes the existence of some natures to wage it, and these natures cannot exist without peace of one kind or other. . . .

God, then, the most wise Creator and most just Ordainer of all natures, who placed the human race upon earth as its greatest ornament, imparted to men some good things adapted to this life, to wit, temporal peace, such as we can enjoy in this life from health and safety and human fellowship, and all things needful for the preservation and recovery of this peace, such as the objects which are accommodated to our outward senses, light, night, the air, and waters suitable for us, and everything the body requires to sustain, shelter, heal, or beautify it: and all under this most equitable condition, that every man who made a good use of these advantages suited to the peace of his mortal condition, should receive ampler and better blessings, namely, the peace of immortality, accompanied by glory and honour in an endless life made fit for the enjoyment of God and of one another in God; but that he who used the present blessings badly should both lose them and should not receive the others.

The whole use, then, of things temporal has a reference to this result of earthly peace in the earthly community, while in the city of God it is connected with eternal peace. And therefore, if we were irrational animals, we should desire nothing beyond the proper arrangement of the parts of the body and the satisfaction of the appetites— nothing, therefore, but bodily comfort and abundance of pleasures, that the peace of the body might contribute to the peace of the soul. For if bodily peace be wanting, a bar is put to the peace even of the irrational soul, since it cannot obtain the gratification of its appetites. And these two together help out the mutual peace of soul and body, the peace of harmonious life and health. For as animals, by shunning pain, show that they love bodily peace, and, by pursuing pleasure to gratify their appetites, show that they love peace of soul, so their shrinking from death is a sufficient indication of their intense love of that peace which binds soul and body in close alliance. But, as man has a rational soul, he subordinates all this which he has in common with the beasts to the peace of his rational soul, that his intellect may have free play and may regulate his actions, and that he may thus enjoy the well-ordered harmony of knowledge and action which constitutes, as we have said, the peace of the rational soul. And for this purpose he must desire to be neither molested by pain, nor disturbed by desire, nor extinguished by death, that he may arrive at some useful knowledge by which he may regulate his life and manners. But, owing to the liability of the human mind to fall into mistakes, this very pursuit of knowledge may be a snare to him unless he has a divine Master, whom he may obey without misgiving, and who may at the same time give him such help as to preserve his own freedom. And because, so long as he is in this mortal body, he is a stranger to God, he walks by faith, not by sight; and he therefore refers all peace, bodily or spiritual or both, to that peace which mortal man has with the immortal God, so that he exhibits the well-ordered obedience of faith to eternal law. But as this divine Master inculcates two precepts—the love of God and the love of our neighbour—and as in these precepts a man finds three things he has to love—God, himself, and his neighbour—and that he who loves God loves himself thereby, it follows that he must endeavour to get his neighbour to love God, since he is ordered to love his neighbour as himself. He ought to make this endeavour in behalf of his wife, his children, his household, all within his reach, even as he would wish his neighbour to do the same for him if he needed it; and consequently he will be at peace, or in well-ordered concord, with all men, as far as in him lies. And this is the order of this concord, that a man, in the first place, injure no one, and, in the second, do good to every one he can reach. Primarily, therefore, his own household are his care, for the law of nature and of society gives him readier access to them and greater opportunity of serving them. And hence the apostle says, "Now, if any provide not for his own, and specially for those of his own house, he hath denied the faith, and is worse than an infidel." [16] This is the origin of domestic peace, or the well-ordered concord of those in the family who rule and those who obey. For they who care for the rest rule—the husband the wife, the parents the children, the masters the servants; and they who are cared for obey—the women their husbands, the children their parents, the servants their masters. But in the family of the just man who lives by faith and is as yet a pilgrim journeying on to the celestial city, even those who rule serve those whom they seem to command; for they rule not

16. 1 Tim. v. 8.

from a love of power, but from a sense of the duty they owe to others—not because they are proud of authority, but because they love mercy.

This is prescribed by the order of nature: it is thus that God has created man. For "let them," He says, "have dominion over the fish of the sea, and over the fowl of the air, and over every creeping thing which creepeth on the earth." [17] He did not intend that His rational creature, who was made in His image, should have dominion over anything but the irrational creation—not man over man, but man over the beasts. And hence the righteous men in primitive times were made shepherds of cattle rather than kings of men, God intending thus to teach us what the relative position of the creatures is, and what the desert of sin; for it is with justice, we believe, that the condition of slavery is the result of sin. And this is why we do not find the word "slave" in any part of Scripture until righteous Noah branded the sin of his son with this name. It is a name, therefore, introduced by sin and not by nature. The origin of the Latin word for slave is supposed to be found in the circumstance that those who by the law of war were liable to be killed were sometimes preserved by their victors, and were hence called servants.[18] And these circumstances could never have arisen save through sin. For even when we wage a just war, our adversaries must be sinning; and every victory, even though gained by wicked men, is a result of the first judgment of God, who humbles the vanquished either for the sake of removing or of punishing their sins. Witness that man of God, Daniel, who, when he was in captivity, confessed

17. Gen. i. 26.
18. *Servus,* "a slave," from *servare,* "to preserve."

to God his own sins and the sins of his people, and declares with pious grief that these were the cause of the captivity.[19] The prime cause, then, of slavery is sin, which brings man under the dominion of his fellow—that which does not happen save by the judgment of God, with whom is no unrighteousness, and who knows how to award fit punishments to every variety of offence. But our Master in heaven says, "Every one who doeth sin is the servant of sin." [20] And thus there are many wicked masters who have religious men as their slaves, and who are yet themselves in bondage; "for of whom a man is overcome, of the same is he brought in bondage." [21] And beyond question it is a happier thing to be the slave of a man than of a lust; for even this very lust of ruling, to mention no others, lays waste men's hearts with the most ruthless dominion. Moreover, when men are subjected to one another in a peaceful order, the lowly position does as much good to the servant as the proud position does harm to the master. But by nature, as God first created us, no one is the slave either of man or of sin. This servitude is, however, penal, and is appointed by that law which enjoins the preservation of the natural order and forbids its disturbance; for if nothing had been done in violation of that law, there would have been nothing to restrain by penal servitude. And therefore the apostle admonishes slaves to be subject to their masters, and to serve them heartily and with good-will, so that, if they cannot be freed by their masters, they may themselves make their slavery in some sort free, by serving not in crafty

19. Dan. ix.
20. John viii. 34.
21. 2 Pet. ii. 19.

fear, but in faithful love, until all unrighteousness pass away, and all principality and every human power be brought to nothing, and God be all in all.

And therefore, although our righteous fathers[22] had slaves, and administered their domestic affairs so as to distinguish between the condition of slaves and the heirship of sons in regard to the blessings of this life, yet in regard to the worship of God, in whom we hope for eternal blessings, they took an equally loving oversight of all the members of their household. And this is so much in accordance with the natural order, that the head of the household was called *paterfamilias;* and this name has been so generally accepted, that even those whose rule is unrighteous are glad to apply it to themselves. But those who are true fathers of their households desire and endeavour that all the members of their household, equally with their own children, should worship and win God, and should come to that heavenly home in which the duty of ruling men is no longer necessary, because the duty of caring for their everlasting happiness has also ceased; but, until they reach that home, masters ought to feel their position of authority a greater burden than servants their service. And if any member of the family interrupts the domestic peace by disobedience, he is corrected either by word or blow, or some kind of just and legitimate punishment, such as society permits, that he may himself be the better for it, and be readjusted to the family harmony from which he had dislocated himself. For as it is not benevolent to give a man help at the expense of some greater benefit he might receive, so it is not innocent to spare a man at the

22. The patriarchs.

risk of his falling into graver sin. To be innocent, we must not only do harm to no man, but also restrain him from sin or punish his sin, so that either the man himself who is punished may profit by his experience, or others be warned by his example. Since, then, the house ought to be the beginning or element of the city, and every beginning bears reference to some end of its own kind, and every element to the integrity of the whole of which it is an element, it follows plainly enough that domestic peace has a relation to civic peace —in other words, that the well-ordered concord of domestic obedience and domestic rule has a relation to the well-ordered concord of civic obedience and civic rule. And therefore it follows, further, that the father of the family ought to frame his domestic rule in accordance with the law of the city, so that the household may be in harmony with the civic order.

But the families which do not live by faith seek their peace in the earthly advantages of this life; while the families which live by faith look for those eternal blessings which are promised, and use as pilgrims such advantages of time and of earth as do not fascinate and divert them from God, but rather aid them to endure with greater ease, and to keep down the number of those burdens of the corruptible body which weigh upon the soul. Thus the things necessary for this mortal life are used by both kinds of men and families alike, but each has its own peculiar and widely different aim in using them. The earthly city, which does not live by faith, seeks an earthly peace, and the end it proposes, in the well-ordered concord of civic obedience and rule, is the combination of men's wills to attain the things which are helpful to this

life. The heavenly city, or rather the part of it
which sojourns on earth and lives by faith, makes
use of this peace only because it must, until this
mortal condition which necessitates it shall pass
away. Consequently, so long as it lives like a captive and a stranger in the earthly city, though it
has already received the promise of redemption,
and the gift of the Spirit as the earnest of it, it
makes no scruple to obey the laws of the earthly
city, whereby the things necessary for the maintenance of this mortal life are administered; and
thus, as this life is common to both cities, so there
is a harmony between them in regard to what belongs to it. But, as the earthly city has had some philosophers whose doctrine is condemned by the
divine teaching, and who, being deceived either
by their own conjectures or by demons, supposed
that many gods must be invited to take an interest
in human affairs, and assigned to each a separate
function and a separate department—to one the
body, to another the soul; and in the body itself,
to one the head, to another the neck, and each of
the other members to one of the gods; and in like
manner, in the soul, to one god the natural capacity was assigned, to another education, to another
anger, to another lust; and so the various affairs
of life were assigned—cattle to one, corn to another, wine to another, oil to another, the woods
to another, money to another, navigation to another, wars and victories to another, marriages to
another, births and fecundity to another, and other
things to other gods: and as the celestial city, on
the other hand, knew that one God only was to
be worshipped, and that to Him alone was due that
service which the Greeks call λατρεία, and which
can be given only to a god, it has come to pass that

the two cities could not have common laws of religion, and that the heavenly city has been compelled in this matter to dissent, and to become obnoxious to those who think differently, and to stand the brunt of their anger and hatred and persecutions, except in so far as the minds of their enemies have been alarmed by the multitude of the Christians and quelled by the manifest protection of God accorded to them. This heavenly city then, while it sojourns on earth, calls citizens out of all nations, and gathers together a society of pilgrims of all languages, not scrupling about diversities in the manners, laws, and institutions whereby earthly peace is secured and maintained, but recognising that, however various these are, they all tend to one and the same end of earthly peace. It therefore is so far from rescinding and abolishing these diversities, that it even preserves and adapts them, so long only as no hindrance to the worship of the one supreme and true God is thus introduced. Even the heavenly city, therefore, while in its state of pilgrimage, avails itself of the peace of earth, and, so far as it can without injuring faith and godliness, desires and maintains a common agreement among men regarding the acquisition of the necessaries of life.

B. *Natural Law and Civil Right*

[a]To all men as it were in an assemblage of mankind, the Truth crieth, *If truly indeed justice ye speak, judge right things, ye sons of men.* For to what unjust man is it not an easy thing to speak justice? or what man if about justice questioned, when he hath not a cause, would not easily answer what is just? In as much as the hand of our

a. *Enarr. in Ps.* LVII [Lat.], 1-2.

Maker in our very hearts hath written this truth, *That which to thyself thou wouldest not have done, do not thou to another.*[1] Of this truth, even before that the Law was given, no one was suffered to be ignorant, in order that there might be some rule whereby might be judged even those to whom Law had not been given. But lest men should complain that something had been wanting for them, there hath been written also in tables that which in their hearts they read not. For it was not that they had it not written, but read it they would not. There hath been set before their eyes that which in their conscience to see they would be compelled; and as if from without the voice of God were brought to them, to his own inward parts hath man been thus driven, the Scripture saying, *For in the thoughts of the ungodly man there will be questioning.*[2] Where questioning is, there is law. But because men, desiring those things which are without, even from themselves have become exiles, there hath been given also a written law: not because in hearts it had not been written, but because thou wast a deserter from thy heart, by Him that is every where thou art seized, and to thyself within art called back. Therefore the written law, what crieth it, to those that have deserted the law written in their hearts? *Return ye transgressors to the heart.*[3] For who hath taught thee that thou wouldest have no other man draw near thy wife? Who hath taught thee, that thou wouldest not have a theft committed upon thee? who hath taught thee, that thou wouldest not suffer wrong, and whatever other thing either universally or particularly might

1. Matt. vii. 12.
2. Wisd. i. 9.
3. Is. xlvi. 8.

be spoken of? For many things there are, of which severally if questioned men with loud voice would answer, that they would not suffer. Come, if thou art not willing to suffer these things, art thou by any means the only man? dost thou not live in the fellowship of mankind? He that together with thee hath been made, is thy fellow; and all men have been made after the image of God, unless with earthly covetings they efface that which He hath formed. That which therefore to thyself thou wilt not have to be done, do not thou to another. For thou judgest that there is evil in that, which to suffer thou art not willing: and this thing thou art constrained to know by an inward law; that in thy very heart is written. Thou wast doing somewhat, and there was a cry raised in thy hands: how art thou constrained to return to thy heart when this thing thou sufferest in the hands of others? Is theft a good thing? No! I ask, is adultery a good thing? All cry, No! Is man-slaying a good thing? All cry, that they abhor it. Is coveting the property of a neighbour a good thing? No! is the voice of all men. Or if yet thou confessest not, there draweth near one that coveteth thy property: be pleased to answer what thou wilt have. All men therefore, when of these things questioned, cry that these things are not good. Again, of doing kindnesses, not only of not hurting, but also of conferring and distributing, any hungry soul is questioned thus; "thou sufferest hunger, another man hath bread, and there is abundance with him beyond sufficiency, he knoweth thee to want, he giveth not: it displeaseth thee when hungering, let it displease thee when full also, when of another's hungering thou shalt have known. A stranger wanting shelter cometh into thy country, he is not taken in: he then crieth that inhuman is that city, at once among barbarians he might have found a home. He feeleth the injustice because he suffereth; thou perchance feelest not, but it is meet that thou imagine thyself also a stranger; and that thou see in what manner he will have displeased thee, who shall not have given that, which thou in thy country wilt not give to a stranger." I ask all men. True are these things? True. Just are these things? Just.

But hear ye the Psalm. *If truly therefore justice ye speak, judge right things, ye sons of men.* Be it not a justice of lips, but also of deeds. For if thou actest otherwise than thou speakest, good things thou speakest, and ill thou judgest. For if thou actest as thou judgest; if asked which is better, gold or faith, thou art not so far perverse and erring from all truth as to answer that gold is better: thou preferrest therefore, when asked, to gold, faith; thou hast spoken justice. Hast thou heard the Psalm? *If truly therefore justice ye speak, judge right things, ye sons of men.* And where shall I prove thee not to judge as thou hast spoken? I already have got thine answer setting faith before gold. Behold from some place or other a friend hath come, and without witness gold he hath entrusted to thee; he alone knoweth this, and thou, as far as regardeth men. There is there another witness, that is not seen, and yet seeth: and the man to thee in a secret place and in thy closet perchance, in the absence of witnesses, gold hath entrusted; the witness that is present, not in a chamber of walls is present, but in the couches of your consciences. He hath entrusted and hath departed, to no one of his friends he hath made it known, hoping himself to return and to receive from his friend that which he had given: such is the uncertainty of things human, he is dead, he hath left an heir, hath left a son: the son knoweth not what his father had, what to thee he entrusted: return thou, return transgressor to the heart, there written the law is: *That which to thyself thou wilt not have to be done, to another do thou not.* Suppose thyself to have entrusted, to none of thy friends to have told it, to have died, to have left a son; what wouldest thou wish to be rendered to him by thine own friend? Answer, judge the case, the judge's tribunal is in thy mind, there is sitting there God, there is at hand for accuser conscience, for torturer fear. Amid things of men thou art, in the fellowship of men thou art engaged: think what thou wouldest have to be rendered to thy son by thy friend. I know what answer thy thought maketh. So judge thou, as thou hearest judge, a voice there will be; the voice of truth holdeth not its peace; not with lips it crieth, but a cry is raised out of the heart: incline thine ear, there be thou with the son of thy friend. Thou seest perchance also a man in need wandering about, knowing not what his father had, where he hath placed it, to whom he entrusted it; think also of thy son, suppose that man to live whom thou despisest as dead, thyself deem dead in order that thou mayest live. But something else covetousness doth enjoin; doth enjoin contrary to God; God one thing, another thing covetousness: one thing in Paradise our Maker, another thing athwart it, the serpent, the deceiver. Let there come into thy mind first thy fall; for this reason mortal thou art, for this reason toiling, for this in the sweat of thy face eating bread, for this reason thorns and thistles for thee the earth beareth: by example learn that which thou wouldest not by precept. But cupidity prevaileth; why not rather truth? And where is that which thou wast speaking? Behold, thou art meditating to deny the deposit of gold; behold, thou art meditating from the heir of thy friend altogether to hide it. I had asked a little before which would be the more precious, and which would be the better, gold, or good faith. Wherefore one thing sayest thou, another thing doest? Fearest thou not this voice, *If truly justice ye speak, judge right things, ye sons of men?* Behold thou hast told me that better is good faith, and in thy judgment better thou hast considered gold to be. Thou hast not judged as thou hast spoken; true things thou hast spoken, and false things thou hast judged: therefore even when thou wast speaking justice, truly thou didst not speak. For *if truly justice ye speak, judge right things, ye sons of men.* When to me concerning justice thou wast making answer, it was for shame, not with openness thou wast speaking.

[b]Lo, this that I am proposing, examine thyself therein, weigh thyself thereon, ascend the tribunal of thy mind thereon, and place thyself before thyself, and judge thyself; and if thou shalt find thyself amiss, amend thyself. I propose then: God saith in His Law, that a thing found must be restored: God saith in His Law, which He gave to His first people, for whom Christ had not yet died, that a thing found as belonging to another must be restored; if anyone, for example, should find on the road a bag of money belonging to another, that he ought to restore it. But he does not know to whom? Ignorance doth not excuse itself, if avarice is not supreme.

b. *Sermons,* CLXXVIII, 8-9.

I will tell you, Beloved, since it was God's gift; and there are among the people of God who do not hear the Word of God in vain; I will tell what a poor man did when I was settled in Milan; so poor was he, as to be a grammarian's usher; but decidedly a Christian, though the grammarian was a heathen; better the vail than the Chair. He found a bag, if the number does not escape me, with about two hundred dollars; mindful of the Law he put up a public notice. For he knew that it ought to be restored; but to whom to restore it, he knew not. He put up a public notice: "Whosoever has lost some pieces of silver, let him come to such a place, and enquire of such a man." The man who was wandering about in lamentation every where, having discovered and read the notice, came to him. And that he might not by some chance be seeking for what was another's, the poor usher asked for proofs, asked the quality of the bag, the seal, the number of pieces too. And when he was faithfully answered in all, he restored what he had found. But the other, filled with joy, and seeking to make him some return, offered him as a tithe twenty pieces; and he would not receive it. He offered him as little as ten; he would not receive it. He asked him at least to receive five; he would not. The man in anger threw down the bag. "I have not lost any thing!" said he: "if you will not receive any thing of me, neither have I lost any thing." What a contest my Brethren, what a contest, what a battle, what a conflict! The theatre, the world; the Spectator, God. At last, being overcome, our poor man received what was offered; he forthwith laid it all out upon the poor, he left not one single piece in his own house.

What is this? If I have made any impression on

your hearts, if the word of God hath settled in you, if it hath found rest in you, do this, my Brethren; do not think you are suffering loss if you shall do it; it is a great gain if you shall do what I am saying. "I have lost twenty pieces of silver, I have lost two hundred, five hundred." What hast thou lost? They were lost out of thine house; another lost them, not thou. The earth is common, ye are in one house, travellers both in this world, ye have entered into the one inn of this road. He laid it by, he forgot it; it fell from him, thou hast found it elsewhere.

ᶜNow, if we look carefully at what is written: "The whole world is the wealth of the faithful man, but the unfaithful one has not a penny," ⁴ do we not prove that those who seem to rejoice in lawfully acquired gains, and do not know how to use them, are really in possession of other men's property? Certainly, what is lawfully possessed is not another's property, but 'lawfully' means justly and justly means rightly. He who uses his wealth badly possesses it wrongfully, and wrongful possession means that it is another's property. You see, then, how many there are who ought to make restitution of another's goods, although those to whom restitution is due may be few; wherever they are, their claim to just possession is in proportion to their indifference to wealth. Obviously, no one possesses justice unlawfully: whoever does not love it does not have it; but money is wrongly possessed by bad men while good men who love it least have the best right to it. In this life the wrong of evil possessors is endured and among them certain laws are established which are called

c. *Letters,* CLIII (Schopp, III, p. 302).
4. Prov. xvii. 6.

civil laws, not because they bring men to make a good use of their wealth, but because those who make a bad use of it become thereby less injurious. This comes about either because some of them become faithful and fervent—and these have a right to all things—or because those who live among them are not hampered by their evil deeds, but are tested until they come to that City where they are heirs to eternity, where the just alone have a place, the wise alone leadership, and those who are there possess what is truly their own.

ᵈBy what right does every man possess what he possesses? Is it not by human right? For by divine right, "The earth is the Lord's, and the fulness thereof." ⁵ The poor and the rich, God made of one clay; the same earth supports alike the poor and the rich. By human right, however, one says, This estate is mine, this house is mine, this servant is mine. By human right, therefore, is by right of the emperors. Why so? Because God has distributed to mankind these very human rights through the emperors and kings of this world. Do you wish us to read the laws of the emperors, and to act by the estates according to these laws? If you will have your possession by human right, let us recite the laws of the emperors; let us see whether they would have [you] possess anything. But what is the emperor to me? thou sayest. It is by right from him that thou possessest the land. Or take away rights created by emperors, and then who will dare say, That estate is mine, or that slave is mine, or this house is mine? If, however, in order to their possessing these things, men have received rights derived from kings, will ye that we read the

d. *In Johan. Evang. Tract VI*, 25, 26.
5. Ps. xxiv. 1.

laws, that you may be glad in having even a single garden, and impute it to nothing but the clemency of the dove that you are permitted to remain in possession even there? . . .

But what have we to do with the emperor? But I have already said that we are treating of human right. And yet the apostle would have us obey kings, would have us honour kings, and said, "Honour the king." [6] Do not say, What have I to do with the king? as in that case, what have you to do with the possession? It is by the rights derived from kings that possessions are enjoyed. Thou hast said, What have I to do with the king? Say not then that the possessions are thine; because it is to those same human rights, by which men enjoy their possessions, thou hast referred them.

## C. The "Just" War

[a]I am aware that Cicero, in the third book of his *De Republica,* if I mistake not, argues that a first-rate power will not engage in war except either for honour or for safety. What he has to say about the question of safety, and what he means by safety, he explains in another place, saying, "Private persons frequently evade, by a speedy death, destitution, exile, bonds, the scourge, and the other pains which even the most insensible feel. But to states, death, which seems to emancipate individuals from all punishments, is itself a punishment; for a state should be so constituted as to be eternal. And thus death is not natural to a republic as to a man, to whom death is not only necessary, but often even desirable. But when a

6. 1 Pet. ii. 17.
a. *City of God,* XXII, 6.

state is destroyed, obliterated, annihilated, it is as if (to compare great things with small) this whole world perished and collapsed." Cicero said this because he, with the Platonists, believed that the world would not perish. It is therefore agreed that, according to Cicero, a state should engage in war for the safety which preserves the state permanently in existence, though its citizens change; as the foliage of an olive or laurel, or any tree of this kind, is perennial, the old leaves being replaced by fresh ones. For death, as he says, is no punishment to individuals, but rather delivers them from all other punishments, but it is a punishment to the state. And therefore it is reasonably asked whether the Saguntines did right when they chose that their whole state should perish rather than that they should break faith with the Roman republic; for this deed of theirs is applauded by the citizens of the earthly republic. But I do not see how they could follow the advice of Cicero, who tells us that no war is to be undertaken save for safety or for honour; neither does he say which of these two is to be preferred, if a case should occur in which the one could not be preserved without the loss of the other. For manifestly, if the Saguntines chose safety, they must break faith; if they kept faith, they must reject safety; as also it fell out. But the safety of the city of God is such that it can be retained, or rather acquired, by faith and with faith; but if faith be abandoned, no one can attain it.

[b]Yet the natural order which seeks the peace of mankind, ordains that a monarch should have the power of undertaking war if he thinks it advisable, and that the soldiers should perform their

b. *Contra Faustum*, XXII, 75.

military duties in behalf of the peace and safety of the community. ᶜWhat is the evil in war? Is it the death of some who will soon die in any case, that others may live in peaceful subjection? This is mere cowardly dislike, not any religious feeling. The real evils in war are love of violence, revengeful cruelty, fierce and implacable enmity, wild resistance, and the lust of power, and such like; and it is generally to punish these things, when force is required to inflict the punishment, that, in obedience to God or some lawful authority, good men undertake wars, when they find themselves in such a position as regards the conduct of human affairs, that right conduct requires them to act, or to make others act, in this way. Otherwise, John, when the soldiers who came to be baptized asked, What shall we do? would have replied, Throw away your arms; give up the service; never strike, or wound, or disable any one. But knowing that such actions in battle were not murderous, but authorized by law, and that the soldiers did not thus avenge themselves, but defend the public safety, he replied, "Do violence to no man, accuse no man falsely, and be content with your wages." [1] But as the Manichæans (who blame Moses for his wars) are in the habit of running down John, let them hear the Lord Jesus Christ Himself ordering this money to be given to Cæsar, which John tells the soldiers to be content with. "Give," He says, "to Cæsar the things that are Cæsar's." [2] For tribute-money is given on purpose to pay the soldiers required for war. Again, in the case of the centurion who said, "I

c. *Contra Faustum*, XXII, 74-79.
1. Luke iii. 14.
2. Matt. xxii. 21.

am a man under authority, and have soldiers under me: and I say to one, Go, and he goeth; and to another, Come, and he cometh; and to my servant, Do this, and he doeth it," Christ gave due praise to his faith;[3] He did not tell him to leave the service. But there is no need here to enter on the long discussion of just and unjust wars.

A great deal depends on the causes for which men undertake wars, and on the authority they have for doing so. . . . When war is undertaken in obedience to God, who would rebuke, or humble, or crush the pride of man, it must be allowed to be a righteous war; for even the wars which arise from human passion cannot harm the eternal well-being of God, nor even hurt His saints; for in the trial of their patience, and the chastening of their spirit, and in bearing fatherly correction, they are rather benefited than injured. No one can have any power against them but what is given him from above. For there is no power but of God,[4] who either orders or permits. Since, therefore, a righteous man, serving it may be under an ungodly king, may do the duty belonging to his position in the State in fighting by the order of his sovereign,—for in some cases it is plainly the will of God that he should fight, and in others, where this is not so plain, it may be an unrighteous command on the part of the king, while the soldier is innocent, because his position makes obedience a duty,—how much more must the man be blameless who carries on war on the authority of God, of whom every one who serves Him knows that He can never require what is wrong?

If it is supposed that God could not enjoin war-

3. Matt. viii. 9-10.
4. Rom. xiii. 1.

fare, because in after times it was said by the Lord Jesus Christ, "I say unto you, That ye resist not evil: but if any one strike thee on the right cheek, turn to him the left also," [5] the answer is, that what is here required is not a bodily action, but an inward disposition. The sacred seat of virtue is the heart, and such were the hearts of our fathers, the righteous men of old. But order required such a regulation of events, and such a distinction of times, as to show first of all that even earthly blessings (for so temporal kingdoms and victory over enemies are considered to be, and these are the things which the community of the ungodly all over the world are continually begging from idols and devils) are entirely under the control and at the disposal of the one true God. Thus, under the Old Testament, the secret of the kingdom of heaven, which was to be disclosed in due time, was veiled, and so far obscured, in the disguise of earthly promises. But when the fulness of time came for the revelation of the New Testament, which was hidden under the types of the Old, clear testimony was to be borne to the truth, that there is another life for which this life ought to be disregarded, and another kingdom for which the opposition of all earthly kingdoms should be patiently borne. Thus the name martyrs, which means witnesses, was given to those who, by the will of God, bore this testimony, by their confessions, their sufferings, and their death. The number of such witnesses is so great, that if it pleased Christ—who called Saul by a voice from heaven, and having changed him from a wolf to a sheep, sent him into the midst of wolves—to unite them all in one army, and to give them success in battle, as He

5. Matt. v. 39.

gave to the Hebrews, what nation could withstand them? what kingdom would remain unsubdued? But as the doctrine of the New Testament is, that we must serve God not for temporal happiness in this life, but for eternal felicity hereafter, this truth was most strikingly confirmed by the patient endurance of what is commonly called adversity for the sake of that felicity. So in fulness of time the Son of God, made of a woman, made under the law, that He might redeem them that were under the law, made of the seed of David according to the flesh, sends His disciples as sheep into the midst of wolves, and bids them not fear those that can kill the body, but cannot kill the soul, and promises that even the body will be entirely restored, so that not a hair shall be lost.[6] Peter's sword He orders back into its sheath, restoring as it was before, the ear of His enemy that had been cut off. He says that He could obtain legions of angels to destroy His enemies, but that He must drink the cup which His Father's will had given Him.[7] He sets the example of drinking this cup, then hands it to His followers, manifesting thus, both in word and deed, the grace of patience. Therefore God raised Him from the dead, and has given Him a name which is above every name; that in the name of Jesus every knee should bow, of things in heaven, and of things in earth, and of things under the earth; and that every tongue should confess that Jesus is Lord, to the glory of God the Father.[8] The patriarchs and prophets, then, have a kingdom in this world, to show that these kingdoms, too, are given and taken away

6. Matt. x. 16, 28, 30.
7. Matt. xxvi. 52, 53; Luke xxii. 42, 51; John xviii. 11.
8. Phil. ii. 9-11.

by God: the apostles and martyrs had no kingdom here, to show the superior desirableness of the kingdom of heaven. The prophets, however, could even in those times die for the truth, as the Lord Himself says, "From the blood of Abel to the blood of Zacharia;[9] and in these days, since the commencement of the fulfilment of what is prophesied in the psalm of Christ, under the figure of Solomon, which means the peacemaker, as Christ is our peace,[10] "All kings of the earth shall bow to Him, all nations shall serve Him," [11] we have seen Christian emperors, who have put all their confidence in Christ, gaining splendid victories over ungodly enemies, whose hope was in the rites of idolatry and devil-worship. There are public and undeniable proofs of the fact, that on one side the prognostications of devils were found to be fallacious, and on the other, the predictions of saints were a means of support; and we have now writings in which those facts are recorded.

If our foolish opponents are surprised at the difference between the precepts given by God to the ministers of the Old Testament, at a time when the grace of the New was still undisclosed, and those given to the preachers of the New Testament, now that the obscurity of the Old is removed, they will find Christ Himself saying one thing at one time, and another at another. "When I sent you," He says, "without scrip, or purse, or shoes, did ye lack anything?" And they said, "Nothing." Then saith He to them, "But now, he that hath a scrip, let him take it, and also a purse; and he that hath not a sword, let him sell his garment, and buy one." If the Manichæans found pas-

9. Matt. xxiii. 35.
10. Eph. ii. 14.
11. Ps. lxxii. 11.

sages in the Old and New Testaments differing in this way, they would proclaim it as a proof that the Testaments are opposed to each other. But here the difference is in the utterances of one and the same person. At one time He says, "I sent you without scrip, or purse, or shoes, and ye lacked nothing;" at another, "Now let him that hath a scrip take it, and also a purse; and he that hath not a sword, let him sell his garments, and buy one." Does not this show how, without any inconsistency, precepts and counsels and permissions may be changed, as different times require different arrangements? If it is said that there was a symbolical meaning in the command to take a scrip and purse, and to buy a sword, why may there not be a symbolical meaning in the fact, that one and the same God commanded the prophets in old times to make war, and forbade the apostles? And we find in the passage that we have quoted from the Gospel, that the words spoken by the Lord were carried into effect by His disciples. For, besides going at first without scrip or purse, and yet lacking nothing, as from the Lord's question and their answer it is plain they did, now that He speaks of buying a sword, they say, "Lo, here are two swords;" and He replied, "It is enough." Hence we find Peter with a weapon when he cut off the assailant's ear, on which occasion his spontaneous boldness was checked, because, although he had been told to take a sword, he had not been told to use it.[12] Doubtless, it was mysterious that the Lord should require them to carry weapons, and forbid the use of them. But it was His part to give the suitable precepts, and it was their part to obey without reserve.

12. Luke xxii. 35-38, 50, 51.

It is therefore mere groundless calumny to charge Moses with making war, for there would have been less harm in making war of his own accord, than in not doing it when God commanded him. And to dare to find fault with God Himself for giving such a command, or not to believe it possible that a just and good God did so, shows, to say the least, an inability to consider that in the view of divine providence, which pervades all things from the highest to the lowest, time can neither add anything nor take away; but all things go, or come, or remain according to the order of nature or desert in each separate case, while in men a right will is in union with the divine law, and ungoverned passion is restrained by the order of divine law; so that a good man wills only what is commanded, and a bad man can do only what he is permitted, at the same time that he is punished for what he wills to do unjustly. Thus, in all the things which appear shocking and terrible to human feebleness, the real evil is the injustice; the rest is only the result of natural properties or of moral demerit. This injustice is seen in every case where a man loves for their own sake things which are desirable only as means to an end, and seeks for the sake of something else things which ought to be loved for themselves. For thus, as far as he can, he disturbs in himself the natural order which the eternal law requires us to observe. Again, a man is just when he seeks to use things only for the end for which God appointed them, and to enjoy God as the end of all, while he enjoys himself and his friend in God and for God. For to love in a friend the love of God is to love the friend for God. Now both justice and injustice, to be acts at all, must be voluntary; otherwise, there can be no just rewards or punishments; which no man in his senses will assert. The ignorance and impotence which prevent a man from knowing his duty, or from doing all he wishes to do, belong to God's secret penal arrangement, and to His unfathomable judgments, for with Him there is no iniquity. Thus we are informed by the sure word of God of Adam's sin; and Scripture truly declares that in him all die, and that by him sin entered into the world, and death by sin.[13] And our experience gives abundant evidence, that in punishment for this sin our body is corrupted, and weighs down the soul, and the clay tabernacle clogs the mind in its manifold activity;[14] and we know that we can be freed from this punishment only by gracious interposition. So the apostle cries out in distress, "O wretched man that I am! who shall deliver me from the body of this death? The grace of God through Jesus Christ our Lord." [15] So much we know; but the reasons for the distribution of divine judgment and mercy, why one is in this condition, and another in that, though just, are unknown. Still, we are sure that all these things are due either to the mercy or the judgment of God, while the measures and numbers and weights by which the Creator of all natural productions arranges all things are concealed from our view. For God is not the author, but He is the controller, of sin; so that sinful actions, which are sinful because they are against nature, are judged and controlled, and assigned to their proper place and condition, in order that they may not bring discord and disgrace on universal nature. This being the case, and as the judgments of God and

13. Rom. v. 12, 19.
14. Wisd. ix. 15.
15. Rom. vii. 24, 25.

the movements of man's will contain the hidden reason why the same prosperous circumstances which some make a right use of are the ruin of others, and the same afflictions under which some give way are profitable to others, and since the whole mortal life of man upon earth is a trial,[16] who can tell whether it may be good or bad in any particular case—in time of peace, to reign or to serve, or to be at ease or to die—or in time of war, to command or to fight, or to conquer or to be killed? At the same time, it remains true, that whatever is good is so by the divine blessing, and whatever is bad is so by the divine judgment.

Let no one, then, be so daring as to make rash charges against men, not to say against God. If the service of the ministers of the Old Testament, who were also heralds of the New, consisted in putting sinners to death, and that of the ministers of the New Testament, who are also interpreters of the Old, in being put to death by sinners, the service in both cases is rendered to one God, who, varying the lesson to suit the times, teaches both that temporal blessings are to be sought from Him, and that they are to be forsaken for Him, and that temporal distress is both sent by Him and should be endured for Him.

[d]It has been said that the Christian doctrine and preaching is in no way consistent with the duties and rights of citizens, because among its precepts we find: "Recompense to no man evil for evil," [17] and, "Whosoever shall smite thee on one cheek, turn to him the other also; and if any man take away thy coat, let him have thy cloak also; and whosoever will compel thee to go a mile with him,

16. Job vii. 4.
d. *Letters,* CXXXVIII, 9-15.
17. Rom. xii. 17.

go with him twain," [18]—all which are affirmed to be contrary to the duties and rights of citizens; for who would submit to have anything taken from him by an enemy, or forbear from retaliating the evils of war upon an invader who ravaged a Roman province? To these and similar statements of persons speaking slightingly, or perhaps I should rather say speaking as inquirers regarding the truth, I might give a more elaborate answer, were it not that the persons with whom the discussion is carried on are men of liberal education. In addressing such, why should we prolong the debate, and not rather begin by inquiring for ourselves how it was possible that the Republic of Rome was governed and aggrandized from insignificance and poverty to greatness and opulence by men who, when they had suffered wrong, would rather pardon than punish the offender;[19] or how Cicero, addressing Cæsar, the greatest statesman of his time, said, in praising his character, that he was wont to forget nothing but the wrongs which were done to him?[20] For in this Cicero spoke either praise or flattery: if he spoke praise, it was because he knew Cæsar to be such as he affirmed; if he spoke flattery, he showed that the chief magistrate of a commonwealth ought to do such things as he falsely commended in Cæsar. But what is "not rendering evil for evil," but refraining from the passion of revenge—in other words, choosing, when one has suffered wrong, to pardon rather than to punish the offender, and to forget nothing but the wrongs done to us?

18. Matt. v. 39-41.
19. "Accepta injuria ignoscere quam persequi malebant."—Sallust, *Catilina*, c. 9.
20. "Oblivisci soles nihil nisi injurias."—Cicero, *pro Ligario*, c. 12.

When these things are read in their own authors, they are received with loud applause; they are regarded as the record and recommendation of virtues in the practice of which the Republic deserved to hold sway over so many nations, because its citizens preferred to pardon rather than punish those who wronged them. But when the precept, "Render to no man evil for evil," is read as given by divine authority, and when, from the pulpits in our churches, this wholesome counsel is published in the midst of our congregations, or, as we might say, in places of instruction open to all, of both sexes and of all ages and ranks, our religion is accused as an enemy to the Republic! Yet, were our religion listened to as it deserves, it would establish, consecrate, strengthen, and enlarge the commonwealth in a way beyond all that Romulus, Numa, Brutus, and all the other men of renown in Roman history achieved. For what is a republic but a commonwealth? Therefore its interests are common to all; they are the interests of the State. Now what is a State but a multitude of men bound together by some bond of concord? In one of their own authors we read: "What was a scattered and unsettled multitude had by concord become in a short time a State." But what exhortations to concord have they ever appointed to be read in in their temples? So far from this, they were unhappily compelled to devise how they might worship without giving offence to any of their gods, who were all at such variance among themselves, that, had their worshippers imitated their quarrelling, the State must have fallen to pieces for want of the bond of concord, as it soon afterwards began to do through civil wars, when the morals of the people were changed and corrupted.

But who, even though he be a stranger to our

religion, is so deaf as not to know many precepts enjoining concord, not invented by the discussions of men, but written with the authority of God, are continually read in the churches of Christ? For this is the tendency even of those precepts which they are much more willing to debate than to follow: "That to him who smites us on one cheek we should offer the other to be smitten; to him who would take away our coat we should give our cloak also; and that with him who compels us to go one mile we should go twain." For these things are done only that a wicked man may be overcome by kindness, or rather that the evil which is in the wicked man may be overcome by good, and that the man may be delivered from the evil— not from any evil that is external and foreign to himself, but from that which is within and is his own, under which he suffers loss more severe and fatal than could be inflicted by the cruelty of any enemy from without. He, therefore, who is overcoming evil by good, submits patiently to the loss of temporal advantages, that he may show how those things, through excessive love of which the other is made wicked, deserve to be despised when compared with faith and righteousness; in order that so the injurious person may learn from him whom he wronged what is the true nature of the things for the sake of which he committed the wrong, and may be won back with sorrow for his sin to that concord, than which nothing is more serviceable to the State, being overcome not by the strength of one passionately resenting, but by the good-nature of one patiently bearing wrong. For then it is rightly done when it seems that it will benefit him for whose sake it is done, by producing in him amendment of his ways and concord with others. At all events, it is to be done with this intention, even though the result may be different from what was expected, and the man, with a view to whose correction and conciliation this healing and salutary medicine, so to speak, was employed, refuses to be corrected and reconciled.

Moreover, if we pay attention to the words of the precept, and consider ourselves under bondage to the literal interpretation, the right cheek is not to be presented by us if the left has been smitten. "Whosoever," it is said, "shall smite thee on thy right cheek, turn to him the other also;" [21] but the left cheek is more liable to be smitten, because it is easier for the right hand of the assailant to smite it than the other. But the words are commonly understood as if our Lord had said: If any one has acted injuriously to thee in respect of the higher possessions which thou hast, offer to him also the inferior possessions, lest, being more concerned about revenge than about forbearance, thou shouldst despise eternal things in comparison with temporal things, whereas temporal things ought to be despised in comparison with eternal things, as the left is in comparison with the right.[22] This has been always the aim of the holy martyrs; for final vengeance is righteously demanded only when there remains no room for amendment, namely, in the last great judgment. But meanwhile we must be on our guard, lest, through desire for revenge, we lose patience itself,—a virtue which is of more value than all which an enemy can, in spite of our resistance, take away from us. For another evangelist, in recording the same precept, makes no mention of the right cheek, but names merely the one and the other;[23] so that, while the

21. Matt. v. 39.
22. Compare vol. viii. p. 48.
23. Luke vi. 29.

duty may be somewhat more distinctly learned from Matthew's gospel, he simply commends the same exercise of patience. Wherefore a righteous and pious man ought to be prepared to endure with patience injury from those whom he desires to make good, so that the number of good men may be increased, instead of himself being added, by retaliation of injury, to the number of wicked men.

In fine, that these precepts pertain rather to the inward disposition of the heart than to the actions which are done in the sight of men, requiring us, in the inmost heart, to cherish patience along with benevolence, but in the outward action to do that which seems most likely to benefit those whose good we ought to seek, is manifest from the fact that our Lord Jesus Himself, our perfect example of patience, when He was smitten on the face, answered: "If I have spoken evil, bear witness of the evil, but if not, why smitest thou me?" [24] If we look only to the words, He did not in this obey His own precept, for He did not present the other side of his face to him who had smitten Him, but, on the contrary, prevented him who had done the wrong from adding thereto; and yet He had come prepared not only to be smitten on the face, but even to be slain upon the cross for those at whose hands He suffered crucifixion, and for whom, when hanging on the cross, He prayed, "Father, forgive them, they know not what they do!" [25] In like manner, the Apostle Paul seems to have failed to obey the precept of his Lord and Master, when he, being smitten on the face as He had been, said to the chief priest: "God shall smite thee, thou whited

24. John xviii. 23.
25. Luke xxiii. 34.

wall, for sittest thou to judge me after the law, and commandest me to be smitten contrary to the law?" And when it was said by them that stood near, "Revilest thou God's high priest?" he took pains sarcastically to indicate what his words meant, that those of them who were discerning might understand that now the whited wall, *i.e.* the hypocrisy of the Jewish priesthood, was appointed to be thrown down by the coming of Christ; for He said: "I wist not, brethren, that he was the high priest, for it is written, Thou shalt not speak evil of the ruler of thy people;" [26] although it is perfectly certain that he who had grown up in that nation, and had been in that place trained in the law, could not but know that his judge was the chief priest, and could not, by professing ignorance on this point, impose upon those to whom he was so well known.

These precepts concerning patience ought to be always retained in the habitual discipline of the heart, and the benevolence which prevents the recompensing of evil for evil must be always fully cherished in the disposition. At the same time, many things must be done in correcting with a certain benevolent severity, even against their own wishes, men whose welfare rather than their wishes it is our duty to consult; and the Christian Scriptures have most unambiguously commended this virtue in a magistrate. For in the correction of a son, even with some sternness, there is assuredly no diminution of a father's love; yet, in the correction, that is done which is received with reluctance and pain by one whom it seems necessary to heal by pain. And on this principle, if the commonwealth observe the precepts of the Christian

26. Acts xxiii. 3-5.

religion, even its wars themselves will not be carried on without the benevolent design that, after the resisting nations have been conquered, provision may be more easily made for enjoying in peace the mutual bond of piety and justice. For the person from whom is taken away the freedom which he abuses in doing wrong is vanquished with benefit to himself; since nothing is more truly a misfortune that that good fortune of offenders, by which pernicious impunity is maintained, and the evil disposition, like an enemy within the man, is strengthened. But the perverse and froward hearts of men think human affairs are prosperous when men are concerned about magnificent mansions, and indifferent to the ruin of souls; when mighty theatres are built up, and the foundations of virtue are undermined; when the madness of extravagance is highly esteemed, and works of mercy are scorned; when, out of the wealth and affluence of rich men, luxurious provision is made for actors, and the poor are grudged the necessaries of life; when that God who, by the public declarations of His doctrine, protests against public vice, is blasphemed by impious communities, which demand gods of such character that even those theatrical representations which bring disgrace to both body and soul are fitly performed in honour of them. If God permit these things to prevail, He is in that permission showing more grievous displeasure: if He leave these crimes unpunished, such impunity is a more terrible judgment. When, on the other hand, He overthrows the props of vice, and reduces to poverty those lusts which were nursed by plenty, He afflicts in mercy. And in mercy, also, if such a thing were possible, even wars might be waged by the good, in order that, by bringing under the yoke the unbridled lusts of men, those vices might be abolished which ought, under a just government, to be either extirpated or suppressed.

For if the Christian religion condemned wars of every kind, the command given in the gospel to soldiers asking counsel as to salvation would rather be to cast away their arms, and withdraw themselves wholly from military service; whereas the word spoken to such was, "Do violence to no man, neither accuse any falsely, and be content with your wages," [27]—the command to be content with their wages manifestly implying no prohibition to continue in the service. Wherefore, let those who say that the doctrine of Christ is incompatible with the State's well-being, give us an army composed of soldiers such as the doctrine of Christ requires them to be; let them give us such subjects, such husbands and wives, such parents and children, such masters and servants, such kings, such judges—in fine, even such tax-payers and tax-gatherers, as the Christian religion has taught that men should be, and then let them dare to say that it is adverse to the State's well-being; yea, rather, let them no longer hesitate to confess that this doctrine, if it were obeyed, would be the salvation of the commonwealth.

[e]Do not think that it is impossible for any one to please God while engaged in active military service. Among such persons was the holy David, to whom God gave so great a testimony; among them also were many righteous men of that time; among them was also that centurion who said to the Lord: "I am not worthy that Thou shouldest

27. Luke iii. 14.
e. *Letters*, CLXXXIX, 4.

come under my roof, but speak the word only, and my servant shall be healed: for I am a man under authority, having soldiers under me: and I say to this man, Go, and he goeth; and to another, Come, and he cometh; and to my servant, Do this, and he doeth it;" and concerning whom the Lord said: "Verily, I say unto you, I have not found so great faith, no, not in Israel." [28] Among them was that Cornelius to whom an angel said: "Cornelius, thine alms are accepted, and thy prayers are heard," [29] when he directed him to send to the blessed Apostle Peter, and to hear from him what he ought to do, to which apostle he sent a devout soldier, requesting him to come to him. Among them were also the soldiers who, when they had come to be baptized by John,—the sacred forerunner of the Lord, and the friend of the Bridegroom, of whom the Lord says: "Among them that are born of women there hath not arisen a greater than John the Baptist," [30]—and had inquired of him what they should do, received the answer, "Do violence to no man, neither accuse any falsely; and be content with your wages." [31] Certainly he did not prohibit them to serve as soldiers when he commanded them to be content with their pay for the service.

They occupy indeed a higher place before God who, abandoning all these secular employments, serve Him with the strictest chastity; but "every one," as the apostle says, "hath his proper gift of God, one after this manner, and another after that." [32] Some, then, in praying for you, fight against your invisible enemies; you, in fighting for

28. Matt. viii. 8-10.
29. Acts x. 4.
30. Matt. xi. 11.
31. Luke iii. 14.
32. I Cor. vii. 7.

them, contend against the barbarians, their visible enemies. Would that one faith existed in all, for then there would be less weary struggling, and the devil with his angels would be more easily conquered; but since it is necessary in this life that the citizens of the kingdom of heaven should be subjected to temptations among erring and impious men, that they may be exercised, and "tried as gold in the furnace," [33] we ought not before the appointed time to desire to live with those alone who are holy and righteous, so that, by patience, we may deserve to receive this blessedness in its proper time.

Think, then, of this first of all, when you are arming for the battle, that even your bodily strength is a gift of God; for, considering this, you will not employ the gift of God against God. For, when faith is pledged, it is to be kept even with the enemy against whom the war is waged, how much more with the friend for whom the battle is fought! Peace should be the object of your desire; war should be waged only as a necessity, and waged only that God may by it deliver men from the necessity and preserve them in peace. For peace is not sought in order to the kindling of war, but war is waged in order that peace may be obtained. Therefore, even in waging war, cherish the spirit of a peace-maker, that, by conquering those whom you attack, you may lead them back to the advantage of peace; for our Lord says: "Blessed are the peacemakers; for they shall be called the children of God." [34] If, however, peace among men be so sweet as procuring temporal safety, how much sweeter is that peace

33. Wisd. iii. 6.
34. Matt. v. 9.

with God which procures for men the eternal felicity of the angels! Let necessity, therefore, and not your will, slay the enemy who fights against you. As violence is used towards him who rebels and resists, so mercy is due to the vanquished or the captive, especially in the case in which future troubling of the peace is not to be feared.

[f]Those warriors are indeed great and worthy of singular honour, not only for their consummate bravery, but also (which is a higher praise) for their eminent fidelity, by whose labours and dangers, along with the blessing of divine protection and aid, enemies previously unsubdued are conquered, and peace obtained for the State, and the provinces reduced to subjection. But it is a higher glory still to stay war itself with a word, than to slay men with the sword, and to procure or maintain peace by peace, not by war. For those who fight, if they are good men, doubtless seek for peace; nevertheless it is through blood.

[g]The growth of kingdoms would certainly have been small if the peace and justice of neighbours had not by any wrong provoked the carrying on of war against them; and human affairs being thus more happy, all kingdoms would have been small, rejoicing in neighbourly concord; and thus there would have been very many kingdoms of nations in the world, as there are very many houses of citizens in a city. Therefore, to carry on war and extend a kingdom over wholly subdued nations seems to bad men to be felicity, to good men necessity.

f. *Letters*, CCXXIX, 2.
g. *City of God*, IV, 15.

# CHAPTER IV

## PERSECUTION OF HERETICS

A. *Early View: The Work of Bad Men*

[a]To my Lords Most Beloved, and Brethren Worthy of all Praise, Eleusius, Glorius, and the Two Felixes [of the Donatist sect], Augustine sends greetings.

In passing through Tubursi on my way to the church of Cirta, though pressed for time, I visited Fortunius, your bishop there, and found him to be, in truth, just such a man as you were wont most kindly to leave me to expect. When I sent him notice of your conversation with me concerning him, and expressed a desire to see him, he did not decline the visit. I therefore went to him, because I thought it due to his age that I should go to him, instead of insisting upon his first coming to me. I went, therefore, accompanied by a considerable number of persons, who, as it happened, were at that time beside me. When, however, we had taken our seats in his house, the thing becoming known, a considerable addition was made to the crowd assembled; but in that whole multitude there appeared to me to be very few who desired the matter to be discussed in a sound and profitable manner, or with the deliberation and solemnity which so great a question demands. All

a. *Letters,* XLIV, 1-2.

the others had come rather in the mood of play-goers, expecting a scene in our debates, than in Christian seriousness of spirit, seeking instruction in regard to salvation. Accordingly they could neither favour us with silence when we spoke, nor speak with care, or even with due regard to decorum and order,—excepting, as I have said, those few persons about whose pious and sincere interest in the matter there was no doubt. Everything was therefore thrown into confusion by the noise of men speaking loudly, and each according to the unchecked impulse of his own feelings; and though both Fortunius and I used entreaty and remonstrance, we utterly failed in persuading them to listen silently to what was spoken.

The discussion of the question was opened notwithstanding, and for some hours we persevered, speeches being delivered by each side in turn, so far as was permitted by an occasional respite from the voices of the noisy onlookers.

[b]Fortunius began to insist upon my answering categorically this question: Whether I thought the persecutor or the persecuted to be in the right? To which I answered, that the question was not fairly stated: it might be that both were in the wrong, or that the persecution might be made by the one who was the more righteous of the two parties; and therefore it was not always right to infer that one is on the better side because he suffers persecution, although that is almost always the case. When I perceived that he still laid great stress upon this, wishing to have the justice of the cause of his party acknowledged as beyond dispute because they had suffered persecution, I asked him whether he believed Ambrose, bishop

b. *Letters*, XLIV, 7-11.

of the Church of Milan, to be a righteous man and a Christian? He was compelled to deny expressly that that man was a Christian and a righteous man; for if he had admitted this, I would at once have objected to him that he esteemed it necessary for him to be rebaptized. When, therefore, he was compelled to pronounce concerning Ambrose that he was not a Christian nor a righteous man, I related the persecution which he endured when his church was surrounded with soldiers. I also asked whether Maximianus, who had made a schism from their party at Carthage, was in his view a righteous man and a Christian. He could not but deny this. I therefore reminded him that he had endured such persecution that his church had been razed to the foundations. By these instances I laboured to persuade him, if possible, to give up affirming that the suffering of persecution is the most infallible mark of Christian righteousness.

He also related that, in the infancy of their schism, his predecessors, being anxious to devise some way of hushing up the fault of Cæcilianus, lest a schism should take place, had appointed over the people belonging to his communion in Carthage an interim bishop before Majorinus was ordained in opposition to Cæcilianus. He alleged that this interim bishop was murdered in his own meeting-house by our party. This, I confess, I had never heard before, though so many charges brought by them against us have been refuted and disproved, while by us greater and more numerous crimes have been alleged against them. After having narrated this story, he began again to insist on my answering whether in this case I thought the murderer or the victim the more righteous man; as if he had already proved that the event had taken place as he had stated. I therefore said that we must first ascertain the truth of the story, for we ought not to believe without examination all that is said; and that even were it true, it was possible either that both were equally bad, or that one who was bad had caused the death of another yet worse than himself. For, in truth, it is possible that his guilt is more heinous who rebaptizes the whole man than his who kills the body only.

After this there was no occasion for the question which he afterwards put to me. He affirmed that even a bad man should not be killed by Christians and righteous men; as if we called those who in the Catholic Church do such things righteous men: a statement, moreover, which it is more easy for them to affirm than to prove to us, so long as they themselves, with few exceptions, bishops, presbyters, and clergy of all kinds, go on gathering mobs of most infatuated men, and causing, wherever they are able, so many violent massacres, and devastations to the injury not of Catholics only, but sometimes even of their own partisans. In spite of these facts, Fortunius, affecting ignorance of their most villanous doings, which were better known by him than by me, insisted upon my giving an example of a righteous man putting even a bad man to death. This was, of course, not relevant to the matter in hand; for I conceded that wherever such crimes were committed by men having the name of Christians, they were not the actions of good men. Nevertheless, in order to show him what was the true question before us, I answered by inquiring whether Elijah seemed to him to be a righteous man; to which he could not but assent. Thereupon I reminded him how many false prophets Elijah slew with his own hand.[1] He saw plainly herein, as indeed he could not but see, that such things were then lawful to righteous men. For they did these things as prophets guided by the Spirit and sanctioned by the authority of God, who knows infallibly to whom it may be even a benefit to be put to death.[2] He therefore required me to show him one who, being a righteous man, had in the New Testament times put any one, even a criminal and impious man, to death.

I then laboured to show that it was not right either for us to reproach them with atrocities of which some of their party had been guilty, or for them to reproach us if any such deeds were found by them to have been done on our side. For I granted that no example could be produced from the New Testament of a righteous man putting any one to death; but I insisted that by the example of our Lord Himself, it could be proved that the wicked had been tolerated by the innocent. For His own betrayer, who had already received the price of His blood, He suffered to remain undistinguished from the innocent who were with Him, even up to that last kiss of peace. He did not conceal from the disciples the fact that in the midst of them was one capable of such a crime; and, nevertheless, He administered to them all alike, without excluding the traitor, the first sacrament of His body and blood.[3]

From this we passed to something else, many on both sides discoursing to the best of their ability.

1. I Kings xviii. 40.
2. Qui novit cui etiam prosit occidi.
3. Matt. xxvi. 20-28.

Among other things it was alleged that our party was still intending to persecute them; and he [Fortunius] said that he would like to see how I would act in the event of such persecution, whether I would consent to such cruelty, or withhold from it all countenance. I said that God saw my heart, which was unseen by them; also that they had hitherto had no ground for apprehending such persecution, which if it did take place would be the work of bad men, who were, however, not so bad as some of their own party; but that it was not incumbent on us to withdraw ourselves from communion with the Catholic Church on the ground of anything done against our will, and even in spite of our opposition (if we had an opportunity of testifying against it), seeing that we had learned that toleration for the sake of peace which the apostle prescribes in the words: "Forbearing one another in love, endeavouring to keep the unity of the Spirit in the bond of peace." [4] I affirmed that they had not preserved this peace and forbearance, when they had caused a schism, within which, moreover, the more moderate among them now tolerated more serious evils, lest that which was already a fragment should be broken again, although they did not, in order to preserve unity, consent to exercise forbearance in smaller things. I also said that in the ancient economy the peace of unity and forbearance had not been so fully declared and commended as it is now by the example of the Lord and the charity of the New Testament; and yet prophets and holy men were wont to protest against the sins of the people, without endeavouring to separate themselves from the unity of the

4. Eph. iv. 2, 3.

Jewish people, and from communion in partaking along with them of the sacraments then appointed.

## B. *Later View: Compel Them to Come In*

[a]To His Brother Emeritus, Beloved and Longed For, Augustine sends greetings.

I know that it is not on the possession of good talents and a liberal education that the salvation of the soul depends; but when I hear of anyone who is thus endowed holding a different view from that which truth imperatively insists upon on a point which admits of very easy examination, the more I wonder at such a man, the more I burn with desire to make his acquaintance, and to converse with him; or if that be impossible, I long to bring his mind and mine into contact by exchanging letters, which wing their flight even between places far apart. . . .

The civil powers defend their conduct in persecuting schismatics by the rule which the apostle laid down: "Whoso resisteth the power, resisteth the ordinance of God; and they that resist shall receive to themselves judgment. For rulers are not a terror to good works, but to the evil. Wilt thou then not be afraid of the power? Do that which is good, and thou shalt have praise of the same: for he is the minister of God to thee for good. But if thou do that which is evil, be afraid; for he beareth not the sword in vain: for he is the minister of God, a revenger to execute wrath upon him that doeth evil." [1] The whole question therefore is, whether schism be not an evil work, or whether you have not caused schism, so that your resistance of the powers that be is in a good cause

a. *Letters,* LXXXVII, 1, 7-9.
1. Rom. xiii. 2-4.

and not in an evil work, whereby you would bring judgment on yourselves. Wherefore with infinite wisdom the Lord not merely said, "Blessed are they who are persecuted," but added, "for righteousness' sake." [2] I desire therefore to know from you, in the light of what I have said above, whether it be a work of righteousness to originate and perpetuate your state of separation from the Church. I desire also to know whether it be not rather a work of unrighteousness to condemn unheard the whole Christian world, either because it has not heard what you have heard, or because no proof has been furnished to it of charges which were rashly believed, or without sufficient evidence advanced by you, and to propose on this ground to baptize a second time the members of so many churches founded by the preaching and labours either of the Lord Himself while He was on earth, or of His apostles; and all this on the assumption that it is excusable for you either not to know the wickedness of your African colleagues who are living beside you, and are using the same sacraments with you, or even to tolerate their misdeeds when known, lest the party of Donatus should be divided, but that it is inexcusable for them, though they reside in most remote regions, to be ignorant of what you either know, or believe, or have heard, or imagine, concerning men in Africa. How great is the perversity of those who cling to their own unrighteousness, and yet find fault with the severity of the civil powers!

You answer, perhaps, that Christians ought not to persecute even the wicked. Be it so; let us admit that they ought not: but is it lawful to lay this objection in the way of the powers which are

2. Matt. v. 10.

ordained for this very purpose? Shall we erase
the apostle's words? Or do your MSS. not contain
the words which I mentioned a little while ago?
But you will say that we ought not to communicate with such persons. What then? Did you withdraw, some time ago, from communion with the
deputy Flavianus, on the ground of his putting
to death, in his administration of the laws, those
whom he found guilty? Again, you will say that
the Roman emperors are incited against you by
us. Nay, rather blame yourselves for this, seeing
that, as was long ago foretold in the promise
concerning Christ, "Yea, all kings shall fall down
before Him," [3] they are now members of the
Church; and you have dared to wound the Church
by schism, and still presume to insist upon rebap-
tizing her members. Our brethren indeed demand
help from the powers which are ordained, not to
persecute you, but to protect themselves against
the lawless acts of violence perpetrated by individuals of your party, which you yourselves, who
refrain from such things, bewail and deplore; just
as, before the Roman Empire became Christian,
the Apostle Paul took measures to secure that the
protection of armed Roman soldiers should be
granted him against the Jews who had conspired
to kill him. But these emperors, whatever the occasion of their becoming acquainted with the
crime of your schism might be, frame against
you such decrees as their zeal and their office
demand. For they bear not the sword in vain; they
are the ministers of God to execute wrath upon
those that do evil. Finally, if some of our party
transgress the bounds of Christian moderation in
this matter, it displeases us; nevertheless, we do

3. Ps. lxxii. 11.

not on their account forsake the Catholic Church because we are unable to separate the wheat from the chaff before the final winnowing, especially since you yourselves have not forsaken the Donatist party on account of Optatus, when you had not courage to excommunicate him for his crimes.

You say, however, "Why seek to have us joined to you, if we be thus stained with guilt?" I reply: Because you still live, and may, if you are willing, be restored. For when you join yourselves to us, *i.e.* to the Church of God, the heritage of Christ, who has the ends of the earth as His possession, you are restored so that you live in vital union with the Root. . . . If deserters carry with them the imperial standards, these standards are welcomed back again as they were, if they have remained unharmed, when the deserters are either punished with a severe sentence, or, in the exercise of clemency, restored. If, in regard to this, any more particular inquiry is to be made, that is, as I have said, another question; for in these things, the practice of the Church of God is the rule of our practice.

---

[b]To Vincentius, My Brother Dearly Beloved, Augustine sends greetings.

You are of opinion that no one should be compelled to follow righteousness; and yet you read that the householder said to his servants, "Whomsoever ye shall find, compel them to come in." [4] You also read how he who was at first Saul, and afterwards Paul, was compelled, by the great violence with which Christ coerced him, to know and to embrace the truth; for you can-

b. *Letters*, XCIII, 5-10.
4. Luke xiv. 23.

not but think that the light which our eyes enjoy
is more precious to men than money or any other
possession. This light, lost suddenly by him when
he was cast to the ground by the heavenly voice,
he did not recover until he became a member of
the Holy Church. You are also of opinion that
no coercion is to be used with any man in order
to his deliverance from the fatal consequences
of error; and yet you see that, in examples which
cannot be disputed, this is done by God, who loves
us with more real regard for our profit than any
other can; and you hear Christ saying, "No man
can come to me except the Father draw him," [5]
which is done in the hearts of all those who,
through fear of the wrath of God, betake themselves to Him. You know also that sometimes the
thief scatters food before the flock that he may
lead them astray, and sometimes the shepherd
brings wandering sheep back to the flock with his
rod.

Did not Sarah, when she had the power, choose
rather to afflict the insolent bondwoman? And
truly she did not cruelly hate her whom she had
formerly by an act of her own kindness made a
mother; but she put a wholesome restraint upon
her pride.[6] Moreover, as you well know, these
two women, Sarah and Hagar, and their two sons
Isaac and Ishmael, are figures representing spiritual and carnal persons. And although we read
that the bondwoman and her son suffered great
hardships from Sarah, nevertheless the Apostle
Paul says that Isaac suffered persecution from
Ishmael: "But as then he that was born after
the flesh persecuted him that was born after the

5. John vi. 44.
6. Gen. xvi. 5.

Spirit, even so it is now;"[7] whence those who have understanding may perceive that it is rather the Catholic Church which suffers persecution through the pride and impiety of those carnal men whom it endeavours to correct by afflictions and terrors of a temporal kind. Whatever therefore the true and rightful Mother does, even when something severe and bitter is felt by her children at her hands, she is not rendering evil for evil, but is applying the benefit of discipline to counteract the evil of sin, not with the hatred which seeks to harm, but with the love which seeks to heal. When good and bad do the same actions and suffer the same afflictions, they are to be distinguished not by what they do or suffer, but by the causes of each: e.g. Pharaoh oppressed the people of God by hard bondage; Moses afflicted the same people by severe correction when they were guilty of impiety:[8] their actions were alike; but they were not alike in the motive of regard to the people's welfare,—the one being inflated by the lust of power, the other inflamed by love. Jezebel slew prophets, Elijah slew false prophets;[9] I suppose that the desert of the actors and of the sufferers respectively in the two cases was wholly diverse.

Look also to the New Testament times, in which the essential gentleness of love was to be not only kept in the heart, but also manifested openly: in these the sword of Peter is called back into its sheath by Christ, and we are taught that it ought not to be taken from its sheath even in Christ's defence.[10] We read, however, not only that the Jews beat the Apostle Paul, but also that the

7. Gal. iv. 29.
8. Ex. v. 9 and xxxii. 27.
9. 1 Kings xviii. 4, 40.
10. Matt. xxvi. 52.

Greeks beat Sosthenes, a Jew, on account of the
Apostle Paul.[11] Does not the similarity of the
events apparently join both; and, at the same
time, does not the dissimilarity of the causes make
a real difference? Again, God spared not His own
Son, but delivered Him up for us all.[12] Of the Son
also it is said, "who loved me, and gave Himself
for me;" [13] and it is also said of Judas that Satan
entered into him that he might betray Christ.[14]
Seeing, therefore, that the Father delivered up His
Son, and Christ delivered up His own body, and
Judas delivered up his Master, wherefore is God
holy and man guilty in this delivering up of Christ,
unless that in the one action which both did, the
reason for which they did it was not the same?
Three crosses stood in one place: on one was the
thief who was to be saved; on the second, the
thief who was to be condemned; on the third, between them, was Christ, who was about to save
the one thief and condemn the other. What could
be more similar than these crosses? what more
unlike than the persons who were suspended on
them? Paul was given up to be imprisoned and
bound,[15] but Satan is unquestionably worse than
any gaoler: yet to him Paul himself gave up one
man for the destruction of the flesh, that the spirit
might be saved in the day of the Lord Jesus.[16]
And what say we to this? Behold, both deliver a
man to bondage; but he that is cruel consigns his
prisoner to one less severe, while he that is com-
passionate consigns his to one who is more cruel.

11. Acts xvi. 22, 23, and xviii. 17.
12. Rom. viii. 32.
13. Gal. ii. 20.
14. John xiii. 2.
15. Acts xxi. 23, 24.
16. I Cor. v. 5.

Let us learn, my brother, in actions which are similar to distinguish the intentions of the agents; and let us not, shutting our eyes, deal in groundless reproaches, and accuse those who seek men's welfare as if they did them wrong. In like manner, when the same apostle says that he had delivered certain persons unto Satan, that they might learn not to blaspheme,[17] did he render to these men evil for evil, or did he not rather esteem it a good work to correct evil men by means of the evil one?

If to suffer persecution were in all cases a praiseworthy thing, it would have sufficed for the Lord to say, "Blessed are they which are persecuted," without adding "for righteousness' sake." [18] Moreover, if to inflict persecution were in all cases blameworthy, it would not have been written in the sacred books, "Whoso privily slandereth his neighbour, him will I persecute [cut off, E. V.]." [19] In some cases, therefore, both he that suffers persecution is in the wrong, and he that inflicts it is in the right. But the truth is, that always both the bad have persecuted the good, and the good have persecuted the bad: the former doing harm by their unrighteousness, the latter seeking to do good by the administration of discipline; the former with cruelty, the latter with moderation; the former impelled by lust, the latter under the constraint of love. For he whose aim is to kill is not careful how he wounds, but he whose aim is to cure is cautious with his lancet; for the one seeks to destroy what is sound, the other that which is decaying. The wicked put prophets to death; prophets also put the wicked to death. The Jews scourged Christ;

17. I Tim. i. 20.
18. Matt. v. 10.
19. Ps. ci. 5.

Christ also scourged the Jews. The apostles were given up by men to the civil powers; the apostles themselves gave men up to the power of Satan. In all these cases, what is important to attend to but this: who were on the side of truth, and who on the side of iniquity; who acted from a desire to injure, and who from a desire to correct what was amiss?

You say that no example is found in the writings of evangelists and apostles, of any petition presented on behalf of the Church to the kings of the earth against her enemies. Who denies this? None such is found. But at that time the prophecy, "Be wise now, therefore, O ye kings; be instructed, ye judges of the earth: serve the Lord with fear," was not yet fulfilled. Up to that time the words which we find at the beginning of the same Psalm were receiving their fulfilment, "Why do the heathen rage, and the people imagine a vain thing? The kings of the earth set themselves, and the rulers take counsel together against the Lord, and against His Anointed." [20] Truly, if past events recorded in the prophetic books were figures of the future, there was given under King Nebuchadnezzar a figure both of the time which the Church had under the apostles, and of that which she has now. In the age of the apostles and martyrs, that was fulfilled which was prefigured when the aforesaid king compelled pious and just men to bow down to his image, and cast into the flames all who refused. Now, however, is fulfilled that which was prefigured soon after in the same king, when, being converted to the worship of the true God, he made a decree throughout his empire, that whosoever should speak against the God of Shadrach,

20. Ps. ii. 1, 2, 10, 11.

Meshach, and Abednego, should suffer the penalty which their crime deserved. The earlier time of that king represented the former age of emperors who did not believe in Christ, at whose hands the Christians suffered because of the wicked; but the later time of that king represented the age of the successors to the imperial throne, now believing in Christ, at whose hands the wicked suffer because of the Christians.

It is manifest, however, that moderate severity, or rather clemency, is carefully observed towards those who, under the Christian name, have been led astray by perverse men, in the measures used to prevent them who are Christ's sheep from wandering, and to bring them back to the flock, when by punishments, such as exile and fines, they are admonished to consider what they suffer, and wherefore, and are taught to prefer the Scriptures which they read to human legends and calumnies.

<sup>c</sup>As to the obtaining or putting in force of edicts of the powers of this world against schismatics and heretics, those from whom you separated yourselves were very active in this matter, both against you, so far as we have heard, and against the followers of Maximianus, as we prove by the indisputable evidence of their own Records; but you had not yet separated yourselves from them at the time when in their petition they said to the Emperor Julian that "nothing but righteousness found a place with him,"—a man whom all the while they knew to be an apostate, and whom they saw to be so given over idolatry, that they must either admit idolatry to be righteousness, or be unable to deny that they had wickedly lied when they said that nothing but righteousness had a

c. *Letters,* XCIII, 12-14.

place with him with whom they saw that idolatry had so large a place. Grant, however, that that was a mistake in the use of words, what say you as to the deed itself? If not even that which is just is to be sought by appeal to an emperor, why was that which was by you supposed to be just sought from Julian?

Do you reply that it is lawful to petition the Emperor in order to recover what is one's own, but not lawful to accuse another in order that he may be coerced by the Emperor? I may remark, in passing, that in even petitioning for the recovery of what is one's own, the ground covered by apostolic example is abandoned, because no apostle is found to have ever done this. But apart from this, when your predecessors brought before the Emperor Constantine, by means of the pro-consul Anulinus, their accusations against Cæcilianus, who was then bishop of Carthage, with whom as a guilty person they refused to have communion, they were not endeavouring to recover something of their own which they had lost, but were by calumnies assailing one who was, as we think, and as the issue of the judicial proceedings showed, an innocent man; and what more heinous crime could have been perpetrated by them than this? If, however, as you erroneously suppose, they did in his case deliver up to the judgment of the civil powers a man who was indeed guilty, why do you object to our doing that which your own party first presumed to do, and for doing which we would not find fault with them, if they had done it not with an envious desire to do harm, but with the intention of reproving and correcting what was wrong. But we have no hesitation in finding fault with you, who think that we are criminal in bringing any complaint before a Christian emperor against the enemies of our communion, seeing that a document given by your predecessors to Anulinus the proconsul, to be forwarded by him to the Emperor Constantine, bore this superscription: "Libellus Ecclesiæ Catholicæ, criminum Cæciliani, traditus a parte Majorini." We find fault, moreover, with them more particularly, because when they had of their own accord gone to the Emperor with accusations against Cæcilianus, which they ought by all means to have in the first place proved before those who were his colleagues beyond the sea, and when the Emperor, acting in a much more orderly way than they had done, referred to bishops the decision of this case pertaining to bishops which had been brought before him, they, even when defeated by a decision against them, would not come to peace with their brethren. Instead of this, they next accused at the bar of the temporal sovereign, not Cæcilianus only, but also the bishops who had been appointed judges; and finally, from a second episcopal tribunal they appealed to the Emperor again. Nor did they consider it their duty to yield either to truth or to peace when he himself inquired into the case and gave his decision.

Now what else could Constantine have decreed against Cæcilianus and his friends, if they had been defeated when your predecessors accused them, than the things decreed against the very men who, having of their own accord brought the accusations, and having failed to prove what they alleged, refused even when defeated to acquiesce in the truth? The Emperor, as you know, in that case decreed for the first time that the property of those who were convicted of schism and obstinately resisted the unity of the Church should be confiscated. If, however, the issue had been that your predecessors who brought the accusations had gained their case, and the Emperor had made some such decree against the communion to which Cæcilianus belonged, you would have wished the emperors to be called the friends of the Church's interests, and the guardians of her peace and unity. But when such things are decreed by emperors against the parties who, having of their own accord brought forward accusations, were unable to substantiate them, and who, when a welcome back to the bosom of peace was offered to them on condition of their amendment, refused the terms, an outcry is raised that this is an unworthy wrong, and it is maintained that no one ought to be coerced to unity, and that evil should not be requited for evil to any one. What else is this than what one of yourselves wrote: "What we wish is holy"? And in view of these things, it was not a great or difficult thing for you to reflect and discover how the decree and sentence of Constantine, which was published against you on the occasion of your predecessors so frequently bringing before the Emperor charges which they could not make good, should be in force against you; and how all succeeding emperors, especially those who are Catholic Christians, necessarily act according to it as often as the exigencies of your obstinacy make it necessary for them to take any measures in regard to you.

[d]You now see therefore, I suppose, that the thing to be considered when any one is coerced, is not the mere fact of the coercion, but the nature of that to which he is coerced, whether it be good

d. *Letters*, XCIII, 16-19.

or bad: not that any one can be good in spite of his own will, but that, through fear of suffering what he does not desire, he either renounces his hostile prejudices, or is compelled to examine truth of which he had been contentedly ignorant; and under the influence of this fear repudiates the error which he was wont to defend, or seeks the truth of which he formerly knew nothing, and now willingly holds what he formerly rejected. Perhaps it would be utterly useless to assert this in words, if it were not demonstrated by so many examples. We see not a few men here and there, but many cities, once Donatist, now Catholic, vehemently detesting the diabolical schism, and ardently loving the unity of the Church; and these became Catholic under the influence of that fear which is to you so offensive by the laws of emperors, from Constantine, before whom your party of their own accord impeached Cæcilianus, down to the emperors of our own time, who most justly decree that the decision of the judge whom your own party chose, and whom they preferred to a tribunal of bishops, should be maintained in force against you.

I have therefore yielded to the evidence afforded by these instances which my colleagues have laid before me. For originally my opinion was, that no one should be coerced into the unity of Christ, that we must act only by words, fight only by arguments, and prevail by force of reason, lest we should have those whom we knew as avowed heretics feigning themselves to be Catholics. But this opinion of mine was overcome not by the words of those who controverted it, but by the conclusive instances to which they could point. For, in the first place, there was set over against my opinion my own town, which, although it was once wholly on the side of Donatus, was brought over to the Catholic unity by fear of the imperial edicts, but which we now see filled with such detestation of your ruinous perversity, that it would scarcely be believed that it had ever been involved in your error. There were so many others which were mentioned to me by name, that from facts themselves, I was made to own that to this matter the word of Scripture might be understood as applying: "Give opportunity to a wise man, and he will be yet wiser." [21] For how many were already, as we assuredly know, willing to be Catholics, being moved by the indisputable plainness of truth, but daily putting off their avowal of this through fear of offending their own party! How many were bound, not by truth—for you never pretended to that as yours—but by the heavy chains of inveterate custom, so that in them was fulfilled the divine saying: "A servant (who is hardened) will not be corrected by words; for though he understand, he will not answer"! [22] How many supposed the sect of Donatus to be the true Church, merely because ease had made them too listless, or conceited, or sluggish, to take pains to examine Catholic truth! How many would have entered earlier had not the calumnies of slanderers, who declared that we offered something else than we do upon the altar of God, shut them out! How many, believing that it mattered not to which party a Christian might belong, remained in the schism of Donatus only because they had been born in it, and no one was compelling them to forsake it and pass over into the Catholic Church!

21. Prov. ix. 9.
22. Prov. xxix. 19.

To all these classes of persons the dread of those laws in the promulgation of which kings serve the Lord in fear has been so useful, that now some say we were willing for this some time ago; but thanks be to God, who has given us occasion for doing it at once, and has cut off the hesitancy of procrastination! Others say: We already knew this to be true, but we were held prisoners by the force of old custom: thanks be to the Lord, who has broken these bonds asunder, and has brought us into the bond of peace! Others say: We knew not that the truth was here, and we had no wish to learn it; but fear made us become earnest to examine it when we became alarmed, lest, without any gain in things eternal, we should be smitten with loss in temporal things: thanks be to the Lord, who has by the stimulus of fear startled us from our negligence, that now being disquieted we might inquire into those things which, when at ease, we did not care to know! Others say: We were prevented from entering the Church by false reports, which we could not know to be false unless we entered it; and we would not enter unless we were compelled: thanks be to the Lord, who by His scourge took away our timid hesitation, and taught us to find out for ourselves how vain and absurd were the lies which rumour had spread abroad against His Church: by this we are persuaded that there is no truth in the accusations made by the authors of this heresy, since the more serious charges which their followers have invented are without foundation. Others say: We thought, indeed, that it mattered not in what communion we held the faith of Christ; but thanks to the Lord, who has gathered us in from a state of schism, and has taught us that it is fitting that the one God be worshipped in unity.

Could I therefore maintain opposition to my colleagues, and by resisting them stand in the way of such conquests of the Lord, and prevent the sheep of Christ which were wandering on your mountains and hills—that is, on the swellings of your pride—from being gathered into the fold of peace, in which there is one flock and one Shepherd? [23] Was it my duty to obstruct these measures, in order, forsooth, that you might not lose what you call your own, and might without fear rob Christ of what is His: that you might frame your testaments according to Roman law, and might by calumnious accusations break the Testament made with the sanction of Divine law to the fathers, in which it was written, "In thy seed shall all the nations of the earth be blessed": [24] that you might have freedom in your transactions in the way of buying and selling, and might be emboldened to divide and claim as your own that which Christ bought by giving Himself as its price: that any gift made over by one of you to another might remain unchallenged, and that the gift which the God of gods has bestowed upon His children, called from the rising of the sun to the going down thereof,[25] might become invalid: that you might not be sent into exile from the land of your natural birth, and that you might labour to banish Christ from the kingdom bought with His blood, which extends from sea to sea, and from the river to the ends of the earth? [26] Nay verily; let the kings of the earth serve Christ by making laws for Him and

23. John xi. 16.
24. Gen. xxvi. 4.
25. Ps. l. 1.
26. Ps. lxxii. 8.

for His cause. Your predecessors ex
anus and his companions to be pu
kings of the earth for crimes with which
falsely charged: let the lions now be turned
break in pieces the bones of the calumniators, and
let no intercession for them be made by Daniel
when he has been proved innocent, and set free
from the den in which they meet their doom;[27]
for he that prepareth a pit for his neighbour shall
himself most justly fall into it.[28]

## C. *Treatise on the Correction of the Donatists*[1]

[A letter to Boniface, who, as we learn from
Letter CCXX, was tribune, and afterwards count
in Africa. In it Augustine shows that the heresy
of the Donatists has nothing in common with that
of Arius; and points out the moderation with which
it was possible to recall the heretics to the communion of the church through awe of the imperial
laws. He adds remarks concerning the savage conduct of the Donatists and Circumcelliones, con-
cluding with a discussion of the unpardonable nature of the sin against the Holy Ghost.]

[a]I must express my satisfaction, and congratulations, and admiration, my son Boniface, in that,

27. Dan. vi. 23, 24.
28. Prov. xxvi. 27.
1. In Book II. c. xlviii. of his *Retractations,* Augustine
says: "About the same time" (as that at which he wrote
his treatise *De Gestis Pelagii, i.e.* about the year 417),
"I wrote also a treatise *De Correctione Donatistarum,*
for the sake of those who were not willing that the
Donatists should be subjected to the correction of the
imperial laws. This treatise begins with the words
"Laudo, et gratulor, et admiror." This letter in the old
editions was No. 50,—the letter which is now No. 4
in the appendix being formerly No. 185.
a. *Letters,* CLXXXV, 1-2.

amid all the cares of wars and arms, you are eagerly anxious to know concerning the things that are of God. From hence it is clear that in you it is actually a part of your military valour to serve in truth the faith which is in Christ. To place, therefore, briefly before your Grace the difference between the errors of the Arians and the Donatists, the Arians say that the Father, the Son, and the Holy Ghost are different in substance; whereas the Donatists do not say this, but acknowledge the unity of substance in the Trinity. And if some even of them have said that the Son was inferior to the Father, yet they have not denied that He is of the same substance; whilst the greater part of them declare that they hold entirely the same belief regarding the Father and the Son and the Holy Ghost as is held by the Catholic Church. Nor is this the actual question in dispute with them; but they carry on their unhappy strife solely on the question of communion, and in the perversity of their error maintain rebellious hostility against the unity of Christ. But sometimes, as we have heard, some of them, wishing to conciliate the Goths, since they see that they are not without a certain amount of power, profess to entertain the same belief as they. But they are refuted by the authority of their own leaders; for Donatus himself, of whose party they boast themselves to be, is never said to have held this belief.

Let not, however, things like these disturb thee, my beloved son. For it is foretold to us that there must needs be heresies and stumbling-blocks, that we may be instructed among our enemies; and that so both our faith and our love may be the more approved,—our faith, namely, that we should not be deceived by them; and our love, that we should take the utmost pains we can to correct the erring ones themselves; not only watching that they should do no injury to the weak, and that they should be delivered from their wicked error, but also praying for them, that God would open their understanding, and that they might comprehend the Scriptures. For in the sacred books, where the Lord Christ is made manifest, there is also His Church declared; but they, with wondrous blindness, whilst they would know nothing of Christ Himself save what is revealed in the Scriptures, yet form their notion of His Church from the vanity of human falsehood, instead of learning what it is on the authority of the sacred books.

[b]For they prefer to the testimonies of Holy Writ their own contentions, because, in the case of Cæcilianus, formerly a bishop of the Church of Carthage, against whom they brought charges which they were and are unable to substantiate, they separated themselves from the Catholic Church,—that is, from the unity of all nations. Although, even if the charges had been true which were brought by them against Cæcilianus, and could at length be proved to us, yet, though we might pronounce an anathema upon him even in the grave, we are still bound not for the sake of any man to leave the Church, which rests for its foundation on divine witness, and is not the figment of litigious opinions, seeing that it is better to trust in the Lord than to put confidence in man.[2] For we cannot allow that if Cæcilianus had erred,—a supposition which I make without prejudice to his integrity,—Christ should therefore have forfeited His inheritance. It is easy for a man to

b. *Letters,* CLXXXV, 4-6.
2. Ps. cxviii. 8.

believe of his fellow-men either what is true or
what is false; but it marks abandoned impudence
to desire to condemn the communion of the whole
world on account of charges alleged against a man,
of which you cannot establish the truth in the
face of the world.

Whether Cæcilianus was ordained by men who
had delivered up the sacred books, I do not know.
I did not see it, I heard it only from his enemies.
It is not declared to me in the law of God, or in
the utterances of the prophets, or in the holy
poetry of the Psalms, or in the writings of any one
of Christ's apostles, or in the eloquence of Christ
Himself. But the evidence of all the several scriptures with one accord proclaims the Church spread
abroad throughout the world, with which the faction of Donatus does not hold communion. . . .

Cæcilianus, the bishop of the Church of Carthage, is accused with the contentiousness of men;
the Church of Christ, established among all nations, is recommended by the voice of God. Mere
piety, truth, and love forbid us to receive against
Cæcilianus the testimony of men whom we do not
find in the Church, which has the testimony of
God; for those who do not follow the testimony
of God have forfeited the weight which otherwise
would attach to their testimony as men.

I would add, moreover, that they themselves,
by making it the subject of an accusation, referred
the case of Cæcilianus to the decision of the Emperor Constantine; and that, even after the bishops
had pronounced their judgment,[3] finding that they
could not crush Cæcilianus, they brought him in
person before the above-named emperor for trial,
in the most determined spirit of persecution. And

3. In the Councils at Rome and Arles.

so they were themselves the first to do what they censure in us, in order that they may deceive the unlearned, saying that Christians ought not to demand any assistance from Christian emperors against the enemies of Christ. And this, too, they did not dare to deny in the conference which we held at the same time in Carthage: nay, they even venture to make it a matter of boasting that their fathers had laid a criminal indictment against Cæcilianus before the emperor; adding furthermore a lie, to the effect that they had there worsted him, and procured his condemnation. How then can they be otherwise than persecutors, seeing that when they persecuted Cæcilianus by their accusations, and were overcome by him, they sought to claim false glory for themselves by a most shameless lie; not only considering it no reproach, but glorying in it as conducive to their praise, if they could prove that Cæcilianus had been condemned on the accusation of their fathers? But in regard to the manner in which they were overcome at every turn in the conference itself, seeing that the records are exceedingly voluminous, and it would be a serious matter to have them read to you while you are occupied in other matters that are essential to the peace of Rome, perhaps it may be possible to have a digest of them read to you, which I believe to be in the possession of my brother and fellow-bishop Optatus; or if he has not a copy, he might easily procure one from the church at Sitifa; for I can well believe that even that volume will prove wearisome enough to you from its lengthiness, amid the burden of your many cares.

<sup>c</sup>But as to the argument of those men who are unwilling that their impious deeds should be

c. *Letters,* CLXXXV, 19-36.

checked by the enactment of righteous laws, when they say that the apostles never sought such measures from the kings of the earth, they do not consider the different character of that age, and that everything comes in its own season. For what emperor had as yet believed in Christ, so as to serve Him in the cause of piety by enacting laws against impiety, when as yet the declaration of the prophet was only in the course of its fulfilment, "Why do the heathen rage, and the people imagine a vain thing? The kings of the earth set themselves, and their rulers take counsel together, against the Lord, and against His Anointed;" and there was as yet no sign of that which is spoken a little later in the same psalm: "Be wise now, therefore, O ye kings; be instructed, ye judges of the earth. Serve the Lord with fear, and rejoice with trembling." [4] How then are kings to serve the Lord with fear, except by preventing and chastising with religious severity all those acts which are done in opposition to the commandments of the Lord? For a man serves God in one way in that he is man, in another way in that he is also king. In that he is man, he serves Him by living faithfully; but in that he is also king, he serves Him by enforcing with suitable rigour such laws as ordain what is righteous, and punish what is the reverse. Even as Hezekiah served Him, by destroying the groves and the temples of the idols, and the high places which had been built in violation of the commandments of God;[5] or even as Josiah served Him, by doing the same things in his turn;[6] or as the king of the Ninevites served Him by compelling all the men of his city

4. Ps. ii. 1, 2, 10, 11.
5. II Kings xviii. 4.
6. *Ibid.,* xxiii. 4, 5.

to make satisfaction to the Lord;⁷ or as Darius served Him, by giving the idol into the power of Daniel to be broken, and by casting his enemies into the den of lions;⁸ or as Nebuchadnezzar served Him, of whom I have spoken before, by issuing a terrible law to prevent any of his subjects from blaspheming God.⁹ In this way, therefore, kings can serve the Lord, even in so far as they are kings, when they do in His service what they could not do were they not kings.

Seeing, then, that the kings of the earth were not yet serving the Lord in the time of the apostles, but were still imagining vain things against the Lord and against His Anointed, that all might be fulfilled which was spoken by the prophets, it must be granted that at that time acts of impiety could not possibly be prevented by the laws, but were rather performed under their sanction. For the order of events was then so rolling on, that even the Jews were killing those who preached Christ, thinking that they did God service in so doing, just as Christ had foretold,¹⁰ and the heathen were raging against the Christians, and the patience of the martyrs was overcoming them all. But so soon as the fulfilment began of what is written in a later psalm, "All kings shall fall down before Him; all nations shall serve Him," ¹¹ what sober-minded man could say to the kings, "Let not any thought trouble you within your kingdom as to who restrains or attacks the Church of your Lord; deem it not a matter in which you should be concerned, which of your subjects may choose

7. Jonah iii. 6-9.
8. Bel and Drag. vv. 22, 42.
9. Dan. iii. 29.
10. John xvi. 2.
11. Ps. lxxii. 11.

to be religious or sacrilegious," seeing that you
cannot say to them, "Deem it no concern of yours
which of your subjects may choose to be chaste,
or which unchaste?" For why, when free-will is
given by God to man, should adulteries be punished by the laws, and sacrilege allowed? Is it a
lighter matter that a soul should not keep faith
with God, than that a woman should be faithless
to her husband? Or if those faults which are committed not in contempt but in ignorance of religious truth are to be visited with lighter punishment, are they therefore to be neglected altogether?

It is indeed better (as no one ever could deny)
that men should be led to worship God by teaching, than that they should be driven to it by fear
of punishment or pain; but it does not follow that
because the former course produces the better
men, therefore those who do not yield to it should
be neglected. For many have found advantage (as
we have proved, and are daily proving by actual
experiment), in being first compelled by fear or
pain, so that they might afterwards be influenced
by teaching, or might follow out in act what they
had already learned in word. Some, indeed, set
before us the sentiments of a certain secular author, who said,

'Tis well, I ween, by shame the young to train,
And dread of meanness, rather than by pain.[12]

This is unquestionably true. But whilst those are
better who are guided aright by love, those are
certainly more numerous who are corrected by
fear. For, to answer these persons out of their own
author, we find him saying in another place,

12. Ter. *Adelph*. I. i. 32, 33.

Unless by pain and suffering thou art taught,
Thou canst not guide thyself aright in aught.[13]

But, moreover, holy Scripture has both said concerning the former better class, "There is no fear in love; but perfect love casteth out fear;" [14] and also concerning the latter lower class, which furnishes the majority, "A servant will not be corrected by words; for though he understand, he will not answer." [15] In saying, "He will not be corrected by words," he did not order him to be left to himself, but implied an admonition as to the means whereby he ought to be corrected; otherwise he would not have said, "He will not be corrected by words," but without any qualification, "He will not be corrected." For in another place he says that not only the servant, but also the undisciplined son, must be corrected with stripes, and that with great fruits as the result; for he says, "Thou shalt beat him with the rod, and shalt deliver his soul from hell;" [16] and elsewhere he says, "He that spareth the rod hateth his son." [17] For, give us a man who with right faith and true understanding can say with all the energy of his heart, "My soul thirsteth for God, for the living God: when shall I come and appear before God?" [18] and for such an one there is no need of the terror of hell, to say nothing of temporal punishments or imperial laws, seeing that with him it is so indispensable a blessing to cleave unto the Lord, that he not only dreads being parted from that happiness as a heavy

13. This is not found in the extant plays of Terence.
14. 1 John iv. 18.
15. Prov. xxix. 19.
16. *Ibid.*, xxiii. 14.
17. *Ibid.*, xiii. 24.
18. Ps. xlii. 2.

punishment, but can scarcely even bear delay in its attainment. But yet, before the good sons can say they have "a desire to depart, and to be with Christ," [19] many must first be recalled to their Lord by the stripes of temporal scourging, like evil slaves, and in some degree like good-for-nothing fugitives.

For who can possibly love us more than Christ, who laid down His life for His sheep? [20] And yet, after calling Peter and the other apostles by His words alone, when He came to summon Paul, who was before called Saul, subsequently the powerful builder of His Church, but originally its cruel persecutor, He not only constrained him with His voice, but even dashed him to the earth with His power; and that He might forcibly bring one who was raging amid the darkness of infidelity to desire the light of the heart, He first struck him with physical blindness of the eyes. If that punishment had not been inflicted, he would not afterwards have been healed by it; and since he had been wont to see nothing with his eyes open, if they had remained unharmed, the Scripture would not tell us that at the imposition of Ananias' hands, in order that their sight might be restored, there fell from them as it had been scales, by which the sight had been obscured.[21] Where is what the Donatists were wont to cry: Man is at liberty to believe or not believe? Towards whom did Christ use violence? Whom did He compel? Here they have the Apostle Paul. Let them recognise in his case Christ first compelling, and afterwards teaching; first striking, and afterwards consoling. For it is won-

19. Phil. i. 23.
20. John x. 15.
21. Acts ix. 1-18.

derful how he who entered the service of the gospel in the first instance under the compulsion of bodily punishment, afterwards laboured more in the gospel than all they who were called by word only;[22] and he who was compelled by the greater influence of fear to love, displayed that perfect love which casts out fear.

Why, therefore, should not the Church use force in compelling her lost sons to return, if the lost sons compelled others to their destruction? Although even men who have not been compelled, but only led astray, are received by their loving mother with more affection if they are recalled to her bosom through the enforcement of terrible but salutary laws, and are the objects of far more deep congratulation than those whom she had never lost. Is it not a part of the care of the shepherd, when any sheep have left the flock, even though not violently forced away, but led astray by tender words and coaxing blandishments, to bring them back to the fold of his master when he has found them, by the fear or even the pain of the whip, if they show symptoms of resistance; especially since, if they multiply with growing abundance among the fugitive slaves and robbers, he has the more right in that the mark of the master is recognised on them, which is not outraged in those whom we receive but do not rebaptize? For the wandering of the sheep is to be corrected in such wise that the mark of the Redeemer should not be destroyed on it. For even if any one is marked with the royal stamp by a deserter who is marked with it himself, and the two receive forgiveness, and the one returns to his service, and the other begins to be in the service in which he had no part

22. 1 Cor. xv. 10.

before, that mark is not effaced in either of the two, but rather it is recognised in both of them, and approved with the honour which is due to it because it is the king's. Since then they cannot show that the destination is bad to which they are compelled, they maintain that they ought not to be compelled by force even to what is good. But we have shown that Paul was compelled by Christ; therefore the Church, in trying to compel the Donatists, is following the example of her Lord, though in the first instance she waited in the hopes of needing to compel no one, that the prediction of the prophet might be fulfilled concerning the faith of kings and peoples.

For in this sense also we may interpret without absurdity the declaration of the blessed Apostle Paul, when he says, "Having in a readiness to avenge all disobedience, when your obedience is fulfilled." [23] Whence also the Lord Himself bids the guests in the first instance to be invited to His great supper, and afterwards compelled; for on His servants making answer to Him, "Lord, it is done as Thou hast commanded, and yet there is room," He said to them, "Go out into the highways and hedges, and compel them to come in." [24] In those, therefore, who were first brought in with gentleness, the former obedience is fulfilled; but in those who were compelled, the disobedience is avenged. For what else is the meaning of "Compel them to come in," after it had previously said, "Bring in," and the answer had been made, "Lord, it is done as Thou commanded, and yet there is room?" If He had wished it to be understood that they were to be compelled by the terrifying force

23. 2 Cor. x. 6.
24. Luke xiv. 22, 23.

of miracles, many divine miracles were rather wrought in the sight of those who were first called, especially in the sight of the Jews, of whom it was said, "The Jews require a sign;" [25] and, moreover, among the Gentiles themselves the gospel was so commended by miracles in the time of the apostles, that had these been the means by which they were ordered to be compelled, we might rather have had good grounds for supposing, as I said before, that it was the earlier guests who were compelled. Wherefore, if the power which the Church has received by divine appointment in its due season, through the religious character and the faith of kings, be the instrument by which those who are found in the highways and hedges—that is, in heresies and schisms—are compelled to come in, then let them not find fault with being compelled, but consider whether they be so compelled. The supper of the Lord is the unity of the body of Christ, not only in the sacrament of the altar, but also in the bond of peace. Of the Donatists themselves, indeed, we can say that they compel no man to any good thing; for whomsoever they compel, they compel to nothing else but evil.

However, before those laws were sent into Africa by which men are compelled to come in to the sacred Supper, it seemed to certain of the brethren, of whom I was one, that although the madness of the Donatists was raging in every direction, yet we should not ask of the emperors to ordain that heresy should absolutely cease to be, by sanctioning a punishment to be inflicted on all who wished to live in it; but that they should rather content themselves with ordaining that those who either preached the Catholic truth with

25. 1 Cor. i. 22.

their voice, or established it by their study, should no longer be exposed to the furious violence of the heretics. And this they thought might in some measure be effected, if they would take the law which Theodosius, of pious memory, enacted generally against heretics of all kinds, to the effect that any heretical bishop or clergyman, being found in any place, should be fined ten pounds of gold, and confirm it in more express terms against the Donatists, who denied that they were heretics; but with such reservations, that the fine should not be inflicted upon all of them, but only in those districts where the Catholic Church suffered any violence from their clergy, or from the Circumcelliones, or at the hands of any of their people; so that, after a formal complaint had been made by the Catholics who had suffered the violence, the bishops or other ministers should forthwith be obliged, under the commission given to the officers, to pay the fine. For we thought that in this way, if they were terrified, and no longer dared do anything of the sort, the Catholic truth might be freely taught and held under such conditions, that while no one was compelled to it, any one might follow it who was anxious to do so without intimidation, so that we might not have false and pretended Catholics. And although a different view was held by other brethren, who either were more advanced in years, or had experience of many states and places where we saw the true Catholic Church firmly established, which had, however, been planted and confirmed by God's great goodness at a time when men were compelled to come in to the Catholic communion by the laws of previous emperors, yet we carried our point, to the effect that the measure which I have described above should be sought in preference from the emperors: it was decreed in our council,[26] and envoys were sent to the court of the count.

But God in His great mercy, knowing how necessary was the terror inspired by these laws, and a kind of medicinal inconvenience for the cold and wicked hearts of many men, and for that hardness of heart which cannot be softened by words, but yet admits of softening through the agency of some little severity of discipline, brought it about that our envoys could not obtain what they had undertaken to ask. For our arrival had already been anticipated by the serious complaints of certain bishops from other districts, who had suffered much ill-treatment at the hands of the Donatists themselves, and had been thrust out from their sees; and, in particular, the attempt to murder Maximianus, the Catholic bishop of the Church of Bagai, under circumstances of incredible atrocity, had caused measures to be taken which left our deputation nothing to do. For a law had already been published, that the heresy of the Donatists, being of so savage a description that mercy towards it really involved greater cruelty than its very madness wrought, should for the future be prevented not only from being violent, but from existing with impunity at all; but yet no capital punishment was imposed upon it, that even in dealing with those who were unworthy, Christian gentleness might be observed, but a pecuniary fine was ordained, and sentence of exile was pronounced against their bishops or ministers.

With regard to the aforesaid bishop of Bagai, in consequence of his claim being allowed in the ordinary courts, after each party had been heard

26. That of Carthage, held June 26, 401.

in turn, in a basilica[27] of which the Donatists had taken possession, as being the property of the Catholics, they rushed upon him as he was standing at the altar, with fearful violence and cruel fury, beat him savagely with cudgels and weapons of every kind, and at last with the very boards of the broken altar. They also wounded him with a dagger in the groin so severely, that the effusion of blood would have soon put an end to his life, had not their further cruelty proved of service for its preservation; for, as they were dragging him along the ground thus severely wounded, the dust forced into the spouting vein stanched the blood, whose effusion was rapidly on the way to cause his death. Then, when they had at length abandoned him, some of our party tried to carry him off with psalms; but his enemies, inflamed with even greater rage, tore him from the hands of those who were carrying him, inflicting grievous punishment on the Catholics, whom they put to flight, being far superior to them in numbers, and easily inspiring terror by their violence. Finally, they threw him into a certain elevated tower, thinking that he was by this time dead, though in fact he still breathed. Lighting then on a soft heap of earth, and being espied by the light of a lamp by some men who were passing by at night, he was recognised and picked up, and being carried to a religious house, by dint of great care, was restored in a few days from his state of almost hopeless danger. Rumour, however, had carried the tidings even across the sea that he had been killed by the violence of the Donatists; and when afterwards he himself went abroad, and was most unexpectedly

27. The basilica of Fundus Calvianensis. See *C. Crescon.* iii. c. 43.

seen to be alive, he showed, by the number, the severity, and the freshness of his wounds, how fully rumour had been justified in bringing tidings of his death.

He sought assistance, therefore, from the Christian emperor, not so much with any desire of revenging himself, as with the view of defending the Church entrusted to his charge. And if he had omitted to do this, he would have deserved not to be praised for his forbearance, but to be blamed for negligence. For neither was the Apostle Paul taking precautions on behalf of his own transitory life, but for the Church of God, when he caused the plot of those who had conspired to slay him to be made known to the Roman captain, the effect of which was, that he was conducted by an escort of armed soldiers to the place where they proposed to send him, that he might escape the ambush of his foes.[28] Nor did he for a moment hesitate to invoke the protection of the Roman laws, proclaiming that he was a Roman citizen, who at that time could not be scourged;[29] and again, that he might not be delivered to the Jews who sought to kill him, he appealed to Cæsar,[30] a Roman emperor, indeed, but not a Christian. And by this he showed sufficiently plainly what was afterwards to be the duty of the ministers of Christ, when in the midst of the dangers of the Church they found the emperors Christians. And hence, therefore, it came about that a religious and pious emperor, when such matters were brought to his knowledge, thought it well, by the enactment of most pious laws, entirely to correct

28. Acts xxiii. 17-32.
29. *Ibid.*, xxii. 25.
30. *Ibid.*, xxv. 11.

the error of this great impiety, and to bring those who bore the standards of Christ against the cause of Christ into the unity of the Catholic Church, even by terror and compulsion, rather than merely to take away their power of doing violence, and to leave them the freedom of going astray, and perishing in their error.

Presently, when the laws themselves arrived in Africa, in the first place those who were already seeking an opportunity for doing so, or were afraid of the raging madness of the Donatists, or were previously deterred by a feeling of unwillingness to offend their friends, at once came over to the Church. Many, too, who were only restrained by the force of custom handed down in their homes from their parents, but had never before considered what was the groundwork of the heresy itself, —had never, indeed, wished to investigate and contemplate its nature,—beginning now to use their observation, and finding nothing in it that could compensate for such serious loss as they were called upon to suffer, became Catholics without any difficulty; for, having been made careless by security, they were now instructed by anxiety. But when all these had set the example, it was followed by many who were less qualified of themselves to understand what was the difference between the error of the Donatists and Catholic truth.

Accordingly, when the great masses of the people had been received by the true mother with rejoicing into her bosom, there remained outside cruel crowds, persevering with unhappy animosity in that madness. Even of these the greater number communicated in feigned reconciliation, and others escaped notice from the scantiness of their numbers. But those who feigned conformity, becoming by degrees accustomed to our communion, and hearing the preaching of the truth, especially after the conference and disputation which took place between us and their bishops at Carthage, were to a great extent brought to a right belief. Yet in certain places, where a more obstinate and implacable body prevailed, whom the smaller number that entertained better views about communion with us could not resist, or where the masses were under the influence of a few more powerful leaders, whom they followed in a wrong direction, our difficulties continued somewhat longer. Of these places there are a few in which trouble still exists, in the course of which the Catholics, and especially the bishops and clergy, have suffered many terrible hardships, which it would take too long to go through in detail, seeing that some of them had their eyes put out, and one bishop his hands and tongue cut off, while some were actually murdered. I say nothing of massacres of the most cruel description, and robberies of houses, committed in nocturnal burglaries, with the burning not only of private houses, but even of churches,—some being found abandoned enough to cast the sacred books into the flames.

But we were consoled for the suffering inflicted on us by these evils, by the fruit which resulted from them. For wherever such deeds were committed by unbelievers, there Christian unity has advanced with greater fervency and perfection, and the Lord is praised with greater earnestness for having deigned to grant that His servants might win their brethren by their sufferings, and might gather together into the peace of eternal salvation through His blood His sheep who were dispersed abroad in deadly error. The Lord is powerful and full of compassion, to whom we daily pray that He will give repentance to the rest as well, that they may recover themselves out of the snare of the devil, by whom they are taken captive at his will,[31] though now they only seek materials for calumniating us, and returning to us evil for good; because they have not the knowledge to make them understand what feelings and love we continue to have towards them, and how we are anxious, in accordance with the injunction of the Lord, given to His pastors by the mouth of the prophet Ezekiel, to bring again that which was driven away, and to seek that which was lost.[32]

But they, as we have sometimes said before in other places, do not charge themselves with what they do to us; while, on the other hand, they charge us with what they do to themselves. For which of our party is there who would desire, I do not say that one of them should perish, but should even lose any of his possessions? But if the house of David could not earn peace on any other terms except that Absalom his son should have been slain in the war which he was waging against his father, although he had most carefully given strict injunctions to his followers that they should use their utmost endeavours to preserve him alive and safe, that his paternal affection might be able to pardon him on his repentance, what remained for him except to weep for the son that he had lost, and to console himself in his sorrow by reflecting on the acquisition of peace for his kingdom?[33] The same, then, is the case with the Catholic Church, our mother; for when war is

31. 2 Tim. ii. 26.
32. Ezek. xxxiv. 4.
33. 2 Sam. xviii. xxii.

waged against her by men who are certainly different from sons, since it must be acknowledged that from the great tree, which by the spreading of its branches is extended over all the world, this little branch in Africa is broken off, whilst she is willing in her love to give them birth, that they may return to the root, without which they cannot have the true life, at the same time if she collects the remainder in so large a number by the loss of some, she soothes and cures the sorrow of her maternal heart by the thoughts of the deliverance of such mighty nations; especially when she considers that those who are lost perish by a death which they brought upon themselves, and not, like Absalom, by the fortune of war. And if you were to see the joy of those who are delivered in the peace of Christ, their crowded assemblies, their eager zeal, the gladsomeness with which they flock together, both to hear and sing hymns, and to be instructed in the word of God; the great grief with which many of them recall to mind their former error, the joy with which they come to the consideration of the truth which they have learned, with the indignation and detestation which they feel towards their lying teachers, now that they have found out what falsehoods they disseminated concerning our sacraments; and how many of them, moreover, acknowledge that they long ago desired to be Catholics, but dared not take the step in the midst of men of such violence,—if, I say, you were to see the congregations of these nations delivered from such perdition, then you would say that it would have been the extreme of cruelty, if, in the fear that certain desperate men, in number not to be compared with the multitudes of those who were rescued, might be burned in fires which they voluntarily kindled for themselves, these others had been left to be lost for ever, and to be tortured in fires which shall not be quenched.

For if two men were dwelling together in one house, which we knew with absolute certainty to be upon the point of falling down, and they were unwilling to believe us when we warned them of the danger, and persisted in remaining in the house; if it were in our power to rescue them, even against their will, and we were afterwards to show them the ruin threatening their house, so that they should not dare to return again within its reach, I think that if we abstained from doing it, we should well deserve the charge of cruelty. And further, if one of them should say to us, Since you have entered the house to save our lives, I shall forthwith kill myself; while the other was not indeed willing to come forth from the house, nor to be rescued, but yet had not the hardihood to kill himself: which alternative should we choose,—to leave both of them to be overwhelmed in the ruin, or that, while one at any rate was delivered by our merciful efforts, the other should perish by no fault of ours, but rather by his own? No one is so unhappy as not to find it easy enough to decide what should be done in such a case. And I have proposed the question of two individuals,—one, that is to say, who is lost, and one who is delivered; what then must we think of the case where some few are lost, and an innumerable multitude of nations are delivered? For there are actually not so many persons who thus perish of their own free will, as there are estates, villages, streets, fortresses, municipal towns, cities, that are delivered

by the laws under consideration from that fatal
and eternal destruction.

But if we were to consider the matter under discussion with yet greater care, I think that if there
were a large number of persons in the house which
was going to fall, and any single one of them could
be saved, and when we endeavoured to effect his
rescue, the other were to kill themselves by jump-
ing out of the windows, we should console ourselves in our grief for the loss of the rest by the
thoughts of the safety of the one; and we should
not allow all to perish without a single rescue, in
the fear lest the remainder should destroy themselves. What then should we think of the work
of mercy to which we ought to apply ourselves, in
order that men may attain eternal life and escape
eternal punishment, if true reason and benevolence compel us to give such aid to men, in order
to secure for them a safety which is not only
temporal, but very short,—for the brief space of
their life on earth?

As to the charge that they bring against us, that
we covet and plunder their possessions, I would
that they would become Catholics, and possess in
peace and love with us, not only what they call
theirs, but also what confessedly belongs to us.
But they are so blinded with the desire of uttering
calumnies, that they do not observe how inconsistent their statements are with one another. At
any rate, they assert, and seem to make it a subject of most invidious complaint among themselves, that we constrain them to come in to our
communion by the violent authority of the laws,
—which we certainly should not do by any means,
if we wished to gain possession of their property.
What avaricious man ever wished for another to

share his possessions? Who that was inflamed with the desire of empire, or elated by the pride of its possession, ever wished to have a partner? Let them at any rate look on those very men who once belonged to them, but now are our brethren joined to us by the bond of fraternal affection, and see how they hold not only what they used to have, but also what was ours, which they did not have before; which yet, if we are living as poor in fellowship with poor, belongs to us and them alike; whilst, if we possess of our private means enough for our wants, it is no longer ours, inasmuch as we do not commit so infamous an act of usurpation as to claim for our own the property of the poor, for whom we are in some sense the trustees.

Everything, therefore, that was held in the name of the churches of the party of Donatus, was ordered by the Christian emperors, in their pious laws, to pass to the Catholic Church, with the possession of the buildings themselves.[34] Seeing, then, that there are with us poor members of those said churches who used to be maintained by these same paltry possessions, let them rather cease themselves to covet what belongs to others whilst they remain outside, and so let them enter within the bond of unity, that we may all alike administer, not only the property which they call their own, but also with it what is asserted to be ours. For it is written, "All are yours; and ye are Christ's; and Christ is God's."[35] Under Him as our Head, let us all be one in His one body; and in all such matters as you speak of, let us follow the example which is recorded in the Acts of the

34. *Cod. Theod.* i. 52, *de Hæreticis.*
35. I Cor. iii. 22, 23.

Apostles: "They were of one heart and of one soul: neither said any of them that ought of the things which he possessed was his own; but they had all things common." [36] Let us love what we sing: "Behold, how good and how pleasant it is for brethren to dwell together in unity!" [37] that so they may know, by their own experience, with what perfect truth their mother, the Catholic Church, calls out to them what the blessed apostle writes to the Corinthians: "I seek not yours, but you." [38]

[d]In this world no one is righteous by his own righteousness,—that is, as though it were wrought by himself and for himself; but as the apostle says, "According as God hath dealt to every man the measure of faith." But then he goes on to add the following: "For as we have many members in one body, and all members have not the same office; so we, being many, are one body in Christ." [39] And according to this doctrine, no one can be righteous so long as he is separated from the unity of this body. For in the same manner as if a limb be cut off from the body of a living man, it cannot any longer retain the spirit of life; so the man who is cut off from the body of Christ, who is righteous, can in no wise retain the spirit of righteousness, even if he retain the form of membership which he received when in the body. Let them therefore come into the framework of this body, and so possess their own labours, not through the lust of lordship, but through the godliness of using them aright. But we, as has been

36. Acts iv. 32.
37. Ps. cxxxiii. 1.
38. II Cor. xii. 14.
d. *Letters,* CLXXXV, 42-44.
39. Rom. xii. 3-5.

said before, cleanse our wills from the pollution of this concupiscence, even in the judgment of any enemy you please to name as judge, seeing that we use our utmost efforts in entreating the very men of whose labours we avail ourselves to enjoy with us, within the society of the Catholic Church, the fruits both of their labours and of our own.

But this, they say, is the very thing which disquiets us,—If we are unrighteous, wherefore do you seek our company? To which question we answer, We seek the company of you who are unrighteous, that you may not remain unrighteous; we seek for you who are lost, that we may rejoice over you as soon as you are found, saying, This our brother was dead, and is alive again; and was lost, and is found.[40] Why, then, he says, do you not baptize me, that you might wash me from my sins? I reply: Because I do not do despite to the stamp of the monarch, when I correct the ill-doing of a deserter. Why, he says, do I not even do penance in your body? Nay truly, except you have done penance, you cannot be saved; for how shall you rejoice that you have been reformed, unless you first grieve that you had been astray? What, then, he says, do we receive with you, when we come over to your side? I answer, You do not indeed receive baptism, which was able to exist in you outside the framework of the body of Christ, although it could not profit you; but you receive the unity of the Spirit in the bond of peace,[41] without which no one can see God; and you receive charity, which, as it is written, "shall cover the multitude of sins." [42] And in regard to this

40. Luke xv. 32.
41. Eph. iv. 3.
42. I Pet. iv. 8.

great blessing, without which we have the apostle's testimony that neither the tongues of men or of angels, nor the understanding of all mysteries, nor the gift of prophecy, nor faith so great as to be able to remove mountains, nor the bestowal of all one's goods to feed the poor, nor giving one's body to be burned, can profit anything;[43] if, I say, you think this mighty blessing to be worthless or of trifling value, you are deservedly but miserably astray; and deservedly you must necessarily perish, unless you come over to Catholic unity.

If, then, they say, it is necessary that we should repent of having been outside, and hostile to the Church, if we would gain salvation, how comes it that after the repentance which you exact from us we still continue to be clergy, or it may be even bishops in your body? This would not be the case, as indeed, in simple truth, we must confess it should not be the case, were it not that the evil is cured by the compensating power of peace itself. But let them give themselves this lesson, and most especially let those feel sorrow in their hearts, who are lying in this deep death of severance from the Church, that they may recover their life even by this sort of wound inflicted on our Catholic mother Church. For when the bough that has been cut off is grafted in, a new wound is made in the tree, to admit of its reception, that life may be given to the branch which was perishing for lack of the life that is furnished by the root. But when the newly-received branch has become identified with the stock in which it is received, the result is both vigour and fruit; but if they do not become identified, the engrafted bough withers, but the life of the tree continues unimpaired. For there is further

43. I Cor. xiii. 1-3.

a mode of grafting of such a kind, that without cutting away any branch that is within, the branch that is foreign to the tree is inserted, not indeed without a wound, but with the slightest possible wound inflicted on the tree. In like manner, then, when they come to the root which exists in the Catholic Church, without being deprived of any position which belongs to them as clergy or bishops after ever so deep repentance of their error, there is a kind of wound inflicted as it were upon the bark of the mother tree, breaking in upon the strictness of her discipline; but since neither he that planteth is anything, neither he that watereth,[44] so soon as by prayers poured forth to the mercy of God peace is secured through the union of the engrafted boughs with the parent stock, charity then covers the multitude of sins.

[e]Let them therefore feel bitter grief for their detestable error of the past, as Peter did for his fear that led him into falsehood, and let them come to the true Church of Christ, that is, to the Catholic Church our mother; let them be in it clergy, let them be bishops unto its profit, as they have been hitherto in enmity against it. We feel no jealousy towards them, nay, we embrace them; we wish, we advise, we even compel those to come in whom we find in the highways and hedges, although we fail as yet in persuading some of them that we are seeking not their property, but themselves. The Apostle Peter, when he denied his Saviour, and wept, and did not cease to be an apostle, had not as yet received the Holy Spirit that was promised; but much more have these men not received Him, when, being severed from the framework of the

44. I Cor. iii. 7.
e. *Letters*, CLXXXV, 46-51.

body, which is alone enlivened by the Holy Spirit, they have usurped the sacraments of the Church outside the Church and in hostility to the Church, and have fought against us in a kind of civil war, with our own arms and our own standards raised in opposition to us. Let them come; let peace be concluded in the virtue of Jerusalem, which virtue is Christian charity,—to which holy city it is said, "Peace be in thy virtue, and plenteousness within thy palaces." [45] Let them not exalt themselves against the solicitude of their mother, which she both has entertained and does entertain with the object of gathering within her bosom themselves, and all the mighty nations whom they are, or recently were, deceiving; let them not be puffed up with pride, that she receives them in such wise; let them not attribute to the evil of their own exaltation the good which she on her part does in order to make peace.

So it has been her wont to come to the aid of multitudes who were perishing through schisms and heresies. This displeased Lucifer,[46] when it was carried out in receiving and healing those who had perished beneath the poison of the Arian heresy; and, being displeased at it, he fell into the darkness of schism, losing the light of Christian charity. In accordance with this principle, the Church of Africa has recognised the Donatists from the very beginning, obeying herein the decree of the bishops who gave sentence in the Church at Rome between Cæcilianus and the party of Donatus; and having condemned one bishop named

45. Ps. cxxii. 6: Fiat pax in virtute tua. The English version is, "Peace be within thy walls."
46. Bishop of Calarita. Comp. *De Agone Christiano,* c. 30.

Donatus,[47] who was proved to have been the author of the schism, they determined that the others should be received, after correction, with full recognition of their orders, even if they had been ordained outside the Church,—not that they could have the Holy Spirit even outside the unity of the body of Christ, but, in the first place, for the sake of those whom it was possible they might deceive while they remained outside, and prevent from obtaining that gift; and, secondly, that their own weakness also being mercifully received within, might thus be rendered capable of cure, no obstinacy any longer standing in the way to close their eyes against the evidence of truth. For what other intention could have given rise to their own conduct, when they received with full recognition of their orders the followers of Maximianus, whom they had condemned as guilty of sacrilegious schism, as their council [48] shows, and to fill whose places they had already ordained other men, when they saw that the people did not depart from their company, that all might not be involved in ruin? And on what other ground did they neither speak against nor question the validity of the baptism which had been administered outside by men whom they had condemned? Why, then, do they wonder, why do they complain, and make it the subject of their calumnies, that we receive them in such wise to promote the true peace of Christ, while yet they do not remember what they themselves have done to promote the false peace of Donatus, which is opposed to Christ? For if this act of theirs be borne in mind, and intelligently

47. The Bishop of Casæ Nigræ.
48. The Council of Bagai.

used in argument against them, they will have no answer whatsoever that they can make.

But as to what they say, arguing as follows: If we have sinned against the Holy Ghost, in that we have treated your baptism with contempt, why is it that you seek us, seeing that we cannot possibly receive remission of this sin, as the Lord says, "Whosoever speaketh against the Holy Ghost, it shall not be forgiven him, neither in this world, neither in the world to come"? [49]—they do not perceive that acording to their interpretation of the passage none can be delivered. For who is there that does not speak against the Holy Ghost and sin against Him, whether we take the case of one who is not yet a Christian, or of one who shares in the heresy of Arius, or of Eunomius, or of Macedonius, who all say that He is a creature; or of Photinus, who denies that He has any substance at all, saying that there is only one God, the Father; or of any of the other heretics, whom it would now take too long a time to mention in detail? Are none, therefore, of these to be delivered? Or if the Jews themselves, against whom the Lord directed His reproach, were to believe in Him, would they not be allowed to be baptized? for the Saviour does not say, Shall be forgiven in baptism; but "Shall not be forgiven, neither in this world, neither in the world to come."

Let them understand, therefore, that it is not every sin, but only some sin, against the Holy Ghost which is incapable of forgiveness. For just as when our Lord said, "If I had not come and spoken unto them, they had not had sin," [50] it is

49. Matt. xii. 32.
50. John xv. 22.

clear that He did not wish it to be understood
that they would have been free from all sin, since
they were filled with many grievous sins, but that
they would have been free from some special sin,
the absence of which would have left them in a
position to receive remission of all the sins which
yet remained in them, viz. the sin of not believing
in Him when He came to them; for they could not
have had this sin, had He not come. In like manner, also, when He said, "Whosoever sinneth
against the Holy Ghost," or, "Whosoever speaketh
against the Holy Ghost;" it is clear that He does
not refer to every sin of whatsoever kind against
the Holy Ghost, in word or deed, but would have
us understand some special and peculiar sin. But
this is the hardness of heart even to the end of
this life, which leads a man to refuse to accept remission of his sins in the unity of the body of
Christ, to which life is given by the Holy Ghost.
For when He had said to His disciples, "Receive
the Holy Ghost," He immediately added, "Whosoever sins ye remit, they are remitted unto them;
and whosoever sins ye retain, they are retained." [51] Whosoever therefore has resisted or
fought against this gift of the grace of God, or has
been estranged from it in any way whatever to
the end of this mortal life, shall not receive the
remission of that sin, either in this world, or in
the world to come, seeing that it is so great a sin
that in it is included every sin; but it cannot be
proved to have been committed by any one, till
he has passed away from life. But so long as he
lives here, "the goodness of God," as the apostle
says, "is leading him to repentance;" but if he
deliberately, with the utmost perseverance in in-

51. John xx. 22, 23.

iquity, as the apostle adds in the succeeding verse,
"after his hardness and impenitent heart, treasures
up unto himself wrath against the day of wrath
and revelation of the righteous judgment of
God,"[52] he shall not receive forgiveness, neither
in this world, neither in that which is to come.

But those with whom we are arguing, or about
whom we are arguing, are not to be despaired of,
for they are yet in the body; but they cannot seek
the Holy Spirit, except in the body of Christ, of
which they possess the outward sign outside the
Church, but they do not possess the actual reality
itself within the Church of which that is the outward sign, and therefore they eat and drink damnation to themselves.[53] For there is but one bread
which is the sacrament of unity, seeing that, as
the apostle says, "We, being many, are one bread,
and one body."[54] Furthermore, the Catholic
Church alone is the body of Christ, of which He
is the Head and Saviour of His body.[55] Outside
this body the Holy Spirit giveth life to no one,
seeing that, as the apostle says himself, "The love
of God is shed abroad in our hearts by the Holy
Ghost which is given unto us;"[56] but he is not a
partaker of the divine love who is the enemy of
unity. Therefore they have not the Holy Ghost
who are outside the Church; for it is written of
them, "They separate themselves, being sensual,
having not the Spirit."[57] But neither does he receive it who is insincerely in the Church, since this
is also the intent of what is written: "For the Holy

52. Rom. ii. 4, 5.
53. I Cor. xi. 29.
54. *Ibid.*, x. 17.
55. Eph. v. 23.
56. Rom. v. 5.
57. Jude 19.

Spirit of discipline will flee deceit." [58] If any one, therefore, wishes to receive the Holy Spirit, let him beware of continuing in alienation from the Church, let him beware of entering it in the spirit of dissimulation; or if he has already entered it in such wise, let him beware of persisting in such dissimulation, in order that he may truly and indeed become united with the tree of life.

I have despatched to you a somewhat lengthy epistle, which may prove burdensome among your many occupations. If, therefore, it may be read to you even in portions, the Lord will grant you understanding, that you may have some answer which you can make for the correction and healing of those men who are commended to you as to a faithful son by our mother the Church, that you may correct and heal them, wherever you can, and howsoever you can, either by speaking and replying to them in your own person, or by bringing them into communication with the doctors of the Church.

58. Wisd. i. 5.

# CHAPTER V

## ECCLESIASTICAL INTERCESSION IN CIVIL AFFAIRS

A. *Mercy for Heretics: Letters to Donatus and Marcellinus*

ᵃTo Donatus, His Noble and Deservedly Honourable Lord, and Eminently Praiseworthy Son, Augustine sends greeting in the Lord.

I would indeed that the African Church were not placed in such trying circumstances as to need the aid of any earthly power. But since, as the apostle says, "there is no power but of God," [1] it is unquestionable that, when by you the sincere sons of your Catholic Mother help is given to her, our help is in the name of the Lord, "who made heaven and earth." [2] For oh, noble and deservedly honourable lord, and eminently praiseworthy son, who does not perceive that in the midst of so great calamities no small consolation has been bestowed upon us by God, in that you, such a man, and so devoted to the name of Christ, have been raised to the dignity of proconsul, so that power allied with your goodwill may restrain the enemies of the Church from their wicked and sacrilegious attempts? In fact, there is only one thing of which

a. *Letters,* C, 1-2.
1. Rom. xiii. 1.
2. Ps. cxxiv. 3.

we are much afraid in your administration of justice, viz., lest perchance, seeing that every injury done by impious and ungrateful men against the Christian society is a more serious and heinous crime than if it had been done against others, you should on this ground consider that it ought to be punished with a severity corresponding to the enormity of the crime, and not with the moderation which is suitable to Christian forbearance. We beseech you, in the name of Jesus Christ, not to act in this manner. For we do not seek to revenge ourselves in this world; nor ought the things which we suffer to reduce us to such distress of mind as to leave no room in our memory for the precepts in regard to this which we have received from Him for whose truth and in whose name we suffer; we "love our enemies," and we "pray for them." [3] It is not their death, but their deliverance from error, that we seek to accomplish by the help of the terror of judges and of laws, whereby they may be preserved from falling under the penalty of eternal judgment; we do not wish either to see the exercise of discipline towards them neglected, or, on the other hand, to see them subjected to the severer punishments which they deserve. Do you, therefore, check their sins in such a way, that the sinners may be spared to repent of their sins.

We beg you, therefore, when you are pronouncing judgment in cases affecting the Church, how wicked soever the injuries may be which you shall ascertain to have been attempted or inflicted on the Church, to forget that you have the power of capital punishment, and not to forget our request. Nor let it appear to you an unimportant

3. Matt. v. 44.

matter and beneath your notice, my most beloved and honoured son, that we ask you to spare the lives of the men on whose behalf we ask God to grant them repentance. For even granting that we ought never to deviate from a fixed purpose of overcoming evil with good, let your own wisdom take this also into consideration, that no person beyond those who belong to the Church is at pains to bring before you cases pertaining to her interests. If, therefore, your opinion be, that death must be the punishment of men convicted of these crimes, you will deter us from endeavouring to bring anything of this kind before your tribunal; and this being discovered, they will proceed with more unrestrained boldness to accomplish speedily our destruction, when upon us is imposed and enjoined the necessity of choosing rather to suffer death at their hands, than to bring them to death by accusing them at your bar. Disdain not, I beseech you, to accept this suggestion, petition, and entreaty from me. For I do not think that you are unmindful that I might have great boldness in addressing you, even were I not a bishop, and even though your rank were much above what you now hold. Meanwhile, let the Donatist heretics learn at once through the edict of your Excellency that the laws passed against their error, which they suppose and boastfully declare to be repealed, are still in force, although even when they know this they may not· be able to refrain in the least degree from injuring us. You will, however, most effectively help us to secure the fruit of our labours and dangers, if you take care that the imperial laws for the restraining of their sect, which is full of conceit and of impious pride, be so used that they may not appear either to themselves or to others to be suffering hardship in any form for the sake of truth and righteousness; but suffer them, when this is requested at your hands, to be convinced and instructed by incontrovertible proofs of things which are most certain, in public proceedings in the presence of your Excellency or of inferior judges, in order that those who are arrested by your command may themselves incline their stubborn will to the better part, and may read these things profitably to others of their party. For the pains bestowed are burdensome rather than really useful, when men are only compelled, not persuaded by instruction, to forsake a great evil and lay hold upon a great benefit.

---

[b]To Marcellinus,[4] My Noble Lord, Justly Distinguished, My Son Very Much Beloved, Augustine sends greeting in the Lord.

I have learned that the Circumcellions and clergy of the Donatist faction belonging to the district of Hippo, whom the guardians of public

b. *Letters*, CXXXIII, 1-3.
4. Marcellinus was commissioned by the Emperor Honorius to convene a conference of Catholic and Donatist bishops, with a view to the final peaceful settlement of their differences. He accordingly summoned both parties to a conference, held in the summer of 411, in which he pronounced the Catholic party to have completely gained their cause in argument. He proceeded to carry out with considerable rigour the laws passed for the repression of the Donatist schism, and thus becoming obnoxious to that faction, fell at length a victim to their revenge when a turn of fortune favoured their plots against his life. The honour of a place among the martyrs of the early Church has been assigned to him. His character may be learned from Letters CXXXVI, CXXXVIII, CXXXIX, and CXLIII, and particularly from the beautiful tribute to his worth given in Letter CLI in which the circumstances of his death are recorded.

order had brought to trial for their deeds, have
been examined by your Excellency, and that the
most of them have confessed their share in the
violent death which the presbyter Restitutus suffered at their hands, and in the beating of Innocentius, another Catholic presbyter, as well as in
digging out the eye and cutting off the finger of the
said Innocentius. This news has plunged me into
the deepest anxiety, lest perchance your Excellency should judge them worthy, according to the
laws, of punishment not less severe than suffering
in their own persons the same injuries as they
had inflicted on others. Wherefore I write this
letter to implore you by your faith in Christ, and
by the mercy of Christ the Lord Himself, by no
means to do this or permit it to be done. For although we might silently pass over the execution
of criminals who may be regarded as brought up
for trial not upon an accusation of ours, but by
an indictment presented by those to whose vigilance the preservation of the public peace is entrusted, we do not wish to have the sufferings
of the servants of God avenged by the infliction
of precisely similar injuries in the way of retaliation. Not, of course, that we object to the removal
from these wicked men of the liberty to perpetrate
further crimes; but our desire is rather that justice
be satisfied without the taking of their lives or the
maiming of their bodies in any part, and that, by
such coercive measures as may be in accordance
with the laws, they be turned from their insane
frenzy to the quietness of men in their sound
judgment, or compelled to give up mischievous
violence and betake themselves to some useful
labour. This is indeed called a penal sentence; but
who does not see that when a restraint is put upon

the boldness of savage violence, and the remedies fitted to produce repentance are not withdrawn, this discipline should be called a benefit rather than vindictive punishment?

Fulfil, Christian judge, the duty of an affectionate father; let your indignation against their crimes be tempered by considerations of humanity; be not provoked by the atrocity of their sinful deeds to gratify the passion of revenge, but rather be moved by the wounds which these deeds have inflicted on their own souls to exercise a desire to heal them. Do not lose now that fatherly care which you maintained when prosecuting the examination, in doing which you extracted the confession of such horrid crimes, not by stretching them on the rack, not by furrowing their flesh with iron claws,[5] not by scorching them with flames, but by beating them with rods,—a mode of correction used by schoolmasters,[6] and by parents themselves in chastising children, and often also by bishops in the sentences awarded by them. Do not, therefore, now punish with extreme severity the crimes which you searched out with lenity. The necessity for harshness is greater in the investigation than in the infliction of punishment; for even the gentlest men use diligence and stringency in searching out a hidden crime, that they may find to whom they may show mercy. Wherefore it is generally necessary to use more rigour in making inquisition, so that when the crime has been brought to light, there may be scope for displaying clemency. For

5. Compare "ungulis sulcantibus latera." *Codex Justin,* ix. 18. 7.
6. Magistris artium liberalium; doubtless the name of Master of Arts was originally connected with the office and work of teaching, instead of being a mere honorary title.

all good works love to be set in the light, not in order to obtain glory from men, but, as the Lord saith, "that they seeing your good works may glorify your Father who is in heaven." [7] And, for the same reason, the apostle was not satisfied with merely exhorting us to practise moderation, but also commands us to make it known: "Let your moderation," he says, "be known unto all men;" [8] and in another place, "Showing all meekness unto all men." [9] Hence, also, that most signal forbearance of the holy David, when he mercifully spared his enemy when delivered into his hand,[10] would not have been so conspicuous had not his power to act otherwise been manifest. Therefore let not the power of executing vengeance inspire you with harshness, seeing that the necessity of examining the criminals did not make you lay aside your clemency. Do not call for the executioner now when the crime has been found out, after having forborne from calling in the tormentor when you were finding it out.

In fine, you have been sent hither for the benefit of the Church. I solemnly declare that what I recommend is expedient in the interests of the Catholic Church, or, that I may not seem to pass beyond the boundaries of my own charge, I protest that it is for the good of the Church belonging to the diocese of Hippo. If you do not hearken to me asking this favour as a friend, hearken to me offering this counsel as a bishop; although, indeed, it would not be presumption for me to say —since I am addressing a Christian, and especially in such a case as this—that it becomes you to

7. Matt. v. 16.
8. Phil. iv. 5.
9. Titus iii. 2.
10. 1 Sam. xxiv. 7.

hearken to me as a bishop commanding with authority, my noble and justly distinguished lord and much-loved son. I am aware that the principal charge of law cases connected with the affairs of the Church has been devolved on your Excellency, but as I believe that this particular case belongs to the very illustrious and honourable proconsul, I have written a letter to him also, which I beg you not to refuse to give to him, or, if necessary, recommend to his attention; and I entreat you both not to resent our intercession, or counsel, or anxiety, as officious. And let not the sufferings of Catholic servants of God, which ought to be useful in the spiritual upbuilding of the weak, be sullied by the retaliation of injuries on those who did them wrong, but rather, tempering the rigour of justice, let it be your care as sons of the Church to commend both your own faith and your Mother's clemency.

May almighty God enrich your Excellency with all good things, my noble and justly distinguished lord and dearly beloved son!

---

ᶜTo Marcellinus, My Lord Justly Distinguished, My Son Very Much Beloved and Longed For, Augustine sends greeting in the Lord.

The Acts[11] which your Excellency promised to send I am eagerly expecting, and I am longing to have them read as soon as possible in the church at Hippo, and also, if it can be done, in all the churches established within the diocese, that all may hear and become thoroughly familiar with the men who have confessed their crimes, not because the fear of God subdued them to repentance, but

c. *Letters,* CXXXIX, 1-2.
11. Gesta—records of judicial procedure.

because the rigour of their judges broke through the hardness of their most cruel hearts,—some of them confessing to the murder of one presbyter [Restitutus], and the blinding and maiming of another [Innocentius]; others not daring to deny that they might have known of these outrages, although they say that they disapproved of them, and persisting in the impiety of schism in fellowship with such a multitude of atrocious villains, while deserting the peace of the Catholic Church on the pretext of unwillingness to be polluted by other men's crimes; others declaring that they will not forsake the schismatics, even though the certainty of Catholic truth and the perversity of the Donatists have been demonstrated to them. The work, which it has pleased God to entrust to your diligence, is of great importance. My heart's desire is, that many similar Donatist cases may be tried and decided by you as these have been, and that in this way the crimes and the insane obstinacy of these men may be often brought to light; and that the Acts recording these proceedings may be published, and brought to the knowledge of all men.

As to the statement in your Excellency's letter, that you are uncertain whether you ought to command the said Acts to be published in Theoprepia,[12] my reply is, Let this be done, if a large multitude of hearers can be gathered there; if this be not the case, some other place of more general resort must be provided; it must not, however, be omitted on any account.

As to the punishment of these men, I beseech you to make it something less severe than sen-

12. This is supposed to be the name of a Donatist church in Carthage.

tence of death, although they have, by their own confession, been guilty of such grievous crimes. I ask this out of a regard both for our own consciences and for the testimony thereby given to Catholic clemency. For this is the special advantage secured to us by their confession, that the Catholic Church has found an opportunity of maintaining and exhibiting forbearance towards her most violent enemies; since in a case where such cruelty was practised, any punishment short of death will be seen by all men to proceed from great leniency. And although such treatment appears to some of our communion, whose minds are agitated by these atrocities, to be less than the crimes deserve, and to have somewhat the aspect of weakness and dereliction of duty, nevertheless, when the feelings, which are wont to be immoderately excited while such events are recent, have subsided after a time, the kindness shown to the guilty will shine with most conspicuous brightness, and men will take much more pleasure in reading these Acts and showing them to others, my lord justly distinguished, and son very much beloved and longed for.

My holy brother and co-bishop Boniface is on the spot, and I have forwarded by the deacon Peregrinus, who travelled along with him, a letter of instructions; accept these as representing me. And whatever may seem in your joint opinion to be for the Church's interest, let it be done with the help of the Lord, who is able in the midst of so great evils graciously to succour you. One of their bishops, Macrobius, is at present going round in all directions, followed by bands of wretched men and women, and has opened for himself the [Donatist] churches which fear, however slight, had moved their owners to close for a time. By the presence, however, of one whom I have commended and again heartily commend to your love, namely, Spondeus, the deputy of the illustrious Celer, their presumption was indeed somewhat checked; but now, since his departure to Carthage, Macrobius has opened the Donatist churches even within his property, and is gathering congregations for worship in them. In his company, moreover, is Donatus, a deacon, rebaptized by them even when he was a tenant of lands belonging to the Church, who was implicated as a ringleader in the outrage [on Innocentius]. When this man is his associate, who can tell what kind of followers may be in his retinue? If the sentence on these men is to be pronounced by the Proconsul,[13] or by both of you together, and if he perchance insist upon inflicting capital punishment, although he is a Christian and, so far as we have had opportunity of observing, not disposed to such severity—if, I say, his determination make it necessary, order those letters of mine, which I deemed it my duty to address to you severally on this subject,[14] to be brought before you while the trial is still going on; for I am accustomed to hear that it is in the power of the judge to mitigate the sentence, and inflict a milder penalty than the law prescribes. If, however, notwithstanding these letters from me, he refuse to grant this request, let him at least allow that the men be remanded for a time; and we will endeavour to obtain this concession from the clemency of the Emperors, so that the sufferings of the martyrs, which ought to shed bright glory on the Church, may not be tarnished

13. Apringius.
14. *Letters* CXXXIII and CXXXIV.

by the blood of their enemies; for I know that in the case of the clergy in the valley of Anaunia,[15] who were slain by the Pagans, and are now honoured as martyrs, the Emperor granted readily a petition that the murderers, who had been discovered and imprisoned, might not be visited with a capital punishment.

B. *The Right of Priestly Intercession: An Exchange of Letters with Macedonius, Vicar of Africa.*

[a]Macedonius[1] to the Deservedly Esteemed Lord, His Uniquely Cherished Father, Augustine.

I received the long-awaited letter of your Holiness through Boniface, bishop of the holy law, whom I was the more delighted to welcome as he brought me my heart's desire—word of your Holiness and of your well-being, deservedly esteemed lord and uniquely cherished father. Therefore, he secured what he asked without delay. But, as the opportunity has arisen, I do not wish to remain without my pay for this same slight service in which I accommodated him at your request. The pay I crave to receive is one which will be a gain to me without loss to the payer, or, rather will be my gain to the glory of the bestower.

You say that it is part of your priestly office to intercede for condemned persons, and to be displeased if you do not succeed, as if you thereby failed to carry out that part of your duty. I have

15. Anaunia, a valley not far from Trent, destined to be so famous for the Council held there. In the month of May, 397 A.D., Martyrius, Sisinnius, and Alexander were killed there by the heathen.
a. *Letters,* XLII (Schopp, III, pp. 279-280).
1. Vicar of Africa, entrusted with the duty of enforcing imperial decrees against the Donatists.

a serious doubt about this, whether it is part of religion. For if sin is so strictly forbidden by the Lord that no opportunity of repentance is granted after the first, how can we argue that any crime, of whatever sort, should be forgiven us, and how can we approve it by wishing it to go unpunished? And if it is a fact that the one who approves a sin is no less involved in all the circumstances of a sin than the one who commits it, it is clear that we are implicated in a share of the guilt as often as we wish the one who is subject to the penalty to go unpunished. Besides, here is another point, which is even more serious. All sins seem to deserve forgiveness when the guilty person promises amendment, but human behavior has now come to this pass that men wish to have the punishment of their crime remitted and at the same time to keep the profit which they gained by their evil deeds. Your priestly office thinks that intercession should be made for these, also, although the fact that the same motive for the crime continues to be present gives no hope at all for them in the future. Whoever holds tenaciously to the object of his sin shows that he will commit the same again when opportunity allows.

This is my reason for consulting your Prudence: I earnestly desire to be freed of the doubt which weighs me down; do not imagine that I am consulting you for any other reason. This is what I have decided to do: to show gratitude to intercessors, especially those as highly esteemed as you are. Often, when I seem unwilling to do something on my own impulse, lest any relaxation of discipline should encourage others to commit crime, I long to give in to good intercessors, so that what I grant willingly may seem to be a con-

cession to another's merit, while the severity of
the verdict is preserved. May the eternal God keep
your Holiness safe for a long time to come, esteemed lord and truly beloved father.

———————

[b]Augustine, Bishop, Servant of Christ and of
His Household, gives greeting in the Lord to His
Beloved Son, Macedonius.

When a man is as much burdened with public
duties and as devoted to the interest of others and
to the public welfare rather than his own, as you
are—and I congratulate you—it is not right for
us to deprive you of our conversation nor to delay
you with a foreword. Here, then, is what you
wanted to learn from me, or to discover whether
I knew the answer. If you judged that it was a
trifling or superfluous matter, you would see that
there was no place for it among such great and
such exigent cares. You ask me why we say that
it is part of our priestly duty to intercede for condemned persons, and to be displeased if we do
not succeed, as if we were failing to carry out that
part of our duty. You then say that you have a
serious doubt about this, whether it is part of religion. Thereupon, you add your reason for being
disturbed and you say: "If sin is so strictly forbidden by the Lord that no opportunity of repentance is granted after the first, how can we
argue that any crime of whatever sort should be
forgiven?" You press the point still more closely
and you say that we approve an act by wishing it
to go unpunished, and, if it is a fact that the one
who approves of a sin is involved in all the circumstances of it no less than the one who com-

b. *Letters*, CLIII (Schopp, III, pp. 281, 293-303).

mits it, it is clear that we are implicated in a share of guilt as often as we wish the one who is subject to the penalty to go unpunished.

Anyone who did not know your gentleness and kindness would be affronted by these words. But we who know that you wrote this in order to raise the question, not to give an opinion, have no hesitation in answering. . . .

Surely, it is not without purpose that we have the institution of the power of kings, the death penalty of the judge, the barbed hooks of the executioner, the weapons of the soldier, the right of punishment of the overlord, even the severity of the good father. All those things have their methods, their causes, their reasons, their practical benefits. While these are feared, the wicked are kept within bounds and the good live more peacefully among the wicked. However, men are not to be called good because they refrain from wrongdoing through their fear of such things—no one is good through dread of punishment but through love of righteousness—even so, it is not without advantage that human recklessness should be confined by fear of the law so that innocence may be safe among evil-doers, and the evil-doers themselves may be cured by calling on God when their freedom of action is held in check by fear of punishment. However, the intercession of bishops is not a violation of this arrangement of human affairs; on the contrary, there would be neither motive nor opportunity for intervention if it were not for this. The more the penalty of the offender is deserved, the more gratefully the bounty of the intercessor and of the one who pardons is received. It is for this reason, as I see it, that a more unyielding justice shines forth in the Old Testament in the time of the ancient Prophets, to show that penalties were levied against the wicked for a good purpose; but in the New Testament we are urged to pardon offenders with mercy, either as a saving remedy by which our own sins may be pardoned, or as a means of commending gentleness, so that truth, when preached by those who pardon, may  not be so much feared as loved.

It is a matter of great importance what intention a man has in showing leniency. Just as it is sometimes mercy to punish, so it may be cruelty to pardon. For, to use a well-worn case as an example, who would not truthfully say that a person is cruel who would allow a child to play with snakes because he was obstinately set on so doing? Who would not call another kind-hearted who would restrain the child even to the extent of beating him if words had no effect? For this reason, restraint should not go so far as death, because there must be someone to whom restraint is beneficial. Yet it makes a great difference when one man is killed by another, whether it happened through a desire of injuring him, or of carrying off something dishonestly, as it might be done by an enemy, a thief; or whether it happened in the course of inflicting punishment or carrying out an order, as by a judge, an executioner; or through self-defense or the rescue of another, as a thief is killed by a traveller or an enemy by a soldier. And sometimes the one who was the cause of death is more at fault than the killer, as would be the case if a man were to default on the one who stood bail for him, and the latter should pay the required penalty instead of the other. Nevertheless, not everyone who causes another's death is guilty. What if a man were to seek to ravish someone and should

kill himself because he did not get his wish? Or if
a son, fearing the blows which he deserved from
his father, should kill himself by falling? Or if
someone should commit suicide because one man
had been set free or to prevent another from being freed? Because these circumstances have been
the cause of another's death, are we to consent to
sin? are we to deprive a father of the authority to
inflict punishment for wrong-doing—which is done
through a desire of correcting, not of injuring—
or are we to forego the works of mercy? When
these things happen, we owe them human regret,
but we have no right for that reason to put restraint on the will of the doers to prevent them
from happening again.

In the same way, when we intercede for an offender who deserves condemnation, there sometimes are consequences which we do not intend,
either in the person who is set free through our intercession, so that he goes rioting about more ex-
travagantly, because his unchecked boldness goes
to greater lengths of passion, being ungrateful for
the leniency shown, and his single escape from
death may be the cause of many other deaths; or
it may be that the object of our kindness changes
for the better and mends his morals, but he may
be the cause of another's perishing as a result of
an evil life, because the latter, seeing that the former has escaped punishment, commits the same
crimes or even worse ones. Yet, I think, these evil
consequences are not to be laid to our charge when
we intercede with you, but, rather, the good aims
which we have in view and which we intend when
we act thus, that is, to commend mildness so as to
win men's love for the word of truth, and to ensure
that those who are freed from temporal death

may so live as not to fall into eternal death from which they can never be freed.

There is good, then, in your severity which works to secure our tranquility, and there is good in our intercession which works to restrain your severity. Do not be displeased at being petitioned by the good, because the good are not displeased that you are feared by the wicked. Even the Apostle Paul used fear to check the evil deeds of men, fear not only of the judgment to come but even of your present instruments of torture, asserting that they form part of the plan of divine providence, when he said: "Let every soul be subject to higher powers, for there is no power but from God; and those that are ordained of God. Therefore he that resisteth the power, resisteth the ordinance of God, and they that resist, purchase to themselves damnation: for princes are not a terror to the good work but to the evil. Wilt thou then not be afraid of the power? Do that which is good and thou shalt have praise for the same; for he is God's minister to thee for good. But if thou do that which is evil, fear, for he beareth not the sword in vain: for he is God's minister, an avenger to execute wrath upon him that doth evil. Wherefore be subject of necessity, not only for wrath but also for conscience sake. For therefore also you pay tribute, for they are the ministers of God, serving unto this purpose. Render therefore to all men their dues, tribute to whom tribute is due, custom to whom custom, fear to whom fear, honor to whom honor. Owe no man anything but to love one another." [2] These words of the Apostle show the usefulness of your severity. Thus, as those who fear are ordered to render love to those who cause

2. Rom. xiii. 1-8.

them fear, so those who cause fear are ordered to render love to those who fear. Let nothing be done through desire of hurting, but all through love of helping, and nothing will be done cruelly, inhumanly. Thus, the sentence of the judge will be feared, but not so as to cause the religious motive of the intercessor to be scorned, because it is only by yielding and pardoning that the good effect of amending a man's life is produced. But, if perversity and impiety are so great that neither punishment nor pardon can avail to correct them, it is still true that, whether severity or leniency is shown, the obligation of charity is fulfilled by the good through their intention and upright conscience which God beholds.

In the following part of your letter where you say: "But now human behavior has come to this pass that men wish to have the punishment of their crime remitted and at the same time to keep the profit which they gained by their evil deeds," you are speaking of the lowest kind of men, who are absolutely unable to be helped by the remedy of repentance. If the offence committed has involved theft, and restitution is not made, although it is possible to make it, there is no repentance but only pretense. If, however, there is true repentance, the sin will not be forgiven unless there is restitution of stolen goods, but, as I said, where restitution is possible. Often, however, the thief dissipates the goods either by connivance with other offenders or by living an evil life himself, and has nothing left with which to make restitution. To him we certainly cannot say: "Pay back what you took," unless we believe that he has it and denies it. But in the case where he suffers some physical punishment at the hands of the offended party, because it is believed that he has the means of paying back, he is free of guilt, because, even if he has no means of paying back what he took, he pays the penalty of the sin by which he wrongfully stole through the corporal pains applied to make him pay back. It is not an uncivilized thing to intercede for such persons, as one does for those convicted of crimes, since it is not done to save them entirely from making restitution, but so that man may not show cruelty to man, especially the one who has already been given satisfaction for the guilty act, but still wants his money and fears to be cheated of it, without seeking to be avenged. Finally, in such cases, if we can convince the injured party that those for whom we intercede do not possess what is demanded, there is a cessation of their importunity on us. Sometimes, indeed, merciful men, in a state of real doubt, are not willing to inflict certain punishment for the sake of uncertain money. This is the mercy which it befits us to challenge and exhort them to show, for it is better for you to lose the money if he has it than to torture or kill him if he does not have it. In this case it is more effective to intercede with creditors than with judges, because the judge who has the power to enforce restitution and does not do it might seem to be a party to the theft, although in using force he must display a regard for honesty without losing human feeling.

This, indeed, I would say with complete assurance, that the one who intercedes for a man to save him from restoring his ill-gotten goods and who fails, when someone has fled to him for refuge, to force him to make restitution as far as he honestly can, is a party to the theft and the guilt. It would be more merciful for us to withhold our

succor from such men than to offer it to them, for
he does not succor who helps someone to sin when
he should hinder him and turn him away from it.
But can we or ought we for that reason either ex-
tort the money from them or hand them over to
another's extortion? We act within the limits of
our episcopal jurisdiction, threatening them sometimes with human, but especially and always with
divine judgment. In the case of those who refuse
to make restitution, of whom we know that they
have stolen and have the means to pay, we rebuke
and reproach them, showing our detestation of
them, some in private, some publicly, according
as the diversity of characters shows the possibility
of reforming them. Yet, in this we avoid rousing
them to greater madness; sometimes, if an aggra-
vation of the fault to be cured is not feared, we
even cut them off from Communion at the holy
altar.

Indeed, it often happens that they deceive us
either by saying that they have not stolen or by
insisting that they have no means of making restitution, but often, too, you are deceived by thinking either that we do not make them pay back or
that they have the means of paying back. All or
almost all of us men love to call or consider our
suspicions knowledge, since we are influenced by
the credible evidence of circumstances; yet some
credible things are false, just as some incredible
ones are true. Therefore, mentioning some who
"wish to have the punishment of their crime remitted and at the same time to keep the profit
which they gained by their evil deeds," you added
something else when you said: "Your priestly
office thinks that intercession should be made for
these, also." It is possible that you might know

something I do not know and that I might think
I ought to intercede for someone in a case where
I could be deceived, but you could not, because
I believed that a man did not possess what you
knew that he did possess. Thus it could be that we
might not have the same idea of a man's guilt, but
neither of us would approve a failure to make
restitution. As men we have different ideas about
a man, but in the concept of justice we are one.
In the same way it is also possible for me to know
that someone has nothing, while you are not too
sure that he has, but you have good grounds for
suspecting him and in this way it seems to you
that I intercede for a man "who wishes to have the
punishment of his crime remitted and to keep the
profit which he gained by his evil deed." To sum
up, then, neither to you, nor to men such as we
rejoice to find you—if any others can be found—
nor to those who "with great eagerness pursue interests foreign to them, utterly unprofitable and
even extremely dangerous and deadly," [3] nor to
my own heart would I dare to say, as I would not
think or decide that intercession should be made
for anyone to enable him to possess unpunished
what he has wrongfully taken, but I hold rather
that he should restore what he has taken, when his
offense has been pardoned, always supposing that
he still has either what he took or some other
means of making restitution.

It is not true, however, that everything which
is taken from an unwilling donor is wrongfully
taken. Most people do not want to give due credit
to their doctor, or to pay a workman his hire, yet
when these receive their due from unwilling debtors they do not acquire anything unlawfully; on

3. Sallust, *Jurgurtha* 1.5.

the contrary, it would be wrong to deprive them of it. But there is no reason for a judge to take money for a just judgment or a witness for true testimony, because the advocate is paid for legal protection and the lawyer for truthful advice; the two former have to make an inquiry into both sides, the latter stand on one side. But when verdicts and testimony are sold, they are unfair and untrue, because just and true ones are not to be sold, and it is much more infamous for money to be taken when it is infamously even if willingly paid. The one who pays for a just verdict usually demands his money back on the ground that it was wrongfully taken from him, since justice ought not to be for sale; while the one who pays for an unjust verdict would like to demand his money back, if he were not afraid or ashamed of having paid it.

There are other personages of lower rank who not uncommonly take pay from both sides, such as a court attendant by whom a service is performed or on whom it devolves. What is extorted by these with excessive dishonesty is usually demanded back, but if paid according to accepted custom it is not asked back, and those who do demand it contrary to custom we disapprove of more vigorously than those who accept it according to custom, since many officials, necessary to human affairs, are influenced or attracted by gains of this kind. If these latter change their way of life and attain to a higher degree of virtuous living, they are more ready to distribute to the poor, as if it were their own, what they have acquired in this way than they are to pay it back to those from whom they have received it as a form of restitution of what is not their own. However, we think that those who have done an injury to human society by theft, rapine, calumny, oppression, housebreaking ought to pay what they owe rather than give it away, following the example of the tax collector, Zacchaeus, in the Gospel, who received the Lord into his house, was suddenly converted to a holy life, and said: "The half of my goods I give to the poor, and if I have wronged any man of anything I restore him fourfold." [4]

If there is to be a more sincere regard for justice, it would be more honest to say to the advocate: "Pay back what you received when you stood against truth, supported evil-doing, deceived the judge, won your case by lying, as you see that many of the most honorable and eloquent men seem to allow themselves to do, not only with safety but even with renown," rather than to say to any minor official struggling to perform some duty: "Pay back what you received when at the judge's order you held a man who was needed for some case, when you tied him so that he could not resist, shut him up so that he could not run away, and finally produced him while the trial was going on, or dismissed him when it was finished." It is easy to see why no one says this to an advocate, because a man naturally does not wish to ask back what he gave a patron to win a bad case, just as he does not wish to pay back what he received from his opponent when he won his case dishonestly. Finally, how hard it is to find an advocate or a truly good man who has been an advocate, who would say to his client: "Take back what you paid me for representing you so dishonestly, and give back to your opponent what you took from him as a result of my dishonest pleading." Yet, anyone who thoroughly repents of his dishonest

4. Luke xix. 8.

former life ought to do even this, so that, if the dishonest litigant is not willing to make amends for his injustice after this warning, he at least will take no pay for the injustice. Otherwise, it might happen that there is an obligation to pay back what is secretly taken from another by theft, but none to pay back what is gotten by deceiving the judge and evading the law in the very court of law where offenses are punished. And what about lending money at interest,[5] which the very laws and judges require to be paid back? Who is more cruel: the one who steals from or cheats a rich man or the one who destroys a poor man by usury? What is acquired this way is certainly ill-gotten gain, and I would wish restitution to be made of it, but it is not possible to sue for it in court . . .

For a long time I seem to have been putting a burden on a busy man by my talk, whereas it would have been possible to explain quickly what was asked by a man as clear-sighted and experienced as you are. I ought to have made an end of this long since, and I would have if I had thought you would be the only one to read what you urged me to write. May you enjoy a happy life in Christ, my dearest son.

---

[c]Macedonius to his Justly Revered Lord and Truly Estimable Father, Augustine.

I am deeply impressed by your wisdom, both in the writings which you have published and in those which you did not refuse to send, taking pity on my anxiety. The former have a superlative degree of penetration, knowledge, and holiness, and the

5. Forbidden by early Church law.
c. *Letters*, CLIV (Schopp, III, pp. 303-304).

latter are so full of moderation that, if I do not do what you advise, I should have to account the fault in myself, not in my office, justly revered lord and estimable father. For you do not insist, as most men in your circle do, on extorting from me whatever any anxious client happens to want, but you suggest what you think can properly be asked of a judge weighed down by many cares, and you do this with a due regard and respect, which is a most successful way of overcoming difficulties among good people. Therefore, I have granted to those you recommended the fulfillment of their desire, having previously opened the way to hope. . . .

I have written this in the midst of my preoccupation with other cares, which may be vain when we think of the end of the world, but are still pressing enough, being part of the consequence of our being born. If I have time, and if my life holds out, I shall write again from Italy, so as to pay my debt to such learning by due if not adequate services. May the almighty God keep your Holiness safe and happy for an extended age, justly revered lord and truly estimable father.

---

⁴Augustine, Bishop, Servant of Christ and of His Family, gives greeting in the Lord to his Beloved Son, Macedonius.

Although I do not recognize in myself the wisdom with which you endow me, I do owe and return the most lively thanks to your great and sincere kindness toward me, and I am delighted that the result of my studies has given pleasure to a man of such character and influence as you are.

d. *Letters*, CLV (Schopp, III, pp. 305, 310-318).

My joy is the greater because I discern the yearning of your mind, with its love for eternal life and truth and charity itself, directed toward that divine and heavenly country whose king is Christ, and in which alone we find eternal happiness if we live uprightly and devoutly in this world, and also because I see you drawing near to that life and I embrace you in your ardent desire to attain it. This is the source from which true friendship flows, not to be valued by temporal advantages, but to be drunk in through freely given love. No one can be a true friend of man unless he is first a friend of Truth; if friendship does not come into being spontaneously, it cannot exist at all.

Since we know that you are devoted to the public welfare, you must see how plainly the sacred writings show that the happiness of the state has no other source than the happiness of man. One of the sacred writers, filled with the Holy Spirit, speaks thus as he prays: 'Rescue me out of the hand of strange children, whose mouth hath spoken vanity: and their right hand is the right hand of iniquity; whose sons are as new plants in their youth: their daughters decked out, adorned round about after the similitude of a temple: their storehouse full, flowing out of this into that, their sheep fruitful in young, abounding in their goings forth: their oxen fat. There is no breach of wall nor passage, nor crying out in their streets. They have called the people happy that hath these things, but happy is the people whose God is the Lord.' [6]

You see that a people is not called happy because of an accumulation of earthly good fortune, except by the strange children, that is, by those who do not belong to the regeneration by which we

6. Ps. cxliii. 11-15.

become sons of God. The Psalmist prays to be rescued out of their hand, lest he be drawn by them into that false opinion and into their impious sins. Truly they speak vanity when they 'have called the people happy that hath these things'—the things which he had listed above, in which that good fortune consisted, the only good fortune which the lovers of this world seek. Therefore, 'their right hand is the right hand of iniquity' because they have preferred those things which should have been set aside, as the right hand is preferred to the left. Happiness in life is not to be attributed to the possession of those things; they should be subordinate, not pre-eminent; they are intended to follow, not to lead. If, then, we were to speak to him who prayed thus and desired to be rescued from the 'strange children' who 'called that people happy that hath these things,' and if we said: 'What is your own opinion? What people do you call happy?' he would not say: 'Happy is the people whose strength is in their own mind.' If he had said this, he would, it is true, distinguish that people from the former which made happiness consist in that visible and corporeal good fortune, but he would not yet have passed beyond all the vanities and lying follies, for, as the same writings teach elsewhere: 'Cursed be everyone that placeth his hope in man.' [7] Therefore, he ought not to place it in himself, because he himself is a man. Thus, in order to pass beyond the boundaries of all vanities and lying follies, and to place happiness where it truly exists, he says: 'Happy is the people whose God is the Lord.'

You see, therefore, where we are to seek what all, both learned and unlearned, desire; but many,

7. Cf. Jer. xvii. 5.

because of their wanderings and their self-suffi-
ciency, do not know where it is to be sought and
found. In a certain divine psalm two classes of
men are held up to scorn: both 'they that trust in
their own strength' and 'they that glory in the
multitude of their riches,' [8] that is, both the philosophers of this world and those who despise even
such a philosophy and call that people happy who
abound in earthly riches. Therefore, let us ask of
the Lord our God, by whom we were created,
both the strength to overcome the evils of this life,
and happiness in the next life, which we may enjoy
in His eternity after this life, so that in the strength
and in the reward of the strength 'he that glories,'
as the Apostle says, 'may glory in the Lord.' [9] Let
us wish this for ourselves, let us wish it for the
state of which we are citizens, for the happiness of
the state has no other source than the happiness of
man, since the state is merely a unified group of
men.

Therefore, if all your prudence which makes
you try to provide against human vicissitudes, if
all the fortitude which keeps you from being
frightened by any wickedness directed against you,
if all the temperance which shields you from corruption in the midst of such foulness of evil conduct on the part of men, if all the justice which
makes you judge rightly as you allot to each one
what is his, aims at this, strives for this, that those
whose welfare you have at heart may be safe in
body and secure from the dishonesty of anyone,
that they may enjoy peace and may have 'sons
established as new plants, daughters decked out
in the similitude of a temple, storehouses full, flow-

8. Ps. xlviii. 7.
9. 2 Cor. x. 17.

ing out of this into that, their sheep fruitful in young, their oxen fat, their property spoiled by no breach of wall, no outcry of quarreling heard in their streets' [10]—in that case, yours are no true virtues, and theirs no true happiness. That respectful attitude of mine which you praised with kind words in your letter should not prevent me from speaking the truth. If, as I say, any administrative act of yours, endowed with the virtues which I have listed, is limited to this end and aim, that men may suffer no undue distress according to the flesh, if you think it is not incumbent on you that they should make a return for that tranquility which you try to secure for them, that is, not to speak in riddles, that they should worship the true God in whom is all the fruition of the peaceful life, such effort on your part will bring you no return in true happiness.

It seems that I am here speaking disrespectfully, and, in a sense, as if I had forgotten the usual form of my intercession. But, if respect is merely a certain fear of displeasing someone, I am not showing respect by fearing in this case. I should first of all, and with good reason, fear to displease God, and secondly to displease that friendship which you have been so kind as to confer on me, if I were less free in warning you where I think a salutary warning is needed. I should certainly be more respectful when I intercede with you for others, when, in fact I intercede for you yourself, if I spoke freely in proportion to my friendship, and the more faithful I am, the better friend I am, yet I would not say this to you if it were not to show my respect. And if this, as you say, 'is a most successful way of overcoming difficulties

10. Cf. Ps. cxliii. 11-15.

among good people,' [11] may it help me with you in your own behalf, that I may enjoy you in Him who has opened for me this door to you, and has given me confidence, especially as what I ask I now think is easy for your mind to accept, supported and strengthened as it is by so many divine helps.

If you recognize that you have received the virtues which you have, and if you return thanks to Him from whom you have received them, directing them to His service even in your secular office; if you rouse the men subject to your authority and lead them to worship God, both by the example of your own devout life and by your zeal for their welfare, whether you rule them by love or by fear if, in working for their greater security, you have no other aim than that they should thus attain to Him who will be their happiness—then yours will be true virtues, then they will be increased by the help of Him whose bounty lavished them on you, and they will be so perfected as to lead you without fail to that truly happy life which is no other than eternal life. In that life, evil will no longer have to be distinguished from good by the virtue of prudence, because there will be no evil there; adversity will not have to be borne with fortitude, because there will be nothing there but what we love; temperance will not be needed to curb our passions, because there will be no enticements to passion there; nor shall we have to practise justice by helping the poor out of our abundance, for there we shall find no poor and no needy. There will be but one virtue there, and it will be the same as the reward of virtue, which the speaker in the sacred writings mentions as the

11. Cf. Letter CLIV.

object of his love: 'But it is good for me to stick close to my God.' [12] This will constitute the perfect and eternal wisdom, as it will constitute the truly happy life, because to attain it is to attain the eternal and supreme good, and to stick close to God forever is the sum of our good. Let this be called prudence because it will cling most providently to the good which cannot be lost, and fortitude because it will cling most stoutly to the good from which it cannot be parted, and temperance because it will cling most chastely to the good in which there is no corruption, and justice because it will cling most uprightly to the good to which it is deservedly subject.

Yet, this virtue consists in nothing else but in loving what is worthy of love; it is prudence to choose this, fortitude to be turned from it by no obstacles, temperance to be enticed by no allurements, justice to be diverted by no pride. Why do we choose what we exclusively love, except that we find nothing better? But this is God, and if we prefer or equal anything to Him in our love, we know nothing about loving ourselves. We are made better by approaching closer to Him than whom nothing is better; we go to Him not by walking, but by loving. We will have Him more present to us in proportion as we are able to purify the love by which we draw near to Him, for He is not spread through or confined by corporeal space, He is everywhere present and everywhere wholly present, and we go to Him not by the motion of our feet but by our conduct. Conduct is not usually discerned by what one knows but by what he loves; good or bad love makes good or bad conduct. By our crookedness we are far from the uprightness

12. Ps. lxxii. 28.

of God; we are made straight by loving what is upright, that we may rightly cling to the upright One.

Let us strive, then, with the greatest possible effort to bring to him those whom we love as ourselves, if we know that we love ourselves by loving Him. For Christ, who is Truth, says that on these two commandments depend the whole Law and the Prophets: that we love God with our whole heart and our whole soul and our whole mind, and that we love our neighbor as ourselves.[13] Obviously, in this passage the neighbor is not to be rated by blood relationship but by the fact that he is a fellow being endowed with reason, which makes all men kin. For if money is a reason which makes men partners, much more is their common nature a reason to draw them together, not for business purposes but because of their birth. Hence, that writer of comedy whose charming genius is not devoid of the splendor of truth composed this speech where one old man speaks to another:

Have you so much time to spare from your own affairs
That you can meddle in other people's business which is none of yours?

and he gives this answer to the other old man:

I am a man: I hold that no human interest is foreign to me.[14]

They say that at that sentence, the whole theatre, though filled with foolish and ignorant people,

13. Cf. Matt. xxii. 37, 39, 40; Mark xii. 30-31; Luke x. 27.
14. Terence, *Heautontimoreumenos* 75-77.

rang with applause. Thus, the kinship of human souls stirs the feeling of all so naturally that every man feels himself a neighbor of every other man.

Therefore, with that love which the divine law commands, a man ought to love God and himself and his neighbor; yet three commandments were not given and it was not said: 'on these three,' but 'on these two commandments dependeth the whole law and the prophets,' that is, on the love of God with the whole heart and the whole soul and the whole mind, and of the neighbor as oneself, doubtless to make it clear that there is no other love by which a man loves himself than that by which he loves God. Whoever loves himself in any other way ought to be said rather to hate himself, since he thus becomes wicked and is deprived of the light of justice, when he turns from a higher and more excellent good and is directed upon himself as to something lower and defective, and what is so truthfully written then takes place in him: 'He that loveth iniquity hateth his own soul.' [15] Thus, as no one loves himself except by loving God, there was no need of man being commanded to love himself, once the commandment to love God has been given. He ought, then, to love God and his neighbor as himself so as to lead whatever men he can to worship God, using as means either the comforting force of kindness, or the imparting of learning, or the restraint of discipline, because he knows that 'on these two commandments dependeth the whole law and the prophets.'

Whoever chooses this with careful discrimination is prudent; whoever is turned from it by no trial is strong; he who is enticed by no other pleasure is temperate; the one who is puffed up by no

15. Ps. x. 6.

self-esteem is just. By means of these virtues which
have been divinely imparted to us by the grace
of the Man, Christ Jesus, the Mediator of God between the Father and us, through whom we are
reconciled to God in the spirit of charity, after the
hostility of our sin, by means of these virtues, I
repeat, which are divinely imparted to us, we now
live the good life, and afterward receive its reward,
the life of happiness, which must necessarily be
eternal. In this life these virtues are seen in action,
in the next in their effect; here they are at work,
there they are our reward; here, their function,
there their final end. Therefore, all good and holy
men, supported by divine help, in the midst of all
kinds of sufferings hear the call of hope of that
blessed end where they will be forever happy; but,
if they were to remain forever in those same sufferings and most bitter pains, even if they had all
possible virtue, no sane or reasonable being could
doubt that they would be anything but wretched.

'Godliness,' then, 'which is the true worship of
God, is profitable to all things,' [16] since it deflects
or blunts the troubles of this life and leads to that
other life, our salvation, where we shall suffer no
evil and enjoy the supreme and everlasting good.
I exhort you as I do myself to pursue this happiness more earnestly and to hold to it with strong
constancy. If you were not even now a sharer in
it, if you did not judge that your earthly honors
should be subordinate to it, you would not have
said to the Donatist heretics in your edict designed
to bring them back to the unity and peace of
Christ: 'This is enacted for your benefit; it is for
you that the priests of the incorrupt faith labor,
that the august emperor and we, his judges, also

16. 1 Tim. iv. 8.

labor,' and many other points which you made in the same edict, so that it is clear that, though you wear the girdle of an earthly judge, you are thinking for the most part of the heavenly country. If I have aimed at speaking to you at too great length about true virtue and true happiness, I beg you not to regard it as an intrusion on your duties, as, indeed, I trust it is not, since you show a disposition so strong and so marvelously worthy of praise that you do not slight the earthly cares while busying yourself more willingly and more intimately with the heavenly ones.

### C. *Advice and Reproof for a Military Commander: Letters to Count Boniface*

ᵃTo Boniface,[1] My Noble Lord and Justly Distinguished and Honourable Son, Augustine sends greetings in the Lord.

a. *Letters,* CLXXXIX, 1-3.

1. Count Boniface, to whom St. Augustine also addressed letters CLXXXV and CCXX, was governor of the province of Africa under Placidia, who for twenty-five years ruled the empire in the name of her son Valentinian. By his perfidious rival Aetius, Boniface was persuaded to disobey the order of Placidia, when, under the instigation of Aetius himself, she recalled him from the government of Africa. The necessity of powerful allies in order to maintain his position led him to invite the Vandals to pass from Spain into Africa. They came, under Genseric, and the fertile provinces of Northern Africa fell an easy prey to their invading armies. When the treachery of Aetius was discovered, Placidia received Boniface again into favour, and he devoted all his military talents to the task of expelling the barbarians whom his own invitation had made masters of North Africa. But it was now too late to wrest this Roman province from the Vandals; defeated in a great battle, Boniface was compelled in 430 to retire into Hippo Regius, where he succeeded in resisting the besieging army for fourteen months. It was during this siege, and after it had continued three months, that Augustine died. Reinforced by troops from Constantinople, Boniface fought one

I had already written a reply to your Charity, but while I was waiting for an opportunity of forwarding the letter, my beloved son Faustus arrived here on his way to your Excellency. After he had received the letter which I had intended to be carried by him to your Benevolence, he stated to me that you were very desirous that I should write you something which might build you up unto the eternal salvation of which you have hope in Christ Jesus our Lord. And, although I was busily occupied at the time, he insisted, with an earnestness corresponding to the love which, as you know, he bears to you, that I should do this without delay. To meet his convenience, therefore, as he was in haste to depart, I thought it better to write, though necessarily without much time for reflection, rather than put off the gratification of your pious desire, my noble lord and justly distinguished and honourable son.

All is contained in these brief sentences: "Love the Lord thy God with all thy heart, and with all thy soul, and with all thy strength: and love thy neighbour as thyself;" [2] for these are the words in which the Lord, when on earth, gave an epitome of religion, saying in the gospel, "On these two commandments hang all the law and the prophets." Daily advance, then, in this love, both by praying and by well-doing, that through the help of Him

---

more desperate but unsuccessful battle, after which he left Hippo in the hands of Genseric, and returned by order of Placidia to Italy. For fuller particulars of his history, see Gibbon's *History of the Decline and Fall of the Roman Empire,* ch. xxxiii. [Editor's note: See also E. A. Freeman, *Western Europe in the Fifth Century,* London, 1904, pp. 305-370; and J. L. M. de Lepper, *De Rebus Gestis Bonifatii Comitis Africae,* Tilburg, 1941.]

2. Matt. xxii. 37-40.

who enjoined it on you, and whose gift it is, it may be nourished and increased, until, being perfected, it render you perfect. "For this is the love which," as the apostle says, "is shed abroad in our hearts by the Holy Ghost, which is given unto us." [3] This is "the fulfilling of the law;" [4] this is the same love by which faith works, of which he says again, "Neither circumcision availeth anything, nor uncircumcision; but faith, which worketh by love." [5]

In this love, then, all our holy fathers, patriarchs, prophets, and apostles pleased God. In this all true martyrs contended against the devil even to the shedding of blood, and because in them it neither waxed cold nor failed, they became conquerors. In this all true believers daily make progress, seeking to acquire not an earthly kingdom, but the kingdom of heaven; not a temporal, but an eternal inheritance; not gold and silver, but the incorruptible riches of the angels; not the good things of this life, which are enjoyed with trembling, and which no one can take with him when he dies, but the vision of God, whose grace and power of imparting felicity transcend all beauty of form in bodies not only on earth but also in heaven, transcend all spiritual loveliness in men, however just and holy, transcend all the glory of the angels and powers of the world above, transcend not only all that language can express, but all that thought can imagine concerning Him. And let us not despair of the fulfilment of such a great promise because it is exceeding great, but rather believe that we shall receive it because He who has promised it

3. Rom. v. 5.
4. *Ibid.*, xiii. 10.
5. Gal. v. 6.

is exceeding great, as the blessed Apostle John says: "Now are we the sons of God; and it doth not yet appear what we shall be: but we know that, when He shall appear, we shall be like Him; for we shall see Him as He is." [6]

[b]Let the manner of your life be adorned by chastity, sobriety, and moderation; for it is exceedingly disgraceful that lust should subdue him whom man finds invincible, and that wine should overpower him whom the sword assails in vain. As to worldly riches, if you do not possess them, let them not be sought after on earth by doing evil; and if you possess them, let them by good works be laid up in heaven. The manly and Christian spirit ought neither to be elated by the accession, nor crushed by the loss of this world's treasures. Let us rather think of what the Lord says: "Where your treasure is, there will your heart be also;" [7] and certainly, when we hear the exhortation to lift up our hearts, it is our duty to give unfeignedly the response which you know that we are accustomed to give.

In these things, indeed, I know that you are very careful, and the good report which I hear of you fills me with great delight, and moves me to congratulate you on account of it in the Lord. This letter, therefore, may serve rather as a mirror in which you may see what you are, than as a directory from which to learn what you ought to be: nevertheless, whatever you may discover, either from this letter or from the Holy Scriptures, to be still wanting to you in regard to a holy life, persevere in urgently seeking it both by effort and by

6. Luke, iii. 14.
b. *Letters,* CLXXXIX, 7-8.
7. Matt. vi. 21.

prayer; and for the things which you have, give thanks to God as the Fountain of goodness, whence you have received them; in every good action let the glory be given to God, and humility be exercised by you, for, as it is written, "Every good gift and every perfect gift is from above, and cometh down from the Father of lights." [8] But however much you may advance in the love of God and of your neighbour, and in true piety, do not imagine, as long as you are in this life, that you are without sin, for concerning this we read in Holy Scripture: "Is not the life of man upon earth a life of temptation?" [9] Wherefore, since always, as long as you are in this body, it is necessary for you to say in prayer, as the Lord taught us: "Forgive us our debts, as we forgive our debtors," [10] remember quickly to forgive, if any one shall do you wrong and shall ask pardon from you, that you may be able to pray sincerely, and may prevail in seeking pardon for your own sins.

These things, my beloved friend, I have written to you in haste, as the anxiety of the bearer to depart urged me not to detain him; but I thank God that I have in some measure complied with your pious wish. May the mercy of God ever protect you, my noble lord and justly distinguished son.

---

[c]To my Lord Boniface,[11] my Son commended to the Guardianship and Guidance of Divine Mercy for Present and Eternal Salvation, Augustine sends greeting.

8. Jas. i. 17.
9. Job vii. 1.
10. Matt. vi. 12.
c. *Letters,* CCXX, 1-12.
11. See note to Letter CLXXXIX.

Never could I have found a more trustworthy man, nor one who could have more ready access to your ear when bearing a letter from me, than this servant and minister of Christ, the deacon Paulus, a man very dear to both of us, whom the Lord has now brought to me in order that I may have the opportunity of addressing you, not in reference to your power and the honour which you hold in this evil world, nor in reference to the preservation of your corruptible and mortal body, —because this also is destined to pass away, and how soon no one can tell,—but in reference to that salvation which has been promised to us by Christ, who was here on earth despised and crucified in order that He might teach us rather to despise than to desire the good things of this world, and to set our affections and our hope on that world which He has revealed by His resurrection. For He has risen from the dead, and now "dieth no more; death hath no more dominion over Him." [12]

I know that you have no lack of friends, who love you so far as life in this world is concerned, and who in regard to it give you counsels, sometimes useful, sometimes the reverse; for they are men, and therefore, though they use their wisdom to the best of their ability in regard to what is present, they know not what may happen on the morrow. But it is not easy for any one to give you counsel in reference to God, to prevent the perdition of your soul, not because you lack friends who would do this, but because it is difficult for them to find an opportunity of speaking with you on these subjects. For I myself have often longed for this, and never found place or time in which

12. Rom. vi. 9.

I might deal with you as I ought to deal with a man whom I ardently love in Christ. You know besides in what state you found me at Hippo, when you did me the honour to come to visit me,— how I was scarcely able to speak, being prostrated by bodily weakness. Now, then, my son, hear me when I have this opportunity of addressing you at least by a letter,—a rare opportunity, for it was not in my power to send such communication to you in the midst of your dangers, both because I apprehended danger to the bearer, and because I was afraid lest my letter should reach persons into whose hands I was unwilling that it should fall. Wherefore I beg you to forgive me if you think that I have been more afraid than I should have been; however this may be, I have stated what I feared.

Hear me, therefore; nay, rather hear the Lord our God speaking by me, His feeble servant. Call to remembrance what manner of man you were while your former wife, of hallowed memory, still lived, and how under the stroke of her death, while that event was yet recent, the vanity of this world made you recoil from it, and how you earnestly desired to enter the service of God. We know and we can testify what you said as to your state of mind and your desires when you conversed with us at Tubunæ. My brother Alypius and I were alone with you. [I beseech you, then, to call to remembrance that conversation], for I do not think that the worldly cares with which you are now engrossed can have such power over you as to have effaced this wholly from your memory. You were then desirous to abandon all the public business in which you were engaged, and to withdraw into sacred retirement, and live like the servants of

God who have embraced a monastic life. And what was it that prevented you from acting according to these desires? Was it not that you were influenced by considering, on our representation of the matter, how much service the work which then occupied you might render to the churches of Christ if you pursued it with this single aim, that they, protected from all disturbance by barbarian hordes, might live "a quiet and peaceable life," as the apostle says, "in all godliness and honesty;" [13] resolving at the same time for your own part to seek no more from this world than would suffice for the support of yourself and those dependent on you, wearing as your girdle the cincture of a perfectly chaste self-restraint, and having underneath the accoutrements of the soldier the surer and stronger defence of spiritual armour.

At the very time when we were full of joy that you had formed this resolution, you embarked on a voyage and you married a second wife. Your embarkation was an act of the obedience due, as the apostle has taught us, to the "higher powers;" [14] but you would not have married again  had you not, abandoning the continence to which you had devoted yourself, been overcome by concupiscence. When I learned this, I was, I must confess it, dumb with amazement; but, in my sorrow, I was in some degree comforted by hearing that you refused to marry her unless she became a Catholic before the marriage, and yet the heresy of those who refuse to believe in the true Son of God has so prevailed in your house, that by these heretics your daughter was baptized. Now, if the report be true (would to God that it were false!)

13. 1 Tim. ii. 2.
14. Rom. xiii. 1.

that even some who were dedicated to God as His handmaids have been by these heretics re-baptized, with what floods of tears ought this great calamity to be bewailed by us! Men are saying, moreover, —perhaps it is an unfounded slander,—that one wife does not satisfy your passions, and that you have been defiled by consorting with some other women as concubines.

What shall I say regarding these evils—so patent to all, and so great in magnitude as well as number—of which you have been, directly or indirectly, the cause since the time of your being married? You are a Christian, you have a conscience, you fear God; consider, then, for yourself some things which I prefer to leave unsaid, and you will find for how great evils you ought to do penance; and I believe that it is to afford you an opportunity of doing this in the way in which it ought to be done, that the Lord is now sparing you and delivering you from all dangers. But if you will listen to the counsel of Scripture, I pray you, "make no tarrying to turn to the Lord, and put not off from day to day." [15] You allege, indeed, that you have good reason for what you have done, and that I cannot be a judge of the sufficiency of that reason, because I cannot hear both sides of the question;[16] but, whatever be your reason, the nature of which it is not necessary at present either to investigate or to discuss, can you, in the presence of God, affirm that you would ever have come into the embarrassments of your present position had you not loved the good things of this world, which, being a servant of God, such as we knew you to be formerly, it was your duty

15. Eccles. v. 8.
16. See note on Letter CLXXXIX.

to have utterly despised and esteemed as of no value,—accepting, indeed, what was offered to you, that you might devote it to pious uses, but not so coveting that which was denied to you, or was entrusted to your care, as to be brought on its account into the difficulties of your present position, in which, while good is loved, evil things are perpetrated,—few, indeed, by you, but many because of you, and while things are dreaded which, if hurtful, are so only for a short time, things are done which are really hurtful for eternity?

To mention one of these things,—who can help seeing that many persons follow you for the purpose of defending your power or safety, who, although they may be all faithful to you, and no treachery is to be apprehended from any of them, are desirous of obtaining through you certain advantages which they also covet, not with a godly desire, but from worldly motives? And in this way you, whose duty it is to curb and check your own passions, are forced to satisfy those of others. To accomplish this, many things which are displeasing to God must be done; and yet, after all, these passions are not thus satisfied, for they are more easily mortified finally in those who love God, than satisfied, even for a time, in those who love the world. Therefore the Divine Scripture says: "Love not the world, nor the things that are in the world. If any man love the world, the love of the Father is not in him. For all that is in the world, the lust of the flesh, and the lust of the eyes, and the pride of life, is not of the Father, but is of the world. And the world passeth away, and the lust thereof: but he that doeth the will of God abideth for ever, as God abideth for ever." [17] Associated, therefore,

17. 1 John ii. 15-17.

as you are with such multitudes of armed men, whose passions must be humoured, and whose cruelty is dreaded, how can the desires of these men who love the world ever be, I do not say satiated, but even partially gratified by you, in your anxiety to prevent still greater wide-spread evils, unless you do that which God forbids, and in so doing become obnoxious to threatened judgment? So complete has been the havoc wrought in order to indulge their passions, that it would be difficult now to find anything for the plunderer to carry away.

But, what shall I say of the devastation of Africa at this hour by hordes of African barbarians, to whom no resistance is offered, while you are engrossed with such embarrassments in your own circumstances, and are taking no measures for averting this calamity? Who would ever have believed, who would have feared, after Boniface had become a Count of the Empire and of Africa, and had been placed in command in Africa with so large an army and so great authority, that the same man who formerly, as Tribune, kept all these barbarous tribes in peace, by storming their strongholds, and menacing them with his small band of brave confederates, should now have suffered the barbarians to be so bold, to encroach so far, to destroy and plunder so much, and to turn into deserts such vast regions once densely peopled? Where were any found who did not predict that, as soon as you obtained the authority of Count, the African hordes would be not only checked, but made tributaries to the Roman Empire? And now, how completely the event has disappointed men's hopes you yourself perceive; in fact, I need say nothing more on this subject, because your own reflection must suggest much more than I can put in words.

Perhaps you defend yourself by replying that the blame here ought rather to rest on persons who have injured you, and, instead of justly requiting the services rendered by you in your office, have returned evil for good. These matters I am not able to examine and judge. I beseech you rather to contemplate and inquire into the matter, in which you know that you have to do not with men at all, but with God; living in Christ as a believer, you are bound to fear lest you offend Him. For my attention is more engaged by higher causes, believing that men ought to ascribe Africa's great calamities to their own sins. Nevertheless, I would not wish you to belong to the number of those wicked and unjust men whom God uses as instruments in inflicting temporal punishments on whom He pleases; for He who justly employs their malice to inflict temporal judgments on others, reserves eternal punishments for the unjust themselves if they be not reformed. Be it yours to fix your thoughts on God, and to look to Christ, who has conferred on you so great blessings and endured for you so great sufferings. Those who desire to belong to His kingdom, and to live for ever happily with Him and under Him, love even their enemies, do good to them that hate them, and pray for those from whom they suffer persecution;[18] and if, at any time, in the way of discipline they use irksome severity, yet they never lay aside the sincerest love. If these benefits, though earthly and transitory, are conferred on you by the Roman Empire,—for that empire itself is earthly, not heavenly, and cannot bestow what it has not in its power,—if, I say,

18. Matt. v. 44.

benefits are conferred on you, return not evil for good; and if evil be inflicted on you, return not evil for evil. Which of these two has happened in  your case I am unwilling to discuss, I am unable to judge. I speak to a Christian—return not either evil for good, nor evil for evil.

You say to me, perhaps: In circumstances so difficult, what do you wish me to do? If you ask counsel of me in a worldly point of view how your safety in this transitory life may be secured, and the power and wealth belonging to you at present may be preserved or even increased, I know not what to answer you, for any counsel regarding things so uncertain as these must partake of the uncertainty inherent in them. But if you consult me regarding your relation to God and the salvation of your soul, and if you fear the word of truth which says: "What is a man profited, if he shall gain the whole world, and lose his own soul?" [19] I have a plain answer to give. I am prepared with advice to which you may well give heed. But what need is there for my saying anything else than what I have already said. "Love not the world, neither the things that are in the world. If any man love the world, the love of the Father is not in him. For all that is in the world, the lust of the flesh, and the lust of the eyes, and the pride of life, is not of the Father, but is of the world. And the world passeth away, and the lust thereof: but he that doeth the will of God abideth for ever." [20] Here is counsel! Seize it and act on it. Show that you are a brave man. Vanquish the desires with which the world is loved. Do penance for the evils of your past life, when, vanquished by your pas-

19. Matt. xvi. 26.
20. 1 John ii. 15-17.

sions, you were drawn away by sinful desires. If
you receive this counsel, and hold it fast, and act
on it, you will both attain to those blessings which
are certain, and occupy yourself in the midst of
these uncertain things without forfeiting the salvation of your soul.

But perhaps you again ask of me how you can
do these things, entangled as you are with so great
worldly difficulties. Pray earnestly, and say to God,
in the words of the Psalm: "Bring Thou me out
of my distresses," [21] for these distresses terminate
when the passions in which they originate are
vanquished. He who has heard your prayer and
ours on your behalf, that you might be delivered
from the numerous and great dangers of visible
wars in which the body is exposed to the danger
of losing the life which sooner or later must end,
but in which the soul perishes not unless it be held
captive by evil passions,—He, I say, will hear your
prayer that you may, in an invisible and spiritual
conflict, overcome your inward and invisible enemies, that is to say, your passions themselves, and
may so use the world, as not abusing it, so that
with its good things you may do good, not become
bad through possessing them. Because these things
are in themselves good, and are not given to men
except by Him who has power over all things in
heaven and earth. Lest these gifts of His should
be reckoned bad, they are given also to the good;
at the same time, lest they should be reckoned
great, or the supreme good, they are given also to
the bad. Further, these things are taken away
from the good for their trial, and from the bad
for their punishment.

For who is so ignorant, who so foolish, as not

21. Ps. xxv. 17.

to see that the health of this mortal body, and the strength of its corruptible members, and victory over men who are our enemies, and temporal honours and power, and all other mere earthly advantages are given both to the good and to the bad, and are taken away both from the good and from the bad alike? But the salvation of the soul, along with immortality of the body, and the power of righteousness, and victory over hostile passions, and glory, and honour, and everlasting peace, are not given except to the good. Therefore love these things, covet these things, and seek them by every means in your power. With a view to acquire and retain these things, give alms, pour forth prayers, practise fasting as far as you can without injury to your body. But do not love these earthly goods, how much soever they may abound to you. So use them as to do many good things by them, but not one evil thing for their sake. For all such things will perish; but good works, yea, even those good works which are performed by means of the perishable good things of this world, shall never perish.

If you had not now a wife, I would say to you what we said at Tubunæ, that you should live in the holy state of continence, and would add that you should now do what we prevented you from doing at that time, namely, withdraw yourself so far as might be possible without prejudice to the public welfare from the labours of military service, and take to yourself the leisure which you then desired for that life in the society of the saints in which the soldiers of Christ fight in silence, not to kill men, but to "wrestle against principalities and powers, and spiritual wickedness," [22] that is, the devil and his angels. For the saints gain their vic-

22. Eph. vi. 12.

tories over enemies whom they cannot see, and yet they gain the victory over these unseen enemies by gaining the victory over things which are the objects of sense. I am, however, prevented from exhorting you to that mode of life by your having a wife, since without her consent it is not lawful for you to live under a vow of continence; because, although you did wrong in marrying again after the declaration which you made at Tubunæ, she, being not aware of this, became your wife innocently and without restrictions. Would that you could persuade her to agree to a vow of continence, that you might without hindrance render to God what you know to be due to Him! If, however, you cannot make this agreement with her, guard carefully by all means conjugal chastity, and pray to God, who will deliver you out of difficulties, that you may at some future time be able to do what is meanwhile impossible. This, however, does not affect your obligation to love God and not to love the world, to hold the faith stedfastly even in the cares of war, if you must still be engaged in them, and to seek peace; to make the good things of this world serviceable in good works, and not to do what is evil in labouring to obtain these earthly good things,—in all these duties your wife is not, or, if she is, ought not to be, a hindrance to you.

These things I have written, my dearly beloved son, at the bidding of the love with which I love you with regard not to this world, but to God; and because, mindful of the words of Scripture, "Reprove a wise man, and he will love thee; reprove a fool, and he will hate thee more," [23] I was bound to think of you as certainly not a fool but a wise man.

23. Prov. ix. 8.

# CHAPTER VI

## CAPTIVITY IN BABYLON

### A. *Power to Crucify and Power to Release*

[a]What Pilate said to Christ, or what He replied to Pilate, has to be considered and handled in the present discourse. For after the words had been addressed to the Jews, "Take ye him, and judge him according to your law," and the Jews had replied, "It is not lawful for us to put any man to death, Pilate entered again into the judgment hall, and called Jesus, and said unto Him, Art thou the King of the Jews? And Jesus answered, Sayest thou this thing of thyself, or did others tell it thee of me?" The Lord indeed knew both what He Himself asked, and what reply the other was to give; but yet He wished it to be spoken, not for the sake of information to Himself, but that what He wished us to know might be recorded in Scripture. "Pilate answered, Am I a Jew? Thine own nation, and the chief priests, have delivered thee unto me: what hast thou done? Jesus answered, My kingdom is not of this world. If my kingdom were of this world, then would my servants fight, that I should not be delivered to the Jews: but now is my kingdom not from hence." This is what the good Master wished us to know; but first there had to be shown us the vain notion that men had

a. *In Johan. Evang. Tract.*, CXV, 1-5.

regarding His kingdom, whether Gentiles or Jews, from whom Pilate had heard it; as if He ought to have been punished with death on the ground of aspiring to an unlawful kingdom; or as those in the possession of royal power usually manifest their ill-will to such as are yet to attain it, as if, for example, precautions were to be used lest His kingdom should prove adverse either to the Romans or to the Jews. But the Lord was able to reply to the first question of the governor, when he asked Him, "Art thou the King of the Jews?" with the words, "My kingdom is not of this world," etc.; but by questioning him in turn, whether he said this thing of himself, or heard it from others, He wished by his answer to show that He had been charged with this as a crime before him by the Jews: laying open to us the thoughts of men, which were all known to Himself, that they are but vain;[1] and now, after Pilate's answer, giving them, both Jews and Gentiles, all the more reasonable and fitting a reply, "My kingdom is not of this world." But had He made an immediate answer to Pilate's question, His reply would have appeared to refer to the Gentiles only, without including the Jews, as entertaining such an opinion regarding Him. But now when Pilate replied, "Am I a Jew? Thine own nation, and the chief priests, have delivered thee to me;" he removed from himself the suspicion of being possibly supposed to have spoken of his own accord, in saying that Jesus was the king of the Jews, by showing that such a statement had been communicated to him by the Jews. And then by saying, "What hast thou done?" he made it sufficiently clear that this was charged against Him as a crime: as if he had said, If thou

1. Ps. xciv. 11.

deniest such kingly claims, what hast thou done to cause thy being delivered unto me? As if there would be no ground for wonder that one should be delivered up to a judge for punishment, who proclaimed himself a king; but if no such assertion were made, it became needful to inquire of Him, what else, if anything, He had done, that He should thus deserve to be delivered unto the judge.

Hear then, ye Jews and Gentiles; hear, O circumcision; hear, O uncircumcision; hear, all ye kingdoms of the earth: I interfere not with your government in this world, "My kingdom is not of this world." Cherish ye not the utterly vain terror that threw Herod the elder into consternation when the birth of Christ was announced, and led him to the murder of so many infants in the hope of including Christ in the fatal number,[2] made more cruel by his fear than by his anger: "My kingdom," He said, "is not of this world." What would you more? Come to the kingdom that is not of this world; come, believing, and fall not into the madness of anger through fear. He says, indeed, prophetically of God the Father, "Yet have I been appointed king by Him upon His holy hill of Zion;"[3] but that hill of Zion is not of this world. For what is His kingdom, save those who believe in Him, to whom He says, "Ye are not of the world, even as I am not of the world"? And yet He wished them to be in the world: on that very account saying of them to the Father, "I pray not that Thou shouldest take them out of the world, but that Thou shouldest keep them from the evil."[4] Hence also He says not here, "My

2. Matt. ii. 3, 16.
3. Ps. ii. 6.
4. John xvii. 16, 15.

kingdom is not" in this world; but, "is not of this world." And when He proved this by saying, "If my kingdom were of this world, then would my servants fight, that I should not be delivered to the Jews," He saith not, "But now is my kingdom not" here, but, "is not from hence." For His kingdom is here until the end of the world, having tares intermingled therewith until the harvest; for the harvest is the end of the world, when the reapers, that is to say, the angels, shall come and gather out of His kingdom everything that offendeth;[5] which certainly would not be done, were it not that His kingdom is here. But still it is not from hence; for it only sojourns as a stranger in the world: because He says to His kingdom, "Ye are not of the world, but I have chosen you out of the world." [6] They were therefore of the world, so long as they were not His kingdom, but belonged to the prince of this world. Of the world therefore are all mankind, created indeed by the true God, but generated from Adam as a vitiated and condemned stock; and there are made into a kingdom no longer of the world, all from thence that have been regenerated in Christ. For so did God rescue us from the power of darkness, and translate us into the kingdom of the Son of His love:[7] and of this kingdom it is that He saith, "My kingdom is not of this world;" or, "My kingdom is not from hence."

"Pilate therefore said unto Him, Art thou a king then? Jesus answered, Thou sayest that I am a king." Not that He was afraid to confess Himself a king, but "Thou sayest" has been so

5. Matt. xiii. 38-41.
6. John xv. 19.
7. Col. i. 13.

balanced that He neither denies Himself to be a king (for He is a king whose kingdom is not of this world), nor does He confess that He is such a king as to warrant the supposition that His kingdom is of this world. For as this was the very idea in Pilate's mind when he said, "Art thou a king then?" so the answer he got was, "Thou sayest that I am a king." For it was said, "Thou sayest," as if it had been said, Carnal thyself, thou sayest it carnally.

Thereafter He adds, "To this end was I born, and for this cause came I into the world, that I should bear witness unto the truth." * * [8] Whence it is evident that He here referred to His own temporal nativity, when by becoming incarnate He came into the world, and not to that which had no beginning, whereby He was God through whom the Father created the world. For this, then, that is, on this account, He declared that He was born, and to this end He came into the world, to wit, by being born of the Virgin, that He might bear witness unto the truth. But because all men have not faith,[9] He still further said, "Every one that is of the truth heareth my voice."

8. The verse quoted reads in Latin, "Ego in hoc natus sum, et ad hoc veni," etc.; and in reference to the words, "in hoc," Augustine goes on to say, in the passage marked * *: "We are not to lengthen the syllable [vowel] of this pronoun when He says, *In hoc natus sum*, as if He meant to say, In this thing was I born; but to shorten it, as if He had said, *Ad hanc rem natus sum, vel ad hoc natus sum* (for this thing was I born), just as He says, *Ad hoc veni in mundum* (for this came I into the world). For in the Greek Gospel there is no ambiguity in this expression," the Greek having εἰς τοῦτο. This passage is interesting only to Latin scholars, as showing that in ordinary *parlance* they marked, in Augustine's time, the distinction between *hŏc* of the abl. and *hŏc* of the nom. or acc.—Tr.

9. 2 Thess. iii. 2.

He heareth, that is to say, with the ears of the inward man, or, in other words, He obeyeth my voice, which is equivalent to saying, He believeth me. When Christ, therefore, beareth witness unto the truth, He beareth witness, of course, unto Himself; for from His own lips are the words, "I am the truth;" [10] as He said also in another place, "I bear witness of myself." [11] But when He said, "Every one that is of the truth heareth my voice," He commendeth the grace whereby He calleth according to His own purpose. Of which purpose the apostle says, "We know that all things work together for good to them that love God, to those who are called according to the purpose of God," [12] to wit, the purpose of Him that calleth, not of those who are called; which is put still more clearly in another place in this way, "Labour together in the gospel according to the power of God, who saveth us and calleth us with His holy calling, not according to our works, but according to His own purpose and grace." [13] For if our thoughts turn to the nature wherein we have been created, inasmuch as we were all created by the Truth, who is there that is not of the truth? But it is not all to whom it is given of the truth to hear, that is, to obey the truth, and to believe in the truth; while in no case certainly is there any preceding of merit, lest grace should cease to be grace. For had He said, Every one that heareth my voice is of the truth, then it would be supposed that he was declared to be of the truth because he conforms to the truth; it is not this, however, that

10. John xiv. 6.
11. *Ibid.*, viii. 18.
12. Rom. viii. 28.
13. 2 Tim. i. 8, 9.

He says, but, "Every one that is of the truth heareth my voice." And in this way he is not of the truth simply because he heareth His voice; but only on this account he heareth, because he is of the truth, that is, because this is a gift bestowed on him of the truth. And what else is this, but that by Christ's gracious bestowal he believeth in Christ?

"Pilate said unto Him, What is truth?" Nor did he wait to hear the answer; but "when he had said this, he went out again unto the Jews, and said unto them, I find in him no fault. But ye have a custom that I should release unto you one at the passover: will ye therefore that I release unto you the King of the Jews?" I believe when Pilate said, "What is truth?" there immediately occurred to his mind the custom of the Jews, according to which he was wont to release unto them one at the passover; and therefore he did not wait to hear Jesus' answer to his question, What is truth? to avoid delay on recollecting the custom whereby He might be released unto them during the passover— a thing which it is clear he greatly desired. It could not, however, be torn from his heart that Jesus was the King of the Jews, but was fixed there, as in the superscription, by the truth itself, whereof he had just inquired what it was. "But on hearing this, they all cried again, saying, Not this man, but Barabbas. Now Barabbas was a robber." We blame you not, O Jews, for liberating the guilty during the passover, but for slaying the innocent; and yet unless that were done, the true passover would not take place. But a shadow of the truth was retained by the erring Jews, and by a mar- vellous dispensation of divine wisdom the truth of that same shadow was fulfilled by deluded men;

because in order that the true passover might be kept, Christ was led as a sheep to the sacrificial slaughter. Hence there follows the account of the injurious treatment received by Christ at the hands of Pilate and his cohort.

ᵇOn the Jews crying out that they did not wish Jesus to be released unto them at the passover, but Barabbas the robber; not the Saviour, but the murderer; not the Giver of life, but the destroyer,—"then Pilate took Jesus and scourged Him." We must believe that Pilate acted thus for no other reason than that the Jews, glutted with the injuries done to Him, might consider themselves satisfied, and desist from madly pursuing Him even unto death. With a similar intention was it that, as governor, he also permitted his cohort to do what follows, or even perhaps ordered them, although the evangelist is silent on the subject? For he tells us what the soldiers did thereafter, but not that Pilate ordered it. "And the soldiers," he says, "platted a crown of thorns, and put it on His head, and they clothed Him with a purple robe. And they came to Him and said, Hail, King of the Jews! And they smote Him with their hands." Thus were fulfilled the very things which Christ had foretold of Himself; thus were the martyrs moulded for the endurance of all that their persecutors should be pleased to inflict; thus, by concealing for a time the terror of His power, He commended to us the prior imitation of His patience; thus the kingdom which was not of this world overcame that proud world, not by the ferocity of fighting, but by the humility of suffering; and thus the grain of corn that was yet to be

b. *In Johan. Evang. Tract.*, CXVI, 1-9.

multiplied was sown amid the horrors of shame, that it might come to fruition amid the wonders of glory.

"Pilate went forth again, and saith unto them, Behold, I bring him forth, that ye may know that I find no fault in him. Then came Jesus forth, wearing the crown of thorns and the purple robe. And he saith unto them, Behold the man!" Hence it is apparent that these things were done by the soldiers not without Pilate's knowledge, whether it was that he ordered them or only permitted them, namely, for the reason we have stated above, that His enemies might all the more willingly drink in the sight of such derisive treatment, and cease to thirst further for His blood. Jesus goes forth to them wearing the crown of thorns and the purple robe, not resplendent in kingly power, but laden with reproach; and the words are addressed to them, Behold the man! If you hate your king, spare him now when you see him sunk so low; he has been scourged, crowned with thorns, clothed with the garments of derision, jeered at with the bitterest insults, struck with the open hand; his ignominy is at the boiling point, let your ill-will sink to zero. But there is no such cooling on the part of the latter, but rather a further increase of heat and vehemence.

"When the chief priests, therefore, and attendants saw Him, they cried out, saying, Crucify, crucify him. Pilate saith unto them, Take ye him and crucify him; for I find no fault in him. The Jews answered him, We have a law, and by the law he ought to die, because he made himself the Son of God." Behold another and still greater ground of hatred. The former, indeed, seemed but a small matter, as that shown towards the usurpation, by an unlawful act of daring, of the royal power; and yet of neither did Jesus falsely claim possession, but each of them is truly His as both the only-begotten Son of God, and by Him appointed King upon His holy hill of Zion; and both might He now have shown to be His, were it not that in proportion to the greatness of His power He preferred to manifest the corresponding greatness of His patience.

"When Pilate, therefore, heard that saying, he was the more afraid; and entered again into the judgment hall, and saith unto Jesus, Whence art thou? But Jesus gave him no answer." It is found, in comparing the narratives of all the evangelists, that this silence on the part of our Lord Jesus Christ took place more than once, both before the chief priests and before Herod, to whom, as Luke intimates, Pilate had sent Him for a hearing, and before Pilate himself;[14] so that it was not in vain that the prophecy regarding Him had preceded, "As the lamb before its shearer was dumb, so He opened not His mouth," [15] especially on those occasions when He answered not His questioners. For although He frequently replied to questions addressed to Him, yet because of those in regard to which He declined making any reply, the metaphor of the lamb is supplied, in order that in His silence He might be accounted not as guilty, but innocent. When, therefore, He was passing through the process of judgment, wherever He opened not His mouth it was in the character of a lamb that He did so; that is, not as one with an evil conscience who was convicted of his sins,

14. Matt. xxvi. 63, xxvii. 14; Mark xiv. 61, xv. 5: Luke xxiii. 7-9; John xix. 9.
15. Isa. liii. 7.

but as one who in His meekness was sacrificed for the sins of others.

"Then saith Pilate unto Him, Speakest thou not unto me? knowest thou not that I have power to crucify thee, and have power to release thee? Jesus answered: Thou wouldest have no power against me, except it were given thee from above: therefore he that delivered me unto thee hath the greater sin." Here, you see, He replied; and yet wherever He replied not, it is not as one who is criminal or cunning, but as a lamb; that is, in simplicity and innocence He opened not His mouth. Accordingly, where He made no answer, He was silent as a sheep; where He answered, He taught as the Shepherd. Let us therefore set ourselves to learn what He said, what He taught also by the apostle, that "there is no power but of God;" [16] and that he is a greater sinner who maliciously delivereth up to the power the innocent to be slain, than the power itself, if it slay him through fear of another power that is greater still. Of such a sort, indeed, was the power which God had given to Pilate, that he should also be under the power of Cæsar. Wherefore "thou wouldest have," He says, "no power against me," that is, even the little measure thou really hast, "except" this very measure, whatever its amount, "were given thee from above." But knowing as I do its amount, for it is not so great as to render thee altogether independent, "therefore he that delivered me unto thee hath the greater sin." He, indeed, delivered me to thy power at the bidding of envy, whilst thou art to exercise thy power upon me through the impulse of fear. And yet not even through the impulse of fear ought one man

16. Rom. xiii. 1.

to slay another, especially the innocent; nevertheless to do so by an officious zeal is a much greater evil than under the constraint of fear. And therefore the truth-speaking Teacher saith not, "He that delivered me to thee," he only hath sin, as if the other had none; but He saith, "hath the greater sin," letting him understand that he himself was not exempt from blame. For that of the latter is not reduced to nothing because the other is greater.

"Hence Pilate sought to release Him." What is to be understood by the word here used, "hence," [17] as if he had not been seeking to do so before? Read what precedes, and thou wilt find that he had already for some time been seeking to release Jesus. By the original word,[17] therefore, we are to understand, *on this account,* that is, *for this reason,* that he might not contract sin by slaying an innocent man who had been delivered into his hands, even though his sin would be less than that of the Jews, who delivered Him to him to be put to death. "From thence," [17] therefore, that is, for this reason, that he might not commit such a sin, "he sought" not now for the first time, but from the beginning, "to release Him."

"But the Jews cried out, saying, If thou let this man go, thou art not Cæsar's friend: whosoever maketh himself a king, speaketh against Cæsar." They thought to inspire Pilate with greater fear by terrifying him about Cæsar, in order that he might put Christ to death, than formerly when they said, "We have the law, and by the law he ought to die, because he made himself the Son of God." It was not their law, indeed, that impelled him through fear to the deed of murder, but rather it was his fear of the Son of God that

17. "Exinde."

held him back from the crime. But now he could not set Cæsar, who was the author of his own power, at nought, in the same way as the law of another nation.

As yet, however, the evangelist proceeds to say: "But when Pilate heard these sayings, he brought Jesus forth, and sat down before the tribunal, in a place that is called the Pavement,[18] but in the Hebrew, Gabbatha. And it was the preparation[19] of the passover, and about the sixth hour." The question, at what hour the Lord was crucified, because of the testimony supplied by another evangelist, who says, "And it was the third hour, and they crucified Him," [20] we shall consider as we can, if the Lord please, when we are come to the passage itself where His crucifixion is recorded. When Pilate, therefore, had sat down before the tribunal, "he saith unto the Jews, Behold your king! But they cried out, Away with him, away with him, crucify him. Pilate said unto them, Shall I crucify your king?" As yet he tries to overcome the terror with which they had inspired him about Cæsar, by seeking to break them from their purpose on the ground of the ignominy it brought on themselves, with the words, "Shall I crucify your king?" when he failed to soften them on the ground of the ignominy done to Christ; but by and by he is overcome by fear.

For "the chief priests answered, We have no king but Cæsar. Then delivered he Him therefore unto them to be crucified." For he would have every appearance of acting against Cæsar if, on their declaration that they had no king but Cæsar,

18. "Lithostrotos."
19. "Parasceve."
20. Mark xv. 25.

he were wishing to impose on them an/
by releasing without punishment one ...
these very attempts they had delivered unto him
to be put to death. "Therefore he delivered Him
unto them to be crucified." But was it, then, anything different that he had previously desired
when he said, "Take ye him, and crucify him;" or
even earlier still, "Take ye him, and judge him
according to your law"? And why did they show
so great reluctance when they said, "It is not lawful for us to put any man to death," and were in
every way urgent to have Him slain not by themselves, but by the governor, and therefore refused
to receive Him for the purpose of putting Him to
death, if now for the same purpose they actually
do receive Him? Or if such be not the case, why
was it said, "Then delivered he Him therefore
unto them to be crucified"? Or is it of any importance? Plainly it is. For it was not said, "Then
delivered he Him therefore unto them" that they
might crucify Him, but "that He might be crucified," that is, that He might be crucified by the
judicial sentence and power of the governor. But
it is for this reason that the evangelist has said
that He was delivered to them, that he might show
that they were implicated in the crime from which
they tried to hold themselves aloof; for Pilate
would have done no such thing, save to implement
what he perceived to be their fixed desire.

## B. *Subject unto the Higher Powers*

[a]We know what persecutions the body of Christ,
that is, the holy Church, suffered from the kings
of the earth. Let us therefore here also recognize
the words of the Church: *Princes have persecuted*

a. *Enarr. in Ps.*, CXVIII (Lat.), xxxi, 1.

*me without a cause; and my heart hath stood in awe of Thee.* For how had the Christians injured the kingdoms of the earth, although their King promised them the kingdom of heaven? How, I ask, had they injured the kingdoms of the earth? Did their King forbid His soldiers to pay and to render due service to the kings of the earth? Saith He not to the Jews who were striving to calumniate Him, *Render unto Caesar the things that are Caesar's, and unto God the things that are God's?*[1] Did he not even in His own Person pay tribute from the mouth of a fish? Did not His forerunner, when the soldiers of this kingdom were seeking what they ought to do for their everlasting salvation, instead of replying, Loose your belts, throw away your arms, desert your king, that ye may wage war for the Lord, answer, *Do violence to no man: neither accuse any falsely: and be content with your wages?*[2] Did not one of His soldiers, His most beloved companion, say to his fellow soldiers, the provincials, so to speak, of Christ, *Let every soul be subject unto the higher powers?* And a little lower he added, *Render to all their dues; tribute to whom tribute is due; custom to whom custom: fear to whom fear: honour to whom honour. Owe no man any thing, but to love one another.*[3] Does he not enjoin the Church to pray for even kings themselves? How then have the Christians offended against them? What due have they not rendered? in what have not Christians obeyed the monarchs of the earth? The kings of the earth therefore have persecuted the Christians without a cause. But heed what he hath sub-

1. Matt. xxii. 21.
2. Luke iii. 14.
3. Rom. xiii. 1, 7, 8.

joined: *And my heart hath stood in awe of Thy word.* They too had their threatening words: I banish, I proscribe, I slay, I torture with claws, I burn with fires, I expose to beasts, I tear the limbs piecemeal: but rather *of Thy word hath my heart stood in awe. Fear not them which kill the body, but are not able to kill the soul: but rather fear Him which is able to destroy both soul and body in hell.*[4] My heart hath stood in awe of these words of Thine; and I have scorned man who persecuteth me, and have overcome the devil that would seduce me.

[b]At present indeed the righteous suffer in some measure, and at present the unrighteous sometimes tyrannize over the righteous. In what ways? Sometimes the unrighteous arrive at worldly honours: when they have arrived at them, and have been made either judges or kings; for God doth this for the discipline of His folk, for the discipline of His people; the honour due to their power must needs be shewn them. For thus hath God ordained His Church, that every power ordained in the world may have honour, and sometimes from those who are better than those in power. For the sake of illustration I take one instance; hence calculate the grades of all powers. The primary and every day relation of authority between man and man is that between master and slave. Almost all houses have a power of this sort. There are masters, there are also slaves; these are different names, but men and men are equal names. And what saith the Apostle, teaching that slaves are subject to their masters? *Servants, be obedient to them that are your masters according to the flesh:* for there

4. Matt. x. 28.
b. *Enarr. in Ps.,* CXXIV (Lat.), 7-8.

is a Master according to the Spirit. He is the true
and everlasting Master; but those temporal masters are for a time only. When thou walkest in the
way, when thou livest in this life, Christ doth not
wish to make thee proud. It hath been thy lot to
become a Christian, and to have a man for thy
master: thou wast not made a Christian, that thou
mightest disdain to be a servant. For when by
Christ's command thou servest a man, thou servest
not the man, but Him who commanded thee. He
saith this also: *Servants, be obedient to them that
are your masters according to the flesh, with fear
and trembling, in singleness of heart, as unto
Christ; not with eye-service, as men-pleasers, but
as the servants of Christ, doing the will of God
from the heart; with good will.*[5] Behold, he hath
not made men free from being servants, but good
servants from bad servants. How much do the
rich owe to Christ, who orders their house for
them! so that if thou hast had an unbelieving
servant, suppose Christ convert him, and say not
to him, Leave thy master, thou hast now known
Him Who is thy true Master: he perhaps is ungodly and unjust, thou art now faithful and
righteous: it is unworthy that a righteous and faithful man should serve an unjust and unbelieving
master. He spoke not thus unto him, but rather,
Serve him: and to confirm the servant, added,
Serve as I served; I before thee served the unjust.
From whom but His servants did the Lord suffer
so much in His Passion? from whom, but evil
servants? For if they had been good servants, they
would honour their Master. But since they were
evil servants, they wronged Him. What did He,
on the other hand? He recompensed love for

5. Eph. vi. 5, 6.

hatred: for He said, *Father, forgive them: for they know not what they do.*[6] If the Lord of heaven and earth, through Whom all things were created, served the unworthy, asked mercy for His furious persecutors, and, as it were, shewed Himself as their Physician at His Advent: (for physicians also, better both in art and health, serve the sick:) how much more ought not a man to disdain, with his whole mind, and his whole good will, with his whole love to serve even a bad master! Behold, a better serveth an inferior, but for a season. Understand what I have said of the master and slave, to be true also of powers and kings, of all the exalted stations of this world. For sometimes they are good powers, and fear God; sometimes they fear not God. Julian was an infidel Emperor, an apostate, a wicked man, an idolater; Christian soldiers served an infidel Emperor; when they came to the cause of Christ, they acknowledged Him only Who was in heaven. If he called upon them at any time to worship idols, to offer incense; they preferred God to him: but whenever he commanded them to deploy into line, to march against this or that nation, they at once obeyed. They distinguished their everlasting from their temporal master; and yet they were, for the sake of their everlasting Master, submissive to their temporal master.

But will it be thus always, that the ungodly have power over the righteous? It will not be so. See what this Psalm saith: *For God will not leave the rod of the ungodly upon the lot of the righteous.* The rod of the ungodly is felt for a season upon the lot of the righteous; but it is not left there, it will not be there for ever. A time will

6. Luke xxiii. 34.

come, when Christ, appearing in his glory, shall
gather all nations before Him; and shall separate
them one from another, as a shepherd divideth
his sheep from the goats: and He shall set the
sheep on His right hand, but the goats on the
left. And thou wilt see there many slaves among
the sheep, and many masters among the goats;
and again many masters among the sheep, many
slaves among the goats. For all slaves are not
good—do not infer this from the consolation we
have given to servants—nor are all masters evil,
because we have thus repressed the pride of masters. There are good masters who believe, and
there are evil: there are good servants who believe, and there are evil. But as long as good
servants serve evil masters, let them endure for a
season. *For God will not leave the rod of the ungodly upon the lot of the righteous.* Why will He
not? *Lest the righteous put forth their hand unto
wickedness:* that the righteous may endure for a
season the domination of the ungodly, and may
understand that this is not for ever, but may pre-
pare themselves to possess their everlasting heritage. What heritage? When all principalities and
powers shall be subdued, *that God may be all in
all.*[7]

[c]The Apostle himself saith, *Let every soul be
subject unto the higher powers, for there is no
power but of God, the powers that be are ordained of God. He then who resisteth the power,
resisteth the ordinance of God.*[8] But what if it enjoin what thou oughtest not to do? In this case

7. 1 Cor. xv. 28.
c. *Sermons,* LXII, 13.
8. Rom. xiii. 1, 2.

by all means disregard the power through fear of the Power.

<sup>d</sup>Run over now the list of those above thee. First are thy father and mother, if they are educating thee aright; if they are bringing thee up for Christ; they are to be heard in all things, they must be obeyed in every command; let them enjoin nothing against one above themselves, and so let them be obeyed. And who, thou wilt say, is above him who begat me? He who created thee. For man begets, but God creates. How it is that man begets, he does not know; and what he shall beget, he does not know. But He who saw thee that He might make thee, before that he whom He made existed, is surely above thy father. Thy country again should be above thy very parents; so that whereinsoever thy parents enjoin aught against thy country, they are not to be listened to.

<sup>e</sup>Consider these several grades of human powers. If the magistrate enjoin any thing, must it not be done? Yet if his order be in opposition to the Proconsul, thou dost not surely despise the power, but choosest to obey a greater power. Nor in this case ought the less to be angry, if the greater be preferred. Again, if the Proconsul himself enjoin any thing, and the Emperor another thing, is there any doubt, that disregarding the former, we ought to obey the latter? So then if the Emperor enjoin one thing, and God another, what judge ye? Pay me tribute, submit thyself to my allegiance. Right, but not in an idol's temple. In an idol's temple He forbids it. Who forbids it? A greater Power. Pardon me then: thou threatenest a prison, He

d. *Sermons,* LXII, 8.
e. *Ibid.,* LXII, 13-15.

threateneth hell. Here must thou at once take to thee thy *faith as a shield, whereby thou mayest be able to quench all the fiery darts of the enemy.*[9]

But one of these powers is plotting, and contriving evil designs against thee. Well: he is but sharpening the razor wherewith to shave the hair, but not to cut the head. Ye have just now heard this that I have said in the Psalm, *Thou hast worked deceit like a sharp razor.*[10] Why did He compare the deceit of a wicked man in power to a razor? Because it does not reach, save to our superfluous parts. As hairs on our body seem as it were superfluous, and are shaven off without any loss of the flesh; so whatsover an angry man in power can take from thee, count only among thy superfluities. He takes away thy poverty; can he take away thy wealth? Thy poverty is thy wealth in thy heart. Thy superfluous things only hath he power to take away, these only hath he power to injure, even though he had license given him so far as to hurt the body. Yea even this life itself to those whose thoughts are of another life, this present life, I say, may be reckoned among the things superfluous. For so the Martyrs have despised it. They did not lose life, but they gained Life.

Be sure, Brethren, that enemies have no power against the faithful, except so far as it profiteth them to be tempted and proved. Of this be sure, Brethren, let no one say aught against it. Cast all your care upon the Lord, throw yourselves wholly and entirely upon Him. He will not withdraw Himself that ye should fall. He Who created us, hath given us security touching our very

9. Eph. vi. 16.
10. Ps. li. 4.

hairs. *Verily I say unto you, even the hairs of your head are all numbered.*[11] Our hairs are numbered by God; how much more is our conduct known to Him to Whom our hairs are thus known? See then, how that God doth not disregard our least things. For if He disregarded them, He would not create them. For he verily created our hairs, and still taketh count of them. But thou wilt say, though they are preserved at present, perhaps they will perish. On this point also hear His word, *Verily I say unto you, there shall not an hair of your head perish.*[12]

Why art thou afraid of man, O man, whose place is in the Bosom of God? Fall not out of His Bosom; whatsoever thou shalt suffer there, will avail to thy salvation, not to thy destruction. Martyrs have endured the tearing of their limbs, and shall Christians fear the injuries of Christian times? He who would do thee an injury now, can only do it in fear. He does not say openly, come to my altars, and banquet there. And if he should say so, and thou wast to refuse, let him make a complaint of it, let him bring it as an accusation and charge against thee: "He would not come to my altars, he would not come to my temple, where I worship." Let him say this. He does not dare; but in his guile he contrives another attack. Make ready thy hair; he is sharpening the razor; he is about to take off thy superfluous things, to shave what thou must soon leave behind thee. Let him take off what shall endure, if he can. This powerful enemy, what has he taken away? What great thing has he taken away? That which a thief or housebreaker could take: in his utmost

11. Matt. x. 30.
12. Luke xxi. 18.

rage, he can but take what a robber can. Even if he should have license given him to the slaying of the very body, what does he take away, but what the robber can take? I did him too much honour, when I said, *a robber.* For be the robber who and what he may, he is a man. He takes from thee what a fever, or an adder, or a poisonous mushroom can take. Here lies the whole power of the rage of men, to do what a mushroom can! Men eat a poisonous mushroom, and they die. Lo! in what frail estate is the life of man; which sooner or later thou must abandon; do not struggle then in such wise for it, as that thou shouldest be abandoned thyself.

[f]All men that earthly things do mind, all men that do choose earthly felicity before God, all men that seek their own things, not the things which are of Jesus Christ, to that one city belong, which is called Babylon mystically, and which hath for king the devil. But all men who mind those things which are above, who on heavenly things do meditate, who with carefulness live in the world that they may not offend God, who are careful not to sin, who if sinning are not ashamed to confess, humble, mild, holy, just, godly, good, all these to that one City do belong, which for King hath Christ. For the former on earth as it were is the greater in age, not by elevation, not by honour. For the former city was first born, the latter city was after born. For that began from Cain, this from Abel. These two Bodies, serving under two kings, to their several cities belonging, are . . . meanwhile mingled, at the end to be severed; against each other mutually in conflict, the one for iniquity, the other for the truth. And

f. *Enarr. in Ps.,* LXI (Lat.), 6, 8.

sometimes this very temporal mingling bringeth
it to pass that certain men belonging to the city
Babylon, do order matters belonging to Jerusalem,
and again certain men belonging to Jerusalem, do
order matters belonging to Babylon. Something
difficult I seem to have propounded. Be ye patient, until it be proved by examples. *For all things
in the old people, as writeth the Apostle, in a
figure used to befall them: but they have been
written for our amendment, upon whom the end
of the world hath come.*[13] Regard therefore that
people as also set to intimate an after people; and
see then what I say. There were great kings in
Jerusalem: it is a known fact, they are enumerated,
are named. They all were, I say, wicked citizens
of Babylon, and they were ordering matters of
Jerusalem: all men from thence to be dissevered
at the end, to no one but to the devil do belong.
Again we find citizens of Jerusalem to have
ordered certain matters belonging to Babylon. For
those three children, Nebuchadnezzar, overcome
by a miracle, made the ministers of his kingdom,
and set them over his Satraps; and so there were
ordering the matters of Babylon citizens of Jerusalem. Observe now how this is being fulfilled
and done in the Church, and in these times. All
they of whom hath been said, *What things they
say do ye, but what things they do, do not,*[14] are
citizens of Babylon, ordering the commonwealth
of the City Jerusalem. For if they were ordering
nothing of the City Jerusalem, whence *What things
they say do ye?* Whence, *In the chair of Moses
they sit?* Again, if citizens they are of Jerusalem
Herself, that shall reign for everlasting with Christ,

13. Cor. x. 11.
14. Matt. xxii. 3.

whence, *What things they do, do not ye,* except
because they too are to hear, *Depart from Me, all
ye that work iniquity?*[15] It is therefore a thing
known to you, that the citizens of the evil
city do order certain doings of the good City. Let
us see if now also citizens of the good City do
order certain doings of the evil city. Every earthly
commonwealth, sometime assuredly to perish,
whereof the kingdom is to pass away, when there
shall come that kingdom, whereof we pray, *Thy
kingdom come;*[16] and whereof hath been foretold,
*And of His kingdom shall be no end:*[17] an earthly
commonwealth, I say, hath our citizens conducting the affairs of it. For how many faithful, how
many good men, are both magistrates in their
cities, and are judges, and are generals, and are
counts, and are kings? All that are just and good
men, having not any thing in heart but the most
glorious things, which of Thee have been said,
City of God. And as if they are doing bond-serv-
ice in the city which is to pass away, even there
by the doctors of the Holy City they are bidden to
keep faith with those set over them, *whether with
the king as supreme, or with governors as though
sent by God for the punishment of evil men, but
for the praise of good men:*[18] or as servants, that
to their masters they should be subject, even
Christians to Heathens, and the better should keep
faith with the worse, for a time to serve, for everlasting to have dominion. For these things do happen until iniquity do pass away. Servants are commanded to bear with masters unjust and capri-

15. Luke xiii. 27.
16. Matt. vi. 10.
17. Luke i. 33.
18. 1 Pet. ii. 13, 14.

cious: the citizens of Babylon are cor
be endured by the citizens of Jerusalem, sh
even more attentions, than if they were citizens of
the same Babylon.

## C. *By the Waters of Babylon*

[a]I think ye have not forgotten, that I brought to
your notice, or rather to your recollection, that
every one who is trained in the holy Church ought
to know of what place we are citizens, and where
we are wandering, and that the cause of our wandering is sin, the gift of our return, the remission
of our sins, and our justification by the grace of
God. Ye have heard and know that there are two
cities, for the present outwardly mingled together,
yet separated in heart, running together through
the course of time until the end; one whose end is
everlasting peace, and it is called Jerusalem; the
other whose joy is peace in this world, and it is
called Babylon. The meanings of these names too
ye remember, that Jerusalem means 'vision of
peace;' Babylon, 'confusion.' Jerusalem was held
captive in Babylon, but not all, for the Angels too
are its citizens. But as regards men predestined to
the glory of God, to become by adoption joint-
heirs with Christ, whom He has redeemed from
this very captivity by His own Blood, that this
part, I say, of the citizens of Jerusalem are held
captive in Babylon on account of sin, but first
begin to go forth from thence in spirit by confession of sin and love of righteousness, and then
afterwards at the end of the world are to be separated in body also; this we set before you in that
Psalm, which we first handled here with you, be-

a. *Enarr. in Ps.*, CXXXVI (Lat.).

loved, which begins thus: *For Thee, O God, a hymn is meet in Sion, and to Thee shall the vow be performed in Jerusalem.* But to-day we have sung, *By the waters of Babylon we sat down and wept, when we remembered Sion.* Observe, that in the former it is said, *For Thee, O God, a hymn is meet in Sion;* but here, *By the waters of Babylon we sat down and wept, when we remembered Sion,* that Sion where a *hymn is meet for God.*

What then are *the waters of Babylon?* and what is our sitting and weeping in remembrance of Sion? For if we be citizens of Sion, we not only chant this, but do it. If we are citizens of Jerusalem, that is Sion, and in this life, in the confusion of this world, in this Babylon, do not dwell as citizens, but are detained as captives, it befits us not only to chant these things, but also to do them, with affectionate regard, with religious longing for our everlasting city. This city too which is called Babylon hath its lovers, who look for peace in this world, and hope for nothing beyond, but fix their whole joy in this, end it in this, and we see them toil exceedingly for their earthly country: but whosoever live faithfully even therein, if they seek not therein pride, and perishable elation, and hateful boasting, but exhibit true faith, such as they can, as long they can, to whom they can, so far as they see earthly things, and understand the nature of their citizenship, God suffereth them not to perish in Babylon; He hath predestinated them to be citizens of Jerusalem. He understandeth their captivity, and sheweth to them another city, for which they ought truly to sigh, for which they ought to use every endeavour, to win which they ought to the utmost of their power to urge their fellow-citizens, now their fellow-wanderers. Therefore saith the Lord Jesus Christ, *He that is faithful in that which is least, is faithful also in much;* and again He saith, *If ye have not been faithful in that which is another man's, who will give you that which is your own?* [1]

However, brethren, observe *the waters of Babylon. The waters of Babylon* are all things which here are loved, and pass away. One man, for example, loveth to practise husbandry, to grow rich thereby, to employ his mind therein, thence to gain pleasure: let him observe the issue, and see that what he hath loved is not a foundation of Jerusalem, but a stream of Babylon. Another saith, It is a grand thing to be a soldier: all husbandmen fear those who are soldiers, obey them, tremble at them: if I be a husbandman, I shall fear soldiers; if a soldier, farmers will fear me. Madman! Thou hast cast thyself headlong into another stream of Babylon, and that still more boisterous and sweeping. Thou wishest to be feared by thine inferior; fear Him that is greater than thou. He who fears thee may on a sudden become greater than thou, but never will He Whom thou oughtest to fear become less. To be a pleader, saith another, is a grand thing, ever to have clients hanging on the tongue of their eloquent advocate, and from his words looking for loss or gain, death or life, ruin or safety. Thou knowest not whither thou hast cast thyself; this too is another stream of Babylon, and its loud sound is the din of the waters dashing against the rocks. Mark that it flows, it glides on; and if thou markest that it flows and glides on, mark also that it carries things along with it. To traverse the seas, saith another, and to trade, is a grand thing, to know

1. Luke xvi. 10, 12.

many lands, to make gains from every quarter, never to be obnoxious in thy country to any powerful man, and to feed thy mind with the various habits of the nations thou visitest, and to return enriched with the increase of thy gains. This too is a stream of Babylon; when will thy gains stop? When wilt thou rely upon and be secure in the gains thou makest? The richer thou art, the more fearful wilt thou be. Once shipwrecked, thou wilt come forth stripped of all, and deservedly wilt thou bewail thyself *in* the rivers of Babylon, because thou wouldest not *sit down and weep by the waters of Babylon.*

But then other citizens of the holy Jerusalem, understanding their captivity, mark how the natural wishes and the various lusts of men hurry and drag them hither and thither, and drive them into the sea; they see this, and they throw not themselves into the waters of Babylon, but *sit down by the waters of Babylon, and by the waters of Babylon weep,* either for those who are being carried away by them, or themselves whose deserts have placed them in Babylon, but sitting, that is, humbling themselves. *By the waters of Babylon* then *we sat down and wept, when we remembered Sion.* O holy Sion, where all stands firm and nothing flows! Who hath thrown us headlong into this? Why have we left thy Founder and thy society? Behold, placed where all things are flowing and gliding away, scarce one, if he can grasp the tree, shall be snatched from the stream and escape. Humbling ourselves then in our captivity, let us *sit by the waters of Babylon,* let us not dare to plunge ourselves in those streams, nor to be proud and lifted up in the evil and sadness of our captivity, but let us sit, and so weep. Let us sit *by* the waters, not beneath the waters, of Babylon; such be our humility, that it overwhelm us not. Sit *by* the waters, not *in* the waters, not *under* the waters; but yet sit, in humble fashion, talk not as thou wouldest in Jerusalem. There thou wilt stand; for of this very hope another Psalm speaketh, singing thus, *Our feet shall stand in the courts of Jerusalem.*[2] There shalt thou be lifted up, if here by penitence and confession thou humble thyself. In the courts then of Jerusalem our feet shall stand, but *by the waters of Babylon we sat down and wept, when we remembered thee, O Sion.* For this reason is it meet that thou weep, for the remembrance of Sion.

For many weep with the weeping of Babylon, because they rejoice also with the joy of Babylon. When men rejoice at gains and weep at losses, both are of Babylon. Thou oughtest to weep, but in the remembrance of Sion. If thou weepest in the remembrance of Sion, thou oughtest to weep even when it is well with thee in Babylon. Therefore it is said in a certain Psalm, *I found trouble and sorrow; then called I upon the name of the Lord.*[3] What meaneth he by saying, *I have found?* He speaketh of some kind of tribulation, as though it were to be sought; he found it, as though he had sought it. And when he had found it, what gained he by finding it? *He called upon the name of the Lord.* Much doth it matter, whether thou findest tribulation, or art found by tribulation. For he saith in another place, *The sorrows of hell found me.*[4] What is, *The sorrows of hell found me?* What is, *I found trouble and sorrow?* When sadness sud-

---

2. Ps. cxxii. 2.
3. *Ibid.,* cxvi. 3, 4.
4. *Ibid.,* xviii. 5.

denly overtaketh thee, through trouble in thy worldly affairs, wherein thou didst delight, when suddenly sadness of her own accord findeth thee, befalleth thee from some point, whence thou didst not think thou couldest be saddened, and thou art made sad, then *the sorrows of hell have found thee.* For thou thoughtest thyself aloft, whereas thou wast beneath; there hast thou found thyself beneath, where thou thoughtest thyself aloft. For thou hast found thyself grievously afflicted with sorrow, through sadness at some evil from a quarter where perchance thou hadst presumed thou wouldest not be made sad: *the sorrows of hell have found thee.* But when it is well with thee, when all earthly things smile on thee, none of thy loved ones hath died, no drought or hail or barrenness hath assailed thy vineyard, thy cask hath not grown sour, thy cattle have not failed, thou hast not been dishonoured in any high position of this world wherein thou hast been placed, thy friends all around thee live and preserve their friendship for thee, dependents are not wanting, thy children obey thee, thy slaves tremble before thee, thy wife liveth in harmony with thee, thy house is called happy,—then find tribulation, if in any way thou canst, that, having found tribulation thou mayest *call on the name of the Lord.* Perversely seemeth the word of God to teach that thou shouldest weep in joy, and rejoice in sorrow. Hear it rejoicing in sorrow, *We glory,* it saith, *in tribulations.*[5] But see it weeping in joy, if it have *found tribulation.* Let each one mark his own happiness, wherein his soul hath exulted and puffed itself up in a manner with joy and elated itself, and said, 'I am happy.' Let him mark whether that happi-

5. Rom. v. 3.

ness floweth not on, if he can be sure of it that it remaineth for ever. But if he be not certain, but seeth that that wherein he rejoices floweth, it is a stream of Babylon; let him *sit down by it, and weep.* He will sit down and weep, if he *remember Sion.* O for that peace which we shall see in the presence of God! O for that holy equality with the Angels! O for that vision, that fair sight! Lo, in Babylon fair are the things which hold thee: let them not hold thee, let them not deceive thee. One thing is the solace of the captive, another the joy of the free. *By the waters of Babylon we sat down and wept, when we remembered Sion.*

*On the willows in the midst thereof we hung up our instruments of music.* The citizens of Jerusalam have their *instruments of music,* God's Scriptures, God's commands, God's promises, meditation on the life to come; but while they are dwelling *in the midst of Babylon,* they *hang up their instruments of music on the willows* thereof. Willows are unfruitful trees, and here so placed, that no good whatever can be understood of them: elsewhere perhaps there may. Here understand barren trees, growing by the waters of Babylon. These trees are watered by the waters of Babylon, and bring forth no fruit; just as there are men greedy, covetous, barren in good works, citizens of Babylon in such wise, that they are even trees of that region; they are fed there by these pleasures of transitory things, as though watered by *the waters of Babylon.* Thou seekest fruit of them, and no where findest it. When we suffer such men as these, we live among those who are *in the midst* of Babylon. For wide is the difference between *the midst of Babylon* and the outside of Babylon. There are some who are not in the midst of it, that is, are not buried entirely in the lust of the world and the delights thereof. But those who, to speak plainly and briefly, are thoroughly bad, are *in the midst of Babylon,* and are barren trees like the willows of Babylon. When we see them, and find them so barren, that with difficulty do we find in them ought whereby they may be led on to true faith and good works, or to hope of a future life, or to desire to be set free from captivity under mortality, then we know indeed the Scriptures which we should address to them; but, because we find in them no fruit upon which to begin, we turn away our face from them, and say, 'As yet they have no taste nor capacity for them; whatever we say to them, they will consider foolish and contrary.' Therefore by deferring to apply the Scriptures to them, *we hang up our instruments of music upon the willows.* For we hold them not worthy to carry our instruments. We do not therefore insert our instruments into them and bind them to them, but defer to use them, and so hang them up. For the willows are the unfruitful trees of Babylon, fed by temporal pleasures, as by the *waters of Babylon.*

And see whether the Psalm do not agree with this. *On the willows in the midst thereof we hung up our instruments of music. For there they that led us captive demanded of us words of songs, and they that led us away, an hymn.* They demanded of us words of songs and an hymn, who led us captive. Who have led us captive, brethren? Whom have we at some time or other experienced as our capturers. Jerusalem of old experienced captivity at the hands of the Babylonians, the Persians, the Chaldeans, and the men of those nations and regions, and that afterwards, not when these

Psalms were composed. But we have already told you, beloved, that all things, which according to the letter befell that city, were our examples, and it can easily be proved that we are captives. For we breathe not the air of that our true liberty: we enjoy not the purity of truth, and that wisdom, that *remaining in herself maketh all things new.*[6] We are tempted by the delights of earthly things, and we struggle daily with the suggestions of unlawful pleasures; scarce do we breathe freely even in prayer: we understand that we are captives. But who led us captive? what men? what race? what king? If we are redeemed, we once were captives. Who hath redeemed us? Christ. From whom hath He redeemed us? From the devil. The devil then and his angels led us captive: and they would not lead us, unless we consented. We were led captive. Who our capturers were, I have said. For they are the thieves who wounded the traveller who went down from Jerusalem to Jericho, and left him wounded and half dead. Him He, our Keeper, that is, Samaritan, (for Samaritan meaneth 'keeper,') whom the Jews found fault with, and said, *Say we not well that Thou art a Samaritan, and hast a devil?*[7] of which two objections, the one He rejected, the other He accepted: *I,* He answered, *have not a devil:* yet He said not, 'I am not a Samaritan:' for had He not been our Samaritan, our Keeper, verily we had perished: —this Samaritan then, I say, passing by, saw the man left by the thieves hurt and wounded, and, as ye know, took care of him. Just as sometimes under the name of thieves are described those who have inflicted on us the wounds of sins, so,

6. Wisd. vii. 27.
7. John viii. 48.

through our consenting to being made captives, are they also called our capturers.

*Those* then *who have led us captive,* the devil and his angels, when have they spoken unto us, and when have they *asked of us the words of songs?* what then do we understand? That, when those in whom the devil worketh ask such things of us, he is to be understood to ask, who worketh in them. The Apostle saith, *And you hath He quickened, who were dead in trespasses and sins; wherein in time past ye walked according to the course of this world, according to the prince of the power of the air, the spirit that now worketh in the children of disobedience: among whom also we all had our conversation in times past.*[8] He sheweth that, having been redeemed, he has already begun to come forth from Babylon. But still what saith he yet? That we contend with our enemies. And that we may not wax wroth with men, who attack us with persecutions, the Apostle has diverted our efforts from hatred of men, and guided them to struggle with certain spirits, whom we see not, and yet we contend with them. For he saith, *We wrestle not against flesh and blood,* that is, against men, *but against principalities, against powers, against the rulers of the darkness of this world.*[9] What means he by 'this world?' The lovers of this world. These he also calleth *darkness,* that is, unjust, wicked, unbelievers, sinners; whom, when they have come to believe, he congratulateth after this fashion, saying, *Ye were sometime darkness, but now are ye light in the Lord.*[10] So then

8. Eph. ii. 1-3.
9. *Ibid.,* vi. 12.
10. Eph. v. 8.

he has laid down that *we wrestle with* those *principalities:* they it is who have led us captive.

But, just as the devil entered into the heart of Judas, to make him betray his Lord, yet would not have entered, unless he had made room for him; so many evil men from the midst of Babylon, by making room in their hearts for the devil and his angels, so that he may work in them and through them, sometimes ask us, and say to us, 'Explain to us the reason.' So too the heathen generally ask us, 'Explain the reason why Christ came, and what benefit Christ hath been to the human race. Have not matters been worse upon earth since Christ came, and was it not better then with men than it is now? Let the Christians tell us, what good Christ hath brought, wherein they think human affairs more happy, for that Christ hath come. For thou seest that if the theatres and amphitheatres and circuses were safe and standing, if no part of Babylon were falling, if men were surrounded by abundance of pleasures, and could sing and dance to lascivious strains, if the impure and whoremongers could indulge their rest in quiet and safety, if a man did not fear famine in his own house who cried out that the dancers should be clothed, if all this went on without discredit, without disturbance, and all these follies could be enjoyed without anxiety, these would be happy times, and Christ would have brought great happiness to human affairs.' But, forasmuch as wickednesses are now being destroyed, in order that that earthly desire being uprooted, the love of Jerusalem may be planted in; forasmuch as bitternesses are being mixed with this passing life, that men may long for the everlasting life; forasmuch as men are being disciplined with scourges, receiving a father's correction, that they may not hereafter receive a judge's sentence; Christ, they say, hath brought nothing good, Christ hath brought troubles. And thou beginnest to tell to one, how much good Christ hath done, and he receives it not. For thou settest before him the example of those who do as ye have just heard in the Gospel, who *sell all that they have, and give to the poor, that they may have treasure in heaven, and follow their Lord.* Thou sayest to him, 'See what Christ hath brought! How many do this, distribute their goods to the needy, and become poor not of necessity, but of free-will, following God, hoping for the kingdom of Heaven.' He mocketh at such men as fools, and saith, 'Is this the good which Christ hath brought, that man lose his own goods, and giving to the needy, remain needy himself?' What then wilt thou do? Thou takest not in the good things of Christ, for another hath filled thee who is the adversary of Christ, to whom thou hast given place in thine heart. Thou lookest back to former times, and those former times seem to thee to have been happier, which were like olives hanging on the tree, swayed by the wind, enjoying their wandering desires like a sort of liberty in the breeze. The time is come for the olive to be put into the press. For they ought not always to hang on the trees: now it is the end of the year. Not without reason are certain Psalms inscribed, 'For the presses:' on the tree is liberty, in the press, pressure. For when human affairs are being crushed and pressed, thou observest that avarice increaseth: observe also that self-denial increaseth. Wherefore art thou so blind that thou seest the lees flowing down the streets, but not the oil flowing into the vats? Yet is not this without reason: for they who live ill, are generally known, they who turn to God and are cleansed from the filth of evil desires are hidden, for in the press, or rather out the press, the lees openly flow, the oil secretly strains off.

At this ye shout, at this ye rejoice, because now ye can *sit down by the waters of Babylon and weep.* But *they who have led us captive,* when they enter into the hearts of men, and ask us by the tongues of them whom they possess, and say to us, *Sing us the words of songs,* give us a reason for the coming of Christ; tell us what is another life: when they say, I will not believe, give me a reason why thou biddest me believe. Such an one I answer and say, 'Man, how it is that thou willest not that I bid thee believe? Thou art full of evil desires; if I tell of those good things of Jerusalem, thou takest them not in; thou must be emptied of that wherewith thou art full, that thou mayest be filled with that whereof thou art empty.'

Be not then ready to say ought to such an one: he is willow: he is barren wood. Strike not the instrument of music that is sound; hang it up rather. But he will say, 'Tell me, sing to me, shew me the reason. Art thou not willing for me to learn?' Thou hearest not with good intent; thou knockest not so as to deserve that it be opened to thee. He hath filled thee who hath led me captive: he asketh of me by thee. He is cunning: he asketh craftily: he asketh not to learn, but to blame. Therefore 1 will not speak to him; *I will hang up my instrument of music.*

But what will he yet say? *Sing us the words of songs: sing us a hymn: sing us one of the songs of Sion.* What answer we? Babylon beareth thee,

Babylon containeth thee, Babylon nourisheth thee, Babylon speaks by thy mouth, thou knowest not to take in save what glitters for the present, thou knowest not how to meditate on things of eternity, thou takest not in what thou askest. *How shall we sing the Lord's song in a strange land?* Truly, brethren, so it is. Begin to wish to preach the truth in such measure as ye know it, and see how needful it is for you to endure such mockers, persecutors of the truth, full of falsehood. Reply to them, when they ask of you what they cannot take in, and say in full confidence of your holy song, *How shall we sing the Lord's song in a strange land!*

But take heed how thou dwellest among them, O people of God, O body of Christ, O high-born band of wanderers, (for thy home is not here, but elsewhere,) lest when thou lovest them who say to thee, *Sing to us the words of songs, sing us an hymn, sing us one of the songs of Sion,* and strivest for their friendship, and fearest to displease such men, Babylon begin to delight thee and thou forget Jerusalem. In fear then of this, see what the Psalmist subjoins, see what follows. For the man who sang thus, (and that man are we if we choose,) endured all around him men who asked these questions and allured him with flattery, who chid with biting words and falsely praised him, who asked what they took not in, were unwilling to empty themselves of that wherewith they were full; and being as it were in danger among crowds of such men, he lifted up his mind to the recollection of Sion, and his soul bound itself with a sort of oath, and said, *If I forget thee, O Jerusalem,* amid the speeches of those who hold me captive, amid the speeches of treacherous men, amid the speeches of men who ask with ill intent, asking, yet unwilling to learn.

Behold, of this number was that rich man, who asked the Lord, *Good Master, what shall I do that I may attain eternal life?* [11] Did he not in asking about eternal life, ask, as it were, for a *song of Sion? Keep the commandments,* said the Lord to him. And he in his pride, when he heard this, said, *All these have I kept from my youth.* And the Lord spake to him *one of the songs of Sion,* and knew that he took it not in; but He gave us an example how that many ask, as it were, counsel concerning eternal life, and praise us so long as we answer what they ask. He gave from him a lesson as though to bid us, that we should afterward say to such men, *How shall we sing the Lord's song in a strange land?* Behold, He saith, *Wilt thou be perfect? Go and sell all that thou hast, and give to the poor, and thou shalt have treasure in Heaven, and come, follow Me.* That he may learn many of the songs of Sion, let him first cast out all hindrances, let him walk without encumbrance, that he may have no burden to weigh him down, and he shall learn somewhat of *the songs of Sion.* But he *went away sorrowing.* Let us say after him, *How shall we sing the Lord's song in a strange land?* He indeed went away, yet the Lord gave hope for the rich. For the disciples were saddened, and said, *Who then can be saved?* And He answered them, *What is impossible for man, is easy for God.* For the rich too have a sort of measure of their own, and have received a song of Sion, a song whereof the Apostle speaketh, *Charge them that are rich in this world that they be not high-minded, nor trust in uncertain riches,*

11. Matt. xix. 16.

*but in the living God, Who giveth us richly all things to enjoy.* And adding what they ought to do, now he toucheth his instrument, and hangeth it not up: *that they be rich in good works, ready to distribute, willing to communicate, laying up in store for themselves a good foundation against the time to come, that they may lay hold on eternal life.* Here is that one of the *songs of Sion* which the rich have received; first of all, *not to be high-minded.* For riches puff up; and whom they puff up, those streams sweep away. What then is enjoined to them? Above all, *not to be high-minded.* What riches do, that let them beware of in riches; in riches let them beware of pride. For that is the very evil which riches bring to men not on their guard. For gold is not evil, which God hath made: but the avaricious man is evil, who leaveth the Creator, and turneth to the creature. This then let him first take care, that he be not proud; let him *sit by the waters of Babylon.* For it is said to him, *Be not high-minded;* therefore let him *sit: nor trust in uncertain riches;* therefore let him *sit by the waters of Babylon;* for if he trust in uncertain riches, he is carried away by a stream of Babylon. But if he humble himself, and be not proud, and trust not in uncertain riches, he sits by the waters, he sighs for the everlasting Jerusalem, remembering Sion; and that he may reach Sion, he spendeth his riches. There thou hast the song which the rich have received from among the *songs of Sion.* Let them work, let them touch their instrument, let them not be idle. When they find one saying to them, 'What art thou doing? Thou art wasting thy substance by spending so much: lay up store for thy children:' when they see that he takes it not in, and understand that it is a *willow,* let them not readily say, why they do so, or what they do, let them *hang up their instruments on the willows of Babylon.* But beside the willows let them sing, let them not rest, let them work. For they lose not what they spend. They trust their riches to a slave, and they are safe: they trust them to Christ, and are they lost?

Thou hast heard the song of Sion for the rich: hear now the song of the poor. The same Paul saith, *We brought nothing into this world, and it is certain we can carry nothing out: and having food and raiment, let us be therewith content. But they that will be rich fall into temptation and a snare, and into many foolish and hurtful lusts, which drown men in destruction and perdition.* These are *waters of Babylon. For the love of money is the root of all evil, which while some coveted after they have erred from the faith, and pierced themselves through with many sorrows.*[12] Are then these songs contradictory? They are not. See what is said to the rich: *not to be high-minded; not to trust in uncertain riches; to do good; to distribute; to lay up in store for themselves a good foundation for the time to come.* But what is said to the poor? *They who will be rich fall into temptation.* He said not, 'They who are rich,' but, *they who will be rich:* for if they were already rich, they should hear the other song. The rich is bid to spend, the poor not to desire.

But while ye live among such as these, who take not in a song of Sion, *hang up,* as I have said, *your instruments upon the willows in the midst thereof:* defer what ye are about to say. If they begin to be fruitful trees, if the trees are changed, and will bear good fruit; now then it is lawful for

12. 1 Tim. vi. 7-10.

us to sing to the ears of them that listen. But while they among whom ye live drown you with clamour, ask with ill purpose, resist the truth, bind yourselves not to be willing to please them, lest ye forget Jerusalem. And let your one soul, made one out of many by the peace of Christ, let captive Jerusalem, dwelling here on earth, say, *If I forget thee, O Jerusalem, let my right hand forget me.* Vehemently hath she bound herself, my brethren, *let my right hand forget me,* sternly hath she tied herself down. Our right hand is life everlasting, our left, life in this world. Whatsoever thou doest for the sake of life everlasting, thy right hand doeth. If in thy works thou mingle with the love of everlasting life desire for the life of this world, or man's praise, or any worldly advantage, thy left hand knoweth what thy right hand doeth. And thou knowest that it is enjoined in the Gospel, *let not thy left hand know what thy right hand doeth.*[13] Therefore saith she, *If I forget thee, O Jerusalem, let my right hand forget me.* And truly so it happens: it is a prophecy she has uttered, not a wish. To them who forget Jerusalem, this happeneth which she hath said, *their right hand forgetteth them.* For life everlasting abideth in itself: they abide in delights of this world, and make that to be *right* to them, which is *left.*

Listen to this, brethren: for the right hand's sake let me press this upon you, for the salvation of all. Ye remember perhaps that I once spoke in this place of some who make what is left to be right, that is, who consider worldly goods of more value (than everlasting goods), and consider happiness to consist in these, not knowing what is true happiness, the true *right hand.* These Scrip-

13. Matt. vi. 3.

ture calleth strange children, as though they were citizens not of Jerusalem, but of Babylon; for the Psalmist saith in a certain place, *Lord, save me from the hand of strange children, whose mouth talketh of vanity, and their right hand is a right hand of iniquity.* For he goeth on and saith, *Their sons are like strong young vine trees, their daughters polished like unto the temple: their garners are full and plenteous with all manner of store, their sheep bring forth thousands and ten thousands in our streets: their oxen are strong to labour, there is no decay, no leading into captivity, and no complaining in their streets.* Is it sin then to enjoy such happiness as this? No: but to make it the right hand when it is the left. And therefore what goeth he on to say? *They called the people blessed that are in such a case.*[14] Behold how *their mouth hath spoken vanity:* they have *called the people blessed that are in such a case.* Thou indeed art a citizen of Jerusalem, who *forgettest not Jerusalem,* lest *thy right hand forget thee:* lo! they *who have spoken vanity* have called *the people blessed who are in such a case;* sing thou to me a song of Sion. *Blessed,* saith he, *is the people that hath the Lord for their God.* Ask your hearts, brethren, whether ye long for the good things of God, whether ye long for that city, Jerusalem, whether ye desire everlasting life. Let all that earthly happiness be to you on the left hand, let that be on the right which ye will have for ever: and, if ye have that which is left, presume not thereupon. Dost thou not chide him, who chooses to eat with the left hand? If thou thinkest that a wrong is done to thy table when a guest eats with the left, how can it but be a wrong to the Table

14. Ps. cxliv. 7-15.

of God, if thou makest what is right to be left, and what is left, right? What then? *If I forget thee, O Jerusalem, let my right hand forget me.*

*Let my tongue cleave to my jaws, if I remember not thee.* That is let me be dumb, he saith, if I remember not thee. For what word, what sound doth he utter, who uttereth not songs of Sion? That is our tongue, the song of Jerusalem. The song of the love of this world is a strange tongue, a barbarous tongue, which we have learnt in our captivity. Dumb then will he be to God, who forgetteth Jerusalem. And it is not enough to remember: for her enemies too remember her, desiring to overthrow her. 'What is that city?' say they; 'who are the Christians? what sort of men are the Christians? would they were not Christians.' Now the captive band hath conquered its capturers; still they murmur, and rage, and desire to slay the holy city that dwells as a stranger among them; just as Pharaoh desired to destroy the people, when he slew the male children, and left the female: he strangled, that is, the virtues; the lusts he nurtured. Not enough then is it to remember: take heed how thou rememberest. For some things we remember in hate, some in love. And so, when he had said, *If I forget thee, O Jerusalem, let my right hand forget me: let my tongue cleave to my jaws, if I remember not thee;* he added at once, *if I prefer not Jerusalem in the height of my joy.* For there is the height of joy where we enjoy God, where we are safe of united brotherhood, and the union of citizenship. There no tempter shall assail us, no one be able so much as to urge us on to any allurement: there nought will delight us but good: there all want will die,

there perfect bliss will dawn on us. *If I prefer not
Jerusalem in the height of my joy.*

Then he turneth to God in prayer against the
enemies of that city. *Remember, O Lord, the children of Edom.* Edom is the same who is also called
Esau: for ye heard just now the words of the
Apostle read, *Jacob have I loved, but Esau have
I hated.*[15] Two sons were there in one womb, both
twins, in the womb of Rebecca, sons of Isaac,
grandsons of Abraham: both were born; one to
inheritance, the other to disinheritance. But Esau
was his brother's enemy, because he, the younger,
forestalled his blessing, and the prophecy was fulfilled, *the younger shall serve the elder.*[16] Who
then the elder is, and who the younger, and who
the elder that shall serve the younger, we now
understand. Elder seemed to be the people of the
Jews, younger in point of time the Christians. And
see how the elder serveth the younger. They carry
our Scriptures, we live by their Scriptures. But
that ye may understand the elder and younger
generally of all mankind, the elder meaneth the
carnal man, the younger the spiritual man, for
first is the carnal, afterward the spiritual. Thou
findest the Apostle saying clearly, *The first man is
of the earth, earthy; the second Man is the Lord
from heaven. As is the earthy, such are they also
that are earthy; and as is the Heavenly, such are
they also that are heavenly. And as we have borne
the image of the earthy, we shall also bear the
image of the heavenly.* But above this he had said,
*Howbeit, that was not first which is spiritual, but
that which is natural, and afterward that which is
spiritual.* By natural he meaneth the same as he

15. Rom. ix. 13.
16. Gen. xxv. 23.

also calleth carnal. Man, when he is born, is at first natural, carnal. If he turn from his captivity in Babylon to return to Jerusalem, he is renewed, and there happeneth a renewal according to the new and inner man, which is younger in time, greater in power. Esau then signifieth all the carnal, Jacob all the spiritual: the younger the elect, the elder the reprobate. Doth he wish himself too to be of the elect? Let him become a younger son. Moreover, he is called Edom, from a certain red pottage of lentils, a red kind of food. Well boiled were the bruised lentils: Esau desired them of his brother Jacob, and, overcome by lust for eating those lentils, yielded to him his birthright. Jacob gave up the pleasant food, received the honour of preeminence. Hence, by a kind of bargain between them, it came to pass that the younger became the elder, the elder the younger, and the elder served the younger. And the elder was called Edom, which meaneth, according to them who know that language, 'blood,' for in Carthaginian too, blood is called 'Edom.' Wonder not: all carnal men belong to blood. *Flesh and blood shall not inherit the kingdom of God.*[17] To that Edom belongeth not: Jacob belongeth, who gave up fleshly food, and received spiritual honour. So the other became his enemy. All carnal persons are enemies to spiritual persons, for all such, desiring present things, persecute those whom they see to long for things eternal. Against these the Psalmist, looking back to Jerusalem, and beseeching God that he may be delivered from captivity, saith—what? *Remember, O Lord, the children of Edom.* Deliver us from carnal men, from those who imitate Esau, who are elder brethren, yet

17. 1 Cor. xv. 50.

enemies. They were first-born, but the last-born have won the preeminence, for the lust of the flesh hath cast down the former, the contempt of lust hath lifted up the latter. The other live, and envy, and persecute.

*Remember, O Lord, the children of Edom in the day of Jerusalem.* The day of Jerusalem, wherein it was tried, wherein it was held captive, or the day of Jerusalem's happiness, wherein it is freed, wherein it reaches its goal, wherein it is made partaker of eternity? *Remember,* saith he, *O Lord, forget* not, *the children of Edom.* Which? Those *who said, Rase it, rase it, even to the foundation thereof.* Remember then, it means, that day wherein they willed to overthrow Jerusalem. For how great persecutions hath the Church suffered! How did the children of Edom, that is, carnal men, servants of the devil and his angels, who worshipped stocks and stones, and followed the lusts of the flesh, how did they say, 'Extirpate the Christians, destroy the Christians, let not one remain, overthrow them even to the foundation!' Have not these things been said? And when they were said, the persecutors were rejected, the martyrs crowned. *They said, Rase it, rase it, even to the foundation thereof.* The sons of Edom say, 'Rase it, rase it:' God saith, 'Serve.' Whose words can prevail, save God's, Who saith, *The elder shall serve the younger? Rase it, rase it, even to the foundation thereof.*

Then he turneth himself to her, *O daughter of Babylon, unhappy;* unhappy in thy very exulting, thy presumption, thine enmity; *unhappy daughter of Babylon!* The city is called both Babylon, and daughter of Babylon: just as they speak of 'Jerusalem' and 'the daughter of Jerusalem,' 'Sion' and 'the daughter of Sion,' 'the Church' and 'the daughter of the Church.' As it succeedeth the other, it is called 'daughter;' as it is preferred before the other, it is called 'mother.' There was a former Babylon; did the people remain in it? Because it succeedeth to Babylon, it is called daughter of Babylon. O daughter of Babylon, *unhappy* thou! *Happy shall he be that payeth thee;* unhappy thou, happy he.

For what hast thou done, and how shalt thou be repaid? Listen: *happy shall he be that repayeth thee, as thou hast served us.* What repayment meaneth he? Herewith the Psalm closeth, *Happy, that taketh and dasheth thy little ones against the rock.* Her he calleth unhappy, but him happy who payeth her as she hath served us. Do we ask, what reward? *Happy,* saith he, *that taketh and dasheth thy little ones against the rock.* This is the repayment. For what hath that Babylon done to us? We have already sung in another Psalm, *The words of the wicked have prevailed against us.*[18] For when we were born, the confusion of this world found us, and choked us while yet infants with the empty notions of divers errors. The infant that is born destined to be a citizen of Jerusalem, and in God's predestination already a citizen, but meanwhile a prisoner for a time, when learneth he to love ought, save what his parents have whispered into his ears? They teach him and train him in avarice, robbery, daily lying, the worship of divers idols and devils, the unlawful remedies of enchantments and amulets. What shall one yet an infant do, a tender soul, observing what its elders do, save follow that which it seeth them doing. Babylon then has persecuted us

18. Ps. lxv. 3.

when little, but God hath given us when grown up knowledge of ourselves, that we should not follow the errors of our parents. And this was foretold by the Prophet, *The nations shall come to thee from the ends of the earth, and shall say, Surely our fathers have inherited lies, vanity which hath not profited them.*[19] So speak they, now grown up, who when little were slain by following these vanities, and then coming to life again increase in union with God, and repay Babylon. How shall they repay her? As she hath served us. Let her little ones be choked in turn: yea let her little ones in turn be dashed, and die. What are the little ones of Babylon? Evil desires at their birth. For there are, who have to fight with inveterate lusts. When lust is born, before evil habit giveth it strength against thee, when lust is little, by no means let it gain the strength of evil habit; when it is little, dash it. But thou fearest, lest though dashed it die not; *Dash it against the Rock; and that Rock is Christ.*[20]

Brethren, let not your instruments of music rest in your work: sing one to another songs of Sion. Readily have ye heard; the more readily do what ye have heard, if ye wish not to be willows of Babylon fed by its streams, and bringing no fruit. But sigh for the everlasting Jerusalem: whither your hope goeth before, let your life follow; there we shall be with Christ. Christ now is our Head; now He ruleth us from above; in that city He will fold us to Himself; we shall be equal to the Angels of God. We should not dare to imagine this of ourselves, did not the Truth promise it. This then desire, brethren, this day and night

19. Jer. xvi. 19.
20. 1 Cor. x. 4.

think on. Howsoever the world shine happily on you, presume not, parley not willingly with your lusts. Is it a grown up enemy? let it be slain upon the Rock. Is it a little enemy? let it be dashed against the Rock. Slay the grown up ones on the Rock, and dash the little ones against the Rock. Let the Rock conquer. Be built upon the Rock, if ye desire not to be swept away either by the stream, or the winds, or the rain. If ye wish to be armed against temptations in this world, let longing for the everlasting Jerusalem grow and be strengthened in your hearts. Your captivity will pass away, your happiness will come; the last enemy shall be destroyed, and we shall triumph with our King, without death.

# APPENDIX

## The Political Ideas of
## St. Augustine[1]

From *The Philosophical and Political Back-grounds of The Divine Comedy,*[2] a series of lectures by Dino Bigongiari, Da Ponte Professor Emeritus of Italian, at Columbia University.

We want to discuss now the by-products—social and political—of the theology of St. Augustine: by-products fully as important as the theological ideas themselves.

The political implications of that theology are not hard to trace. All depends, of course, on the profound pessimism of his theory of predestination, which one cannot dismiss by saying that it is a Lutheran or Jansenist misinterpretation, for it is too clearly present in his own pages. The doctrine hinges on two facts, both very hard to scrutinize: one, the contamination of the whole species by one man; the other, the determination of the Creator to save some and not the others. Long

1. Printed with the author's permission. Readers interested in comparing the political ideas of St. Augustine with those of St. Thomas Aquinas will find Professor Bigongiari's introduction (pp. vii-xxxvii) to *The Political Ideas of St. Thomas Aquinas,* New York, 1953, very illuminating.
2. These lectures are currently being prepared for publication.

before Adam was created, St. Augustine says, interpreting the words of St. Paul, God knew that Adam would sin, and that all mankind would be corrupted by that sin. But out of that corrupt mass of humanity to come, God picked out certain souls whom he saved by sending them grace in the form of a summons or call of irresistible force—irresistible grace, that is the phrase St. Augustine uses. The persons thus chosen have to be saved. They are not good, and therefore saved. They are good because God has sent His irresistible saving grace.

That, briefly, is the doctrine of predestination. And as a result of it you have St. Augustine's entire political structure. God has predestined very few for salvation; the rest, the great majority, are to be damned. Of course, the word predestination is rarely used for the damned. The commonest use reserves it only for salvation; but, obviously, that leaves us to conclude that those who are not to be saved will be forever damned. These latter, always the majority of human beings, act immorally because they have no grace. They are all filled with lusts, desires for wealth, power, and pleasure. St. Augustine goes through the long pageant of their desires. They are the ones whose needs have called into existence the political state. The state is necessary because these people, with all their greed, with all their desires, would otherwise soon have exterminated themselves. To prevent such extermination, God permitted—he did not create, but permitted—the constitution of states. The one advantage that the state has is that it guarantees some kind of peace. And for what purpose is peace necessary? St. Augustine says, so that these people may satisfy some of their greed. That is what polity means; that is what the state is.

If we forget the theology for a moment, and consider merely the picture of the world St. Augustine gives us, we can easily see that his political pessimism has roots that extend way back into pagan antiquity. To approach St. Augustine's position in this way, we have only to recall a famous statement of Lucian, the satirist. The gods, according to Lucian, are primarily humorists. They have built this world as a stage for their own entertainment. Man finds his way on to that stage, and he comes with an infinite capacity to create, to produce all sorts of things. This ingenuity he uses all for the purpose of making himself happy; yet he finds that his desires are always one step ahead of his capacity to produce. In other words, man is destined to be always running after something he desires that is always beyond his reach; he cannot be satisfied, because his desires go on to infinity. As a result of this constitution of his, man, according to Lucian, is incapable of acting justly.

To understand the political significance of a statement of this sort, you have to recall some of the positions we touched upon in studying the Greek authors; particularly those of the Sophists and Epicureans. We noted that some of the best Greek philosophers, as well as Cicero, and many Christian thinkers, including Dante, held a very different view. It was their boast—we may call it a boast—that the state exists by divine providence in order that there may be justice in this world; that as long as there is justice, a community will be able to maintain itself, and as soon as justice goes—I'm quoting Cicero here—the community goes, collapses, and anarchy sets in. Now this view of man's condition is very different from the Sophist or Epicurean view; and it is the very opposite of the one St. Augustine holds.

In a violent debate with Cicero across the centuries, St. Augustine says: Not only does the removal of justice not lead to the breaking up of a state, but in fact there never has been a state that was maintained by justice. Behind this is Lucian's idea that man is incapable of justice because of his infinite desires, and also the Sophistic and Epicurean position according to which justice comes into existence as a result of a contract—a social contract. Those thinkers, especially the Epicurean philosophers of pleasure, held that all men had it in their hearts to satisfy to the uttermost, to infinity, all their desires, whatever they might be. By experience, however, they have come to realize that if they were to go all out to get such satisfaction, they would probably end up in such disorder that nobody would get anything. They concluded, therefore, that in order to have at least some satisfaction, we have to give up the possibility of satisfying all our desires, and concentrate on enjoying the maximum amount of pleasure our fellow-citizens will permit us to have. Through the centuries ideas of this sort have been presented again and again by serious thinkers. We have only to recall the name of Thomas Hobbes and his doctrine of *bellum omnium contra omnes*.

Let us see how St. Augustine's political philosophy fits into this series of pessimistic views of man. For him, too, men (though not all, not those destined for salvation) are animated with unquenchable desires for goods that are such that as you increase the share of one, the quantity that remains to be shared among the others diminishes. This is true, surely, of sexual pleasure, the possession of a woman, the attainment of glory on the battlefield or in the arena. Are there any pleasures of which it is not true? Long before St. Augustine's time the ancients had pointed out some of them. Seneca, for instance, had noted that our pleasure in contemplation, in singing, in dancing, increases the more people share in it. But it is not so with material goods. As civilization advances, and men learn how to produce more and more wealth, so that all might have more material goods, instead of diminishing, strife mounts. It seems that men contend more, the more there is to be had.

Against this argument, of course, you have the Baconian idea that has dominated our popular thinking for the last few centuries—the idea that we can remove the occasion for struggle over material goods not by limiting our desires but by forcing nature to do our bidding. That's the Baconian attitude: force nature to supply all needs, to supply the means of satisfying all desires, and thereby put an end to this economic and political striving that has characterized the life of man on earth. Look around you, and judge for yourselves whether Lucian or Bacon was right.

Well, our interest in this sort of Baconian utopianism is limited to St. Augustine's criticism. To be sure, St. Augustine has given us some indication as to how we may live happily in the enjoyment of goods which give greater pleasure the more people share in them. The moral principle is clear and rather easy to apply individually. But how to socialize the principle is the problem. Suggestions had been heard even before St. Augustine's time as thinking people, like Plotinus, became alarmed at the progress of material civilization, or rather, at the strife that accompanies it. Centuries later we will hear St. Francis express a similar pessimism about material progress. In a Marxian vein, though to a very opposite purpose, St. Francis reduced all the evil desires that lead mankind away from goodness to a common denominator: the desire for wealth. Wealth, or rather, the desire for wealth is the source of all evil. It is in poverty, therefore, that we should seek salvation. And if we seek it there, St. Francis believed, we will surely find it.

You know how much of his time, of his genius, St. Francis dedicated to singing, in Italy and out of Italy, the praises of Lady Poverty. And strangely enough, occasionally he had a response. We know of whole communities that responded, acting as if they were indeed all to be counted among those few who—St. Augustine would say —are predestined for salvation. Yet it was a response and a happiness that was obviously not to be of great duration. Dante, who sings of that response in the eleventh canto of the *Paradiso,* the canto devoted to St. Francis, grasps why it could not last on the social level. Realizing how destructive of individuals and communities the insatiable desire for wealth is, Dante begins the canto with a terrible invective that has shocked many of his readers. It is a very Augustinian moment in the *Divine Comedy.* He bundles together rulers, doctors, pharmacists, lawyers, corrupt priests, prostitutes, idlers—all who have set for themselves as an aim the satisfaction, the beatitude, the happiness that comes from material goods. Whether they strive for the satisfactions of political rule, or sexual indulgence, or banqueting, these people, Dante says, are all alike, all equally bad.

St. Augustine does not go quite that far. These people are not all the same, he says, though they are all of one camp. When there is a struggle for the goods they desire, and a struggle is always forthcoming, all these people will do what the old Sophists said: they will transform themselves into the powers that constitute the political order. They will form a state.

By state, remember, St. Augustine does not mean any given city or kingdom. When he speaks of the *civitas terrena,* the city of the earth, which he also calls the *civitas diaboli,* the diabolical city, he means all who through all the centuries have striven for the sort of goods I have described. It began in Adam's time, with the first fratricide, Cain, and continues through the time of Remus and Romulus, the reconstituted fratricide, down to the present. All of these people who strive for self-satisfaction in this way, as they are grouped in different states, under different rulers, constitute the city of the devil. God in His mercy has given them, as we said, this utilitarian suggestion or insight: give up that boundless lust for wealth, come to terms; take a little, let others have a little; otherwise nobody will have anything—you will all be dead. And when men, following this utilitarian suggestion, agree to give up their absolute lust, to accept a share of the common good, and to punish those who exceed their shares, we call the result a state—an association dictated by utility for the purpose of enabling a group of people to enjoy, without destroying one another, whatever goods they like best. Some people will

like one thing and some will like another. We
will have, therefore, a hierarchy of states, some
not as bad as others, yet all corrupt to some degree, for the original sin contaminates them all.
Whatever it may be that they want, it is still self-
seeking that moves them to form a political community, the self-seeking that St. Augustine calls
*cupiditas.* The Romans, who sacrificed enjoyment
of the pleasures of the flesh that they might enjoy the satisfaction of dominating as a nation,
might have been less ignoble than Sardanapolis,
who said he wished he had thirty stomachs and as
many genital organs so that he might indulge himself as much as he wanted; but they were not more
just in the eyes of God. Their motive was that
same *cupiditas* on a higher level. That's one pole
of the Augustinian ethics. The other pole, the
sharing of spiritual goods, is *caritas.* Everybody
who has read a page of St. Augustine knows these
two.

Men need the state, St. Augustine emphasizes,
because they need coercion, in two ways. They
need it, first of all, within the bounds of this city
of the devil, to keep within proper confines the
desires for material goods. And they need it, also,
to keep other states from invading the territory
of the commonwealth to secure by violence the
goods on which they have set their hearts. That is
the *civitas terrena.* It provides those who are to
have no peace in eternity with a certain degree of
peace on earth. It restrains civil war. When one
state, at peace internally, comes up against another that it cannot coerce, the war of greed continues on a higher level, until one or the other is
overcome.

In the midst of this *civitas terrena* live also

those few who are predestined for salvation.
Should they try to separate themselves and form a
state of their own, apart from the others? They
cannot, says St. Augustine; and the reason is that,
if all men in a state were really such as these, you
wouldn't need a state. The state is like a hospital.
If mankind were to become physically perfect,
you would not have a perfect hospital; you would
have no hospital at all. The state exists because
of the immorality of human beings. If people were
not immoral, if—taking the impossible—all people
were noble, there would not be any state.

And so those who are predestined to be saved
—who they are nobody knows, or rather, God
knows—will stay in the midst of this city of the
devil, as foreigners, *peregrini, viatori,* until they
are called to their true home, which is not of this
world. While they are here, they are to obey the
laws of the state, doing all it commands them
to do, provided what it commands does not go
against the commandments of God. If, in the re-
lations of individuals to the state, or of one state
to another, the constituted power should order
you to do something that is against the commandments of God, then refuse, then assert yourselves;
but refuse, St. Augustine insists, not by doing, but
by not doing. Refuse by clinging to your duty before God to the point of martyrdom and self-
sacrifice. The wars for Christ are won, St. Augustine reminds his readers, not by killing, but by
dying.

That is the Augustinian scheme. It is important,
even for those of us who do not accept its theological basis, because of its very powerful criticism
of this life of ours. All of us, more or less, share
in, or admire that certain kind of virtue—civic

spirit, patriotism, world-brotherhood, call it what you will—which is built up in the hearts of people who willingly associate themselves together to pursue happiness in this world. Whether it be a tiny city-state, or a large nation-state, or empire, or some dreamed-of world community, your willing association with it makes this peace-enforcing institution dear to you. You don't want to see it fail, you don't want to see it die. You would rather die yourself. And you may wonder why everyone in the world has not rushed to associate himself willingly with your group, which you think is so wonderfully suited for the task of securing peace and happiness.

It is the general tendency of all mankind to resort to such flattering self-justification, is it not? How can those Russians—you hear some people ask—be so enthusiastic in the public square, when they have before them, in our way of life, a picture of almost perfect goodness, justice, welfare, and freedom? We can say the same for the little state of Israel, or the Arab states on its borders, for England, Spain, China, India; all are disposed to flatter themselves in this way. That is how the world goes. A certain group of people invade and occupy certain lands, arm themselves, and set about protecting the lands. Today the image of some ugly imperialist power comes to our mind when we say this. But it is true of all societies that hold or occupy territory and defend it: Switzerland, Cuba, India, Israel, as well as England, Russia, or the United States. Immediately this group of people begins to say: this is our land—these beautiful frontiers, these beautiful bays, these rivers—this is God's country, God has given it to us. So the defense of these lands and these rivers comes to seem just, and the willingness to defend them comes to seem a virtue. But in reality, the only justification, St. Augustine would say, is that the people from whom you took these lands had taken them equally unjustly. Our only real excuse for what we do is that there has been an infinite series of plunders, of iniquities behind ours. But, the other line of argument is more flattering. Here is a man on his own soil; obviously he has a perfect right to protect it against attack. It is his soil; God has given it to him. Well, if there is a fight, under these circumstances, and our side wins, we call it a "just" defense, a just war. You are familiar with the term, I am sure. You hear it and read it daily, coming from people in all parts of the world. Their wars are all *just* wars.

Of course, we must not forget that St. Augustine himself has given us the Christian theory of a just war. That is certainly true. Those knights, crusaders, of the Middle Ages—when they spoke of war, endeavoring to see if there might be a way to make wars and fighting less brutal—invariably cited the arguments of the Augustinian doctrine of a just war. Those arguments were later taken up by St. Thomas, and he did not add anything to them or take anything away. We can say, therefore, that the Roman Catholic Church today has a doctrine of just war that comes entirely out of the pages of St. Augustine.

But now we ought to ask: How can a man who says there can be no just state hold that there can be a just war? We can ask the same question with regard to his doctrine of property. We can speak of justice in the administration of property rights, St. Augustine says, provided we recall that these rights are not administered according to the law of God, but according to the law of the emperor. By divine law there should not be private property. And if some great wealth were to fall into the hands of an individual, it should immediately be used as God commands, by those who want to be perfect or, if not perfect, good. For those who want to be perfect—what does Christ say? If you want to be perfect, sell all your goods and give all to the poor. And if you want to be just good, live in such a way that all people around you will love you for having permitted them to share in the goods of the world that made you happy. Property rights exist for the peace of the city of the devil; but we cannot say they are *just* in terms of the divine law.

And the same is true of wars. Wars occur, St. Augustine tells us clearly, only in this earthly city. What he says of war, therefore, applies only to his *civitas terrena*. As with the laws of property, so with the rules of war. The main point is that the situation of man would be much worse without such rules.

What are the justifications for war? The world being what it is, defensive war is obviously justified, for what happens in defensive war is better than what would happen if a nation under attack did not defend itself. What is important in this doctrine, what chivalry saw and what people no longer see, unfortunately, is that the cruel necessities of war can be mitigated in certain things by applying a few realistic rules that can serve to confine the fighting to its proper objectives. One rule is: Never pursue a war beyond the treaty of peace; when a war is ended, let it be really ended. But above all, see to it that you never fight a war with a feeling of thoroughgoing hatred in your heart. Of all the people I can think of, the man who, I'm sure, would have been most horrified by the trials at Nuremberg is St. Augustine. The enemy may have been as brutal as you like, may have been wholly wrong in his conduct of the war; but, however horribly he has comported himself, the only way to make your defensive war *just* in any sense is to show mercy when victory is won. St. Thomas holds this, and he says himself that he takes it out of St. Augustine.

Related to his doctrine of a just war is St. Augustine's teaching—and here we must touch upon something you are not apt to like—concerning the use of force in matters of faith. You know how the Roman Empire used its civil power to combat heresy by force, as it had used force against the Christians before the time of Constantine. St. Augustine for a long time fought against it. Then, suddenly, for reasons we cannot go into deeply here, he changes his mind. He ceases to be the advocate of adherence according to conscience, and becomes the apostle of compulsion. *Compelle intrare.* To support his position he gives the example from the gospels of the celebration to which some who were invited did not come; the feast was then opened to the maimed, the poor, the halt, and the blind, but still there was room. The Saviour then said: compel them to come in, that my house may be filled. St. Augustine interprets it to mean: force these heretics to come in. Thus he completely reverses his original position, going from day to night, from white to black. You can imagine how many people were resentful and disturbed by this change. And he did not try to conceal the fact that he had reversed himself. Whatever else you may want to say, you have to admit of St. Augustine that he was a most honest thinker.

And remember, he distinctly said: no death penalty for heretics. Many critics have forgotten that. His attitude was that coercion is to be merely a device for facilitating eventual voluntary adherence. It is like the breaking of the shell of an egg. Once these people who have been misled into heresy come out of the broken shell, they will see how magnificent is the orthodox faith, and how much they have almost lost. We must remember that St. Augustine wrote thousands of pages on the subject. Unfortunately, many critics cite only some isolated statement, without noticing all the qualifications and limitations placed upon it, or any of St. Augustine's arguments in justification of his position.

In conclusion we must say a word about St. Augustine's philosophy of history, or rather, about his idea of the relation between providence and history. For here we see the culmination of something that had been preparing itself for a long time in the course of ancient thought. We discussed the question of teleology in connection with the Greeks. Aristotle had established that there is teleology or purpose not only in the volitional acts of man but also in nature. All that we see around us, the animal, vegetable, and mineral kingdoms, is regulated by purpose. The purpose is not conscious, not felt, not regulated by these things themselves; yet what happens is purposeful, because they are activated by a higher being which is called nature. This is, of course, the great Aristotelian doctrine of the teleology of nature. It has often been criticized, repeatedly challenged, sometimes apparently completely rejected, but always it comes back. And even today great scientists have come forward to acknowledge that it cannot be totally rejected, even in their sphere. It does not suffice to explain all phenomena; yet there are obviously large areas of natural phenomena that cannot be sufficiently explained without it.

Well, St. Augustine opened the sphere of history to teleology. There is a design in history, even though individuals have not intended the result accomplished. Historians are always talking as if the sequence of historical events were meaningful, are they not? For example: here comes the philosophical enlightenment of the eighteenth century; that, of course, was the intellectual preparation for the French Revolution; and that in turn was the basis for the appearance of Napoleon, who became, with his arms, the means of spreading the revolutionary ideas throughout Europe. And that, again, was the basis for the resurgence of nationalism in Germany and Italy—and so on. But the question is, was the enlightenment aiming at the Revolution? Did Voltaire want the Revolution? Obviously not. Did the Revolution plan Napoleon? Obviously not. Read the records of the Revolutionary Conventions. And did the France of Napoleon want the rise of the various nationalities—Italian, German? You can answer that for yourselves. Yet, if there is this concatenation, not willed by the agents involved—agents who often aimed at the very opposite effect—who shall we say willed it?

For St. Augustine and his contemporaries the sequence of events under examination was the history of Rome from the legendary fall of Troy to the attacks of the Germanic barbarians. The fall of Troy, whether it be fiction or not, and the consequent development of the Mediterranean world—the rise of Rome—was willed by divine providence. Hector fought as he did for Troy so that Aeneas would have to do what he did. It was the way to realize God's purposes. The players, the agents, had to be, like puppets, unconscious of their true roles.

In other words, externally at least, this Augustinian historical teleology resembles the modern doctrine of Hegel on the cunning of reason in history, does it not? You might say that this conception of history, which has gained a certain amount of notoriety through the Marxian version of it, is full of difficulties. Some people say it is all nonsense. And yet, admitting that the individuals involved were not conscious of the results toward which their deeds tended, how are you going to be able to see any logic in the sequence of political, economic, and social events—unless there is meaning on a higher level? If you deny providence, or the cunning of reason, it is pretty hard to justify what we are all prone to do— namely, to discern some plan in the sequence of historical events in this world.

Well, whether you are prepared to accept it or not, this Augustinian doctrine we have touched upon in our study of his political thought has made its impression.